MICROCONTROLLERS AND APPLICATIONS

AUTHOR

Prof. Santanu Chattopadhyay

Professor,

Dept. of Electronics and Electrical Communication Engineering

IIT Kharagpur, West Bengal

REVIEWER

Dr. C.H. Vithalani

Professor,

Electronics and Communication Engineering (ECE),

Gujarat Technological University,

L.D. College of Engineering, Navarangpura, Ahmedabad, Gujarat

KHANNA BOOK PUBLISHING CO. (P) Ltd.

4C/4344, Ansari Road, Darya Ganj, New Delhi, India

All India Council for Technical Education

Nelson Mandela Marg, Vasant Kunj, New Delhi, India

Dear Readers,

To prevent the piracy, this book is secured with HIGH SECURITY HOLOGRAM on the front title cover. In case you don't find the hologram on the front cover title, please write us to at contact@khannabooks.com or whatsapp us at +91-99109 09320 and avail special gift voucher for yourself.

Specimen of Hologram on front Cover title:

Enlargement Of Overlay

Moreover, there is a SPECIAL DISCOUNT COUPON for you with EVERY HOLOGRAM.

How to avail this SPECIAL DISCOUNT:

Step 1: Scratch the hologram
Step 2: Under the scratch area, your "coupon code" is available
Step 3: Logon to www.khannabooks.com
Step 4: Use your "coupon code" in the shopping cart and get your copy at a special discount
Step 5: Enjoy your reading!

ISBN: 978-93-5538-506-2
Book Code: DIP463EN

Microcontrollers and Applications
by Dr. Santanu Chattopadhyay

First Edition: 2026

Originally Published by:
All India Council for Technical Education, Ministry of Education, GOI

Exclusively Published & Distributed by:
Khanna Book Publishing Co. (P) Ltd.
4C/4344, Ansari Road, Daryaganj,
New Delhi (INDIA)

Visit us at: **www.khannabooks.com**
Write us at: **contact@khannabooks.com**

To view complete list of books, Please scan the QR Code: KPH

Printed in Bharat.

प्रो. टी. जी. सीताराम
अध्यक्ष
Prof. T. G. Sitharam
Chairman

सत्यमेव जयते

आज़ादी का अमृत महोत्सव

अखिल भारतीय तकनीकी शिक्षा परिषद्
(भारत सरकार का एक सांविधिक निकाय)
(शिक्षा मंत्रालय, भारत सरकार)
नेल्सन मंडेला मार्ग, वसंत कुंज, नई दिल्ली–110070
दूरभाष : 011–26131498
ई–मेल : chairman@aicte-india.org

ALL INDIA COUNCIL FOR TECHNICAL EDUCATION
(A STATUTORY BODY OF THE GOVT. OF INDIA)
(Ministry of Education, Govt. of India)
Nelson Mandela Marg, Vasant Kunj, New Delhi-110070
Phone : 011-26131498
E-mail : chairman@aicte-india.org

FOREWORD

Engineers are the backbone of any modern society. They are the ones responsible for the marvels as well as the improved quality of life across the world. Engineers have driven humanity towards greater heights in a more evolved and unprecedented manner.

The All India Council for Technical Education (AICTE), have spared no efforts towards the strengthening of the technical education in the country. AICTE is always committed towards promoting quality Technical Education to make India a modern developed nation emphasizing on the overall welfare of mankind.

An array of initiatives has been taken by AICTE in last decade which have been accelerated now by the National Education Policy (NEP) 2020. The implementation of NEP under the visionary leadership of Hon'ble Prime Minister of India envisages the provision for education in regional languages to all, thereby ensuring that every graduate becomes competent enough and is in a position to contribute towards the national growth and development through innovation & entrepreneurship.

One of the spheres where AICTE had been relentlessly working since past couple of years is providing high quality original technical contents at Under Graduate & Diploma level prepared and translated by eminent educators in various Indian languages to its aspirants. For students pursuing 2nd year of their Engineering education, AICTE has identified 87 books, which shall be translated into 12 Indian languages - Hindi, Tamil, Gujarati, Odia, Bengali, Kannada, Urdu, Punjabi, Telugu, Marathi, Assamese & Malayalam. In addition to the English medium, books in different Indian Languages are going to support the students to understand the concepts in their respective mother tongue.

On behalf of AICTE, I express sincere gratitude to all distinguished authors, reviewers and translators from the renowned institutions of high repute for their admirable contribution in a record span of time.

AICTE is confident that these outcomes based original contents shall help aspirants to master the subject with comprehension and greater ease.

(Prof. T. G. Sitharam)

ACKNOWLEDGEMENT

The author is grateful to the authorities of AICTE, particularly *Prof. T. G. Sitharam*, Chairman; *Prof. M. P. Poonia*, Vice-Chairman; *Prof. Rajive Kumar*, Member-Secretary and *Dr. Amit Kumar Srivastava*, Director, Faculty Development Cell for their planning to publish the book on *Microcontrollers and Applications.* I sincerely acknowledge the valuable contributions of the reviewer of the book *Dr. Chandulal Vithalani*, Professor, Department of Electronics and Communication Engineering, L.D. College of Engineering, Ahmedabad for going through the entire manuscript line-by-line and providing valuable suggestions for content improvements. My sincere thanks to my wife *Santana* for being the constant source of inspiration to write this, as well as, several other books in the past. I would also like to mention about our son *Sayantan*, who always pushes me to newer challenges to put my knowledge into black and white – leading to this book as well.

This book is an outcome of various suggestions of AICTE members, experts and authors who shared their opinion and thought to further develop the engineering education in our country. Acknowledgements are due to the contributors and different workers in this field whose published books, review articles, papers, photographs, footnotes, references and other valuable information enriched me at the time of writing the book.

Santanu Chattopadhyay

PREFACE

In electronic system design, microcontrollers have become a very important component. Digital systems interacting with the environment need computation power for signal processing or for executing a control algorithm. As an electronic system designer, particularly in the digital domain, one should have a good grasp on the features, architectures, programming techniques and interfacing requirements of various microcontrollers, available in the market. Though it is a difficult task to have very good knowledge on each of the alternatives available, one should be able to select the best possible solution for a given application and go ahead with the design and development task without much inconvenience.

To address the issue of application development using microcontrollers, this book attempts to provide a deep understanding for the microcontroller 8051. In order to introduce the concepts related to microcontrollers, first some basic topics on computer organization, 8085 and 8086 microprocessors have been discussed. This will help the reader to prepare the background to initiate the study on microcontrollers. The features of generic microcontrollers have been elaborated to establish their requirement, over and above the existing microprocessors. The architecture, programming and interfacing issues of the 8051 have been elaborated in sufficient detail. Connecting keyboard, LEDs, 7-segment displays, LCDs to the 8051 have been illustrated. To interact with the world, which is analog in nature, analog-to-digital and digital-to-analog converter (ADC and DAC) interfacing techniques have been enumerated. The 8051 supports both the parallel and the serial modes of communication. Both the modes have been illustrated for data transfer to/from the 8051 chip. Apart from assembly language programming for interfacing and control algorithms, Embedded C language has been explored. Along with that, some commonly used advanced microcontrollers, such as, PIC, AVR and ARM have also been introduced to provide a working knowledge of those processors.

Processor architectures could be classified into two main categories – CISC (Complex Instruction Set Computer) and RISC (Reduced Instruction Set Computer). Features of both the RISC and the CISC architectures have been detailed. This has been followed by the discussion on advanced microcontrollers (PIC, AVR, and ARM) that attempt to mix the good features of both RISC and CISC architectures. Most of the advanced processors possess built-in peripherals, such as, timers, ADCs etc. They also possess several communication standards supported and different power-down modes suitable for low-power applications. Discussions have been included to enumerate such options.

The book is an outcome of the author's experience of handling the theory and laboratory courses on subjects like Microprocessors, Microcontrollers and Embedded Systems for more than two decades. It is expected that the book will be highly useful to the students and the subject teachers, for whom it has been primarily meant for. It may also be useful to anybody starting a career as an embedded system designer. Any constructive suggestion to improve the quality of the book in its future editions is most welcome.

Santanu Chattopadhyay

OUTCOME BASED EDUCATION

For the implementation of an outcome based education the first requirement is to develop an outcome based curriculum and incorporate an outcome based assessment in the education system. By going through outcome based assessments, evaluators will be able to evaluate whether the students have achieved the outlined standard, specific and measurable outcomes. With the proper incorporation of outcome based education there will be a definite commitment to achieve a minimum standard for all learners without giving up at any level. At the end of the programme running with the aid of outcome based education, a student will be able to arrive at the following outcomes:

Programme Outcomes (POs) are statements that describe what students are expected to know and be able to do upon graduating from the program. These relate to the skills, knowledge, analytical ability attitude and behaviour that students acquire through the program. The POs essentially indicate what the students can do from subject-wise knowledge acquired by them during the program. As such, POs define the professional profile of an engineering diploma graduate.

National Board of Accreditation (NBA) has defined the following seven POs for an Engineering diploma graduate:

PO1. Basic and Discipline specific knowledge: Apply knowledge of basic mathematics, science and engineering fundamentals and engineering specialization to solve the engineering problems.

PO2. Problem analysis: Identify and analyses well-defined engineering problems using codified standard methods.

PO3. Design/ development of solutions: Design solutions for well-defined technical problems and assist with the design of systems components or processes to meet specified needs.

PO4. Engineering Tools, Experimentation and Testing: Apply modern engineering tools and appropriate technique to conduct standard tests and measurements.

PO5. Engineering practices for society, sustainability and environment: Apply appropriate technology in context of society, sustainability, environment and ethical practices.

PO6. Project Management: Use engineering management principles individually, as a team member or a leader to manage projects and effectively communicate about well-defined engineering activities.

PO7. Life-long learning: Ability to analyse individual needs and engage in updating in the context of technological changes.

COURSE OUTCOMES

By the end of the course the students will be able to:

CO-1: Understand and Compare Fundamentals of Microprocessors and Microcontrollers.
CO-2: Illustrate Architecture of AT 8051Microcontroller.
CO-3: Implement C- Language Programs for Data Manipulation and Interfacing.
CO-4: Interface I/O and Peripheral Devices with AT 8051 Microcontroller.
CO-5: Implement Communication Standards and Protocols.
CO-6: Understand Architecture of ARM (RISC) Microcontroller.

Mapping of Course Outcomes with Programme Outcomes to be done according to the matrix given below:

Course Outcomes	Expected Mapping with Programme Outcomes (1- Weak Correlation; 2- Medium correlation; 3- Strong Correlation)						
	PO-1	PO-2	PO-3	PO-4	PO-5	PO-6	PO-7
CO-1	3	3	3	3	1	1	3
CO-2	3	2	2	2	1	1	3
CO-3	3	2	2	2	1	1	3
CO-4	3	2	2	3	1	1	3
CO-5	3	3	3	3	1	1	3
CO-6	3	3	3	3	1	1	3

GUIDELINES FOR TEACHERS

To implement Outcome Based Education (OBE) knowledge level and skill set of the students should be enhanced. Teachers should take a major responsibility for the proper implementation of OBE. Some of the responsibilities (not limited to) for the teachers in OBE system may be as follows:

- Within reasonable constraint, they should manoeuvre time to the best advantage of all students.
- They should assess the students only upon certain defined criterion without considering any other potential ineligibility to discriminate them.
- They should try to grow the learning abilities of the students to a certain level before they leave the institute.
- They should try to ensure that all the students are equipped with the quality knowledge as well as competence after they finish their education.
- They should always encourage the students to develop their ultimate performance capabilities.
- They should facilitate and encourage group work and team work to consolidate newer approach.
- They should follow Blooms taxonomy in every part of the assessment.

Bloom's Taxonomy

Level	Teacher should Check	Student should be able to	Possible Mode of Assessment
Create	Students ability to create	Design or Create	Mini project
Evaluate	Students ability to justify	Argue or Defend	Assignment
Analyse	Students ability to distinguish	Differentiate or Distinguish	Project/Lab Methodology
Apply	Students ability to use information	Operate or Demonstrate	Technical Presentation/ Demonstration
Understand	Students ability to explain the ideas	Explain or Classify	Presentation/Seminar
Remember	Students ability to recall (or remember)	Define or Recall	Quiz

GUIDELINES FOR STUDENTS

Students should take equal responsibility for implementing the OBE. Some of the responsibilities (not limited to) for the students in OBE system are as follows:

- Students should be well aware of each UO before the start of a unit in each and every course.
- Students should be well aware of each CO before the start of the course.
- Students should be well aware of each PO before the start of the programme.
- Students should think critically and reasonably with proper reflection and action.
- Learning of the students should be connected and integrated with practical and real life consequences.
- Students should be well aware of their competency at every level of OBE.

LIST OF ABBREVIATIONS

AC	Auxiliary Carry
ADC	Analog to Digital Converter
ALE	Address Latch Enable
ALU	Arithmetic Logic Unit
AVR	Advanced Virtual RISC
BIU	Bus Interface Unit
BP	Base Pointer
CAN	Controller Area Network
CCP	Capture Compare Pulse width modulation
CISC	Complex Instruction Set Computer
CLK	Clock
CPU	Central Processing Unit
CS	Code Segment
CY	Carry
DAC	Digital to Analog Converter
DB	Define Byte
DI	Destination Index
DS	Data Segment
EA	External Access
EOC	End of Conversion
ES	Extra Segment
EU	Execution Unit
FIQ	Fast Interrupt Processing
GPR	General Purpose Register
GUI	Graphical User Interface
IDE	Integrated Development Environment
IE	Interrupt Enable
IIC, I2C	Inter Integrated Circuit
IP	Instruction Pointer, Interrupt Priority
IR	Instruction Register
kB	Kilobytes
kHz	Kilohertz
LCD	Liquid Crystal Diode
LED	Light Emitting Diode
LSB	Least Significant Bit
MHz	Megahertz
MSB	Most Significant Bit
OE	Output Enable
OTP	One Time Programmable
PC	Program Counter
PCB	Printed Circuit Board
PIC	Programmable Interface Controller
PPI	Programmable Peripheral Interface
PSEN	Program Strobe Enable
PWM	Pulse Width Modulation
RAM	Random Access Memory
RD	Read
RISC	Reduced Instruction Set Computer
ROM	Read Only Memory
RS	Register Select
SC	Start Conversion
SCI	Serial Communication Interface
SI	Source Index
SID	Serial Input Data
SoC	System-on-Chip
SOD	Serial Output Data
SP	Stack Pointer
SPI	Serial Peripheral Interface
SS	Stack Segment
WR	Write
Z	Zero

LIST OF FIGURES

Unit 1 Fundamentals of Microprocessors and Microcontrollers

Unit 2 The 8051 Architecture

LIST OF TABLES

CONTENTS

1 Fundamentals of Microprocessors and Microcontrollers

UNIT SPECIFICS

Through this unit we have discussed the following aspects:

- *A program logic getting translated into actions of modules in a computer;*
- *Internal configuration of a computer;*
- *Concepts of address-, data- and control buses;*
- *Internal architecture of a generic CPU – registers, ALU, instruction decoding and execution process;*
- *An overview of the 8085 microprocessor – pin diagram, internal architecture and programming;*
- *An overview of the 8086/88 microprocessor – architecture, summary of instructions;*
- *Microcomputer systems and distinction between microprocessors and microcontrollers;*
- *An overview of 8-bit microcontrollers with a comparison between the popular ones;*
- *Integrated Development Environment (IDE) for microcontroller based system development.*

The overall discussion in the unit is to give an overview of CPU architectures, starting with the basic knowledge of components in a computer system. It has been assumed that the reader has a good understanding of Digital Electronics with topics like logic gates, memory elements, registers, counters etc. Also a basic understanding of programming will be helpful. A good number of examples have been included to explain the concepts, wherever needed.

A large number of multiple choice questions have been provided with their answers. Apart from that, subjective questions of short and long answer type have been included. A few numerical problems with answers have been provided. A list of references and suggested readings have been given, so that, one can go through them for more details. The section "Know More" has been carefully designed so that the supplementary information provided in this part becomes beneficial for the users of the book. This section mainly highlights the initial activity, history of the development of microcontrollers, recent developments and application areas.

RATIONALE

This unit on fundamentals of microprocessors and microcontrollers helps the reader to understand the basic architecture of a computer system, its components, interfacing between them and the working principle. Starting with the block diagram level representation of a computing system with CPU, memory and peripherals, it goes into the details of functioning of the CPU to co-ordinate between all the components. The unit explains how a typical CPU works by getting instructions and data from memory and I/O devices interfaced with it. It shows the internal of a CPU at register level with ALU and bus interfaces. The unit takes the reader through an overview of the 8085 and 8086/88 microprocessors. This acquaints the reader with the basic philosophy behind developing electronic systems around microprocessors and microcontrollers. This, in turn, leads to discussion on microcomputers and finally takes the reader to microcontrollers, which are single-chip microcomputers. The unit discusses on microcontroller architecture, comparison between available microcontrollers, how to select a microcontroller for a specific application, etc. For microcontroller based system design, the unit introduces the reader to the integrated development environment (IDE). Thus, the unit gives bird's-eye-view of microcontroller based system design.

PRE-REQUISITES

Electronics: Digital Electronics

Programming: Basic Computer Programming

UNIT OUTCOMES

List of outcomes of this unit is as follows:

U1-O1: List the modules inside a processor

U1-O2: Draw the block-level interfacing of memory to processors

U1-O3: State the internal architecture of 8085 and 8086

U1-O4: Compare between microprocessors and microcontrollers

UI-O5: Distinguish between high- and low-level languages

UI-O6: State the role of tools present in an Integrated Development Environment

Unit-1 Outcomes	***EXPECTED MAPPING WITH COURSE OUTCOMES*** *(1- Weak Correlation; 2- Medium correlation; 3- Strong Correlation)*					
	CO-1	***CO-2***	***CO-3***	***CO-4***	***CO-5***	***CO-6***
U1-O1	*3*	*2*	*1*	-	-	-
U1-O2	*2*	-	-	-	-	-
U1-O3	*3*	*1*	-	-	-	-
U1-O4	*3*	*1*	-	-	-	-
U1-O5	*1*	-	*1*	-	-	-
UI-O6	*2*	-	-	-	-	-

1.1 Introduction

A computing system contains one or more *processors* as its primary component. The job of the processor is to carry out the computation intended by the user of the system. The intended computation is the *program* to be executed by the processor. The program is designed by the user and made available to the processor through the *memory* modules present in the system. Apart from the program, some input values, needed for computation, are to be provided to the processor and the outputs produced from the computation are to be made available to the user. This entire relationship between the modules in a computing system could be understood by the following example.

Example 1.1: To illustrate the role of processor, memory and input-output devices in a computing system, consider the problem of determining roots of a quadratic equation $ax^2 + bx + c = 0$, with $a \neq 0$.The flowchart corresponding to the computation of roots has been shown in Fig 1.1. The flowchart is converted into a program by the user which is further translated into a machine-understandable form. The translated machine-language program is put into the memory. The processor accesses the memory locations to fetch those machine language instructions, one by one. Once an instruction reaches the processor, it is decoded to get the intended action for it. The action may be to do some computation (for example, $d \leftarrow b^2 - 4ac$, $d < 0$ check etc.), get inputs from an input device (such as "Input a, b, c") or output some computed value/message (such as, "Output r_1, r_2"). The input devices (such as, keyboard) work under the command of the processor to get inputs from the outside world/user. Similarly, the output devices (like screen, printer) also work, controlled by the processor.

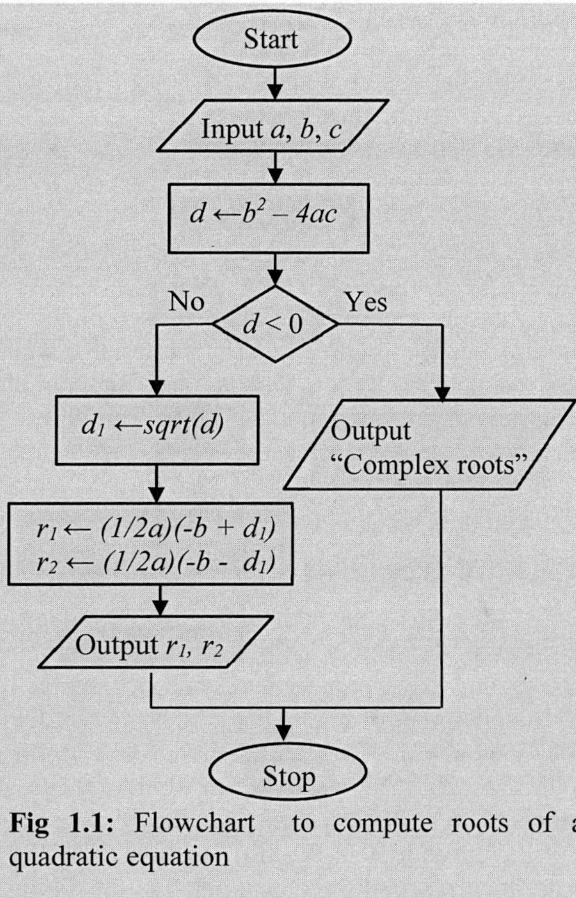

Fig 1.1: Flowchart to compute roots of a quadratic equation

Microprocessors and microcontrollers are semiconductor chips that can function as a processor in a computing system. In the process of familiarizing the readers with an overview of their operations and the commonly available processing platforms, the next section will highlight the basic organization of modules in a computing system.

1.2 Basic Computer Organization

Any computing system consists of three different components: Central Processing Unit (CPU), memory and peripheral devices (primarily the I/O devices). The CPU needs to communicate with the memory modules and peripherals to accomplish its computational task. This communication takes place via a strips of wire, called a *bus*. A bus may typically be of width 8-bits, 16-bits, 32-bits etc. having number of wires equal to its bit-width. For a bus of, say 16-bits, 16 bits of data could be transferred from CPU to memory/peripherals, or vice versa, at a time. This enhances the speed of data transfer, compared to single-wire connections. Transfer of information over a bus may be unidirectional or bidirectional in nature. For a unidirectional bus, transfer is from a master device (for example, CPU) to a slave device (for example, memory/peripherals), while for a bidirectional bus, flow of information may also be from the slave device to the master. In any computer system, there are three types of buses: address bus, data bus and control bus. Out of these, address bus and control bus are generally unidirectional, while the data bus is bidirectional. A typical bus connection in a computer system has been shown in Fig 1.2.

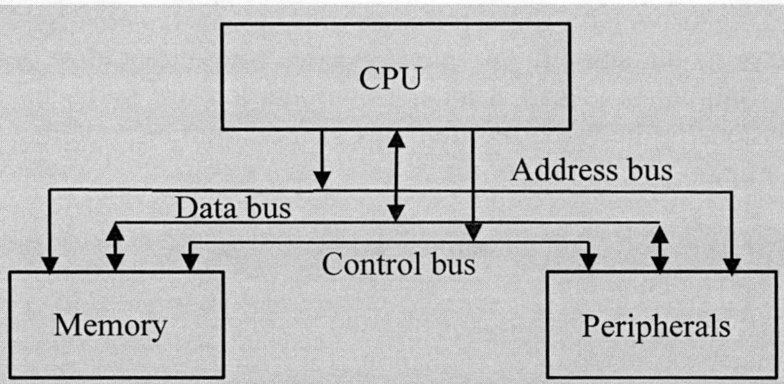

Fig 1.2: A typical computer system

1.2.1 Address Bus

CPU uses the address bus lines to identify a memory location or a peripheral that it wants to access. A memory chip consists of a number of addressable locations. Each location may correspond to one or more bytes of space, typically known as *word size* of the memory. Availability of more number of bits in the address bus of CPU enables it to refer to more number of memory locations and/or I/O devices. For a CPU with *x*-bit address bus, the total number of distinct addresses that it can generate is 2^x. Out of these, some may correspond to memory locations, while others to identify peripherals. On the other hand, a typical memory chip has a set of address lines. For a chip with 1024 (1 kilo) locations, number of address lines is 10 (as $2^{10} = 1024$). If the bit pattern corresponding to *m* appears in the address lines, the location *m* in the chip gets accessed. Apart from that, each memory chip contains a *chip select* input which needs to be enabled to access the chip. This helps in combining more than one memory chips with smaller capacities to cover the full address range of a processor. It has been illustrated in the following example.

Example 1.2: Suppose that the CPU has 16-bit address bus. Thus, total memory space accessible by it is 2^{16} = 64k. Consider each memory chip to be of size 16k with 14 address lines. To get 64k memory, four such chips need to be connected. To develop the system, as shown in Fig 1.3, least significant 14 address lines (A_0 to A_{13}) are connected directly to all the four memory chips. The next two higher order address lines A_{14} and A_{15} are passed through a 2-to-4 decoder to generate 4 chip select signals for the memory chips. Thus, for the addresses generated by the CPU in the range of 0000H-3FFFH Memory 1 is accessed. For addresses 4000H-7FFFH, 8000H-BFFFH, and C000H-FFFFH, Memory 2, Memory 3 and Memory 4 are accessed, respectively.

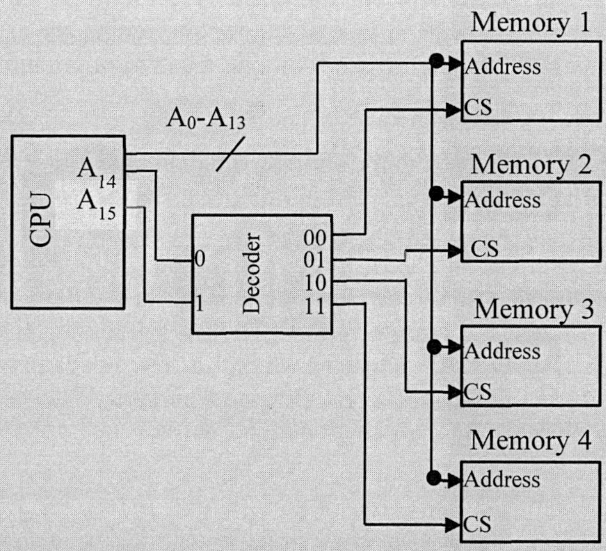

Fig 1.3: Memory interfacing with CPU

In Example 1.2, if some I/O devices need to be connected as well, some of the decoder output lines may be connected to enable those devices. This, of course, will reduce the amount of memory that could be attached in the system.

1.2.2 Data Bus

This is used to transport data between the CPU and memory and/or I/O devices. More the width of the data bus, more data can be transferred at a single go. However, having more number of lines in a data bus (or, any other bus) also means more required area on the board (housing the full system) to route them between the modules, increasing the cost of the system. Typical size of data bus varies between 8 to 64 bits. Processing power of the CPU is often guided by the width of the data bus. If the data bus width is 8-bits, modules internal to the CPU are generally designed to do operations (such as, addition, subtraction, multiplication etc.) on 8-bit operands only. It may be noted that data bus of individual memory chips may be of lesser width than the CPU data bus. A

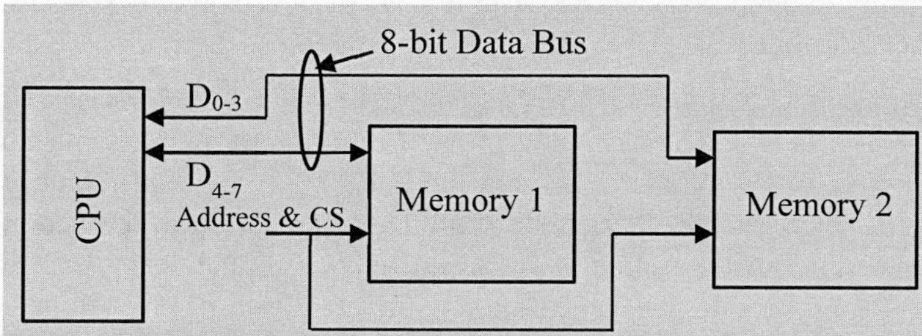

Fig 1.4: Connecting memory modules in parallel

number of memory chips may be operated in parallel to match the data bus lines of the CPU. For example, in Fig 1.4, individual memory chips are of 4-bit data bus. Two such chips are connected in parallel to cater to the 8-bit data bus requirement of the CPU.

1.2.3 Control Bus

Apart from the address and data bus lines, CPU also need several control signals connected to the memory chips and I/O devices. Further, it needs to check the status of devices connected to the system. Sometimes, devices need to contact the CPU proactively on occurrence of some event, for example, the user pressing a key on the keyboard. These control and status lines, from and to the CPU, collectively form the control bus. There cannot be any typical sizes for the control bus. However, two very important control signals for any CPU is the *Read* (RD) and the *Write* (WR). The signal RD is activated when the CPU needs to read the content of a memory location or input device. Similarly, WR is activated when the CPU wants to modify the content of a memory location or output some data to an output device.

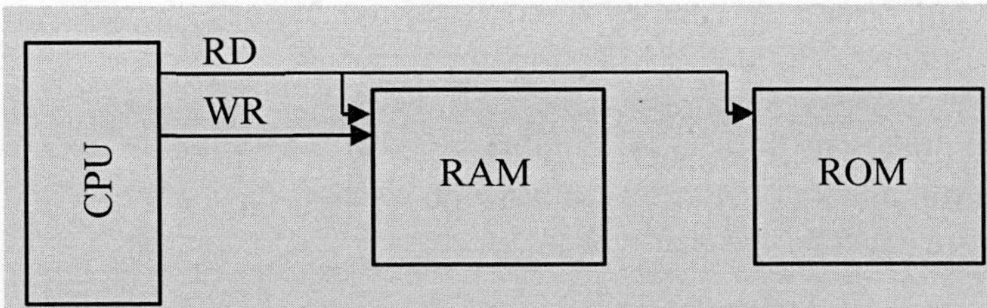

Fig 1.5: RD, WR signals to memory

A computer system normally contains two types of memory modules – Random Access Memory (RAM) and Read Only Memory (ROM). Content of ROM is permanent in nature and is used to hold program/data that is not going to change frequently. Examples of such content include booting program of the system, some specific bit pattern that may be used to display some pattern in output device, etc. ROM content could be reprogrammed only by using some additional devices, commonly known as *Programmer*. On the other hand, content of RAM is volatile. It is used to keep user programs and data. The CPU can only read the contents of ROM, however, may do both read and write operations for RAM. The control lines RD and WR are to be connected accordingly, as shown in Fig 1.5.

Example 1.3: Fig 1.6 shows a computer system with a processor having 16-bit address bus and 8-bit data bus. The system has a total of 64kB of memory interfaced with the processor. Out of these 64kB, 16kB is ROM and 48kB RAM. Individual memory chips are of capacity 16k×4-bits. Thus, each 8-bit memory word has been configured by connecting two such memory chips in parallel. Address lines A_0 to A_{13} have been connected to the address lines of the memory chips. A 2-to-4 decoder has been used to generate the chip select signals from the highest order address bits, A_{14} and A_{15}. The RAM chips have got both the RD and WR control signals connected to them, as their locations may both be read and written by the CPU. On the other hand, only the RD line has been connected to the ROM chips, as the ROM locations could only be read by the CPU. It may be noted that the data lines of ROM are unidirectional, coming out of the memory chip. For RAM chips, the data lines are bidirectional, as data may both be read or written onto them. Processor generates address in the range of 0 to 64k that get mapped onto pair of memory chips to give 8-bit data.

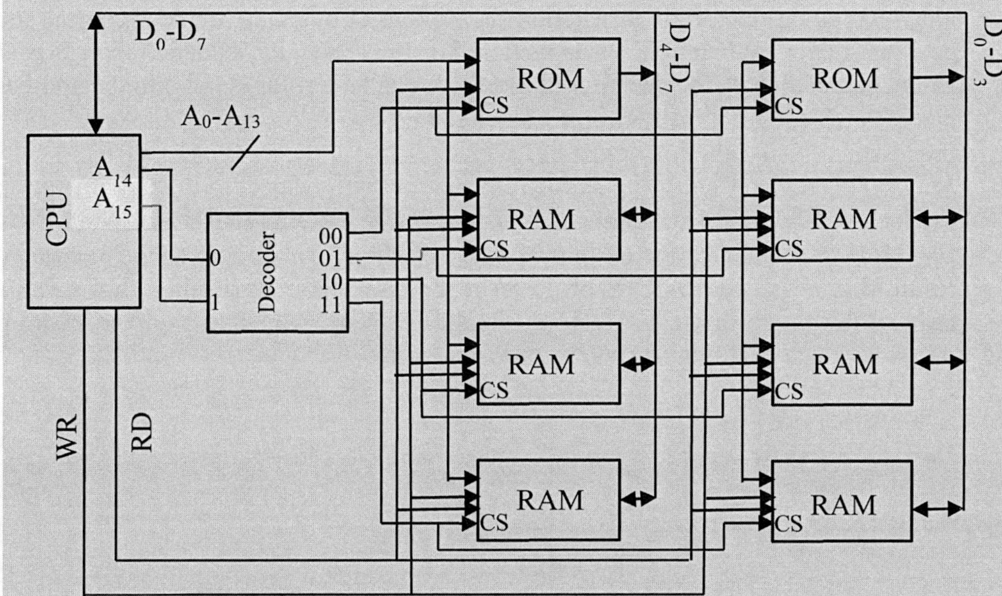

Fig 1.6: Interfacing 16KB ROM and 48KB RAM with CPU

1.2.4 CPU Internals

After looking into the interfacing of CPU with other components in the system, next, let us go into internal structure of the CPU. Fig 1.7 shows the structure of a typical CPU. It consists of the following components.

1. A set of *Registers* to store information temporarily. The information stored may be the data on which the CPU needs to operate, or the address of a memory location containing the data to be fetched into CPU, for operation. The registers could be of sizes 8-bit, 16-bit, 32-bit, 64-bit etc. in different CPUs. More the number of registers in a CPU, it is better. As in that case, for most of the operations, CPU will find the corresponding data within itself and thus does not need additional time to fetch from memory. Wider registers enable larger data size. However, to limit the size and cost of the CPU, number of registers in a CPU is restricted. For most of the contemporary processors, it is not more than 64.
2. An *Arithmetic Logic Unit* (*ALU*) to carry out to carry out the arithmetic and logic operations intended by the program instructions. Examples of arithmetic operations are ADD, SUBTRACT, MULTIPLY, DIVIDE etc. Logic operations include AND, OR, NOT as the most common ones.

3. Some special function registers are often put into the CPU, as noted next.
   a. *Program Counter* (*PC*): It points to the address of the next instruction to be executed. After fetching the next instruction from memory to CPU, PC is incremented by size of the instruction (in number of bytes), to make it point to the next instruction. When the CPU is powered on or is reset, PC is loaded with a fixed value, predecided by the designer of the CPU. Content of PC is put into the address bus to fetch the next instruction to be executed by the processor. In some of the processors, PC is called *Instruction Pointer* (*IP*).
   b. *Flags*: This register holds the status information with respect to the last operation carried out by the ALU. It contains bits named as ZERO, CARRY etc. The ZERO flag bit is set if the last operation performed by the ALU has zero as the computed result. Similarly, the CARRY bit is set if the last operation resulted into a value beyond the range that can be stored in the registers. The flags help in making decisions regarding the instruction sequence to follow.

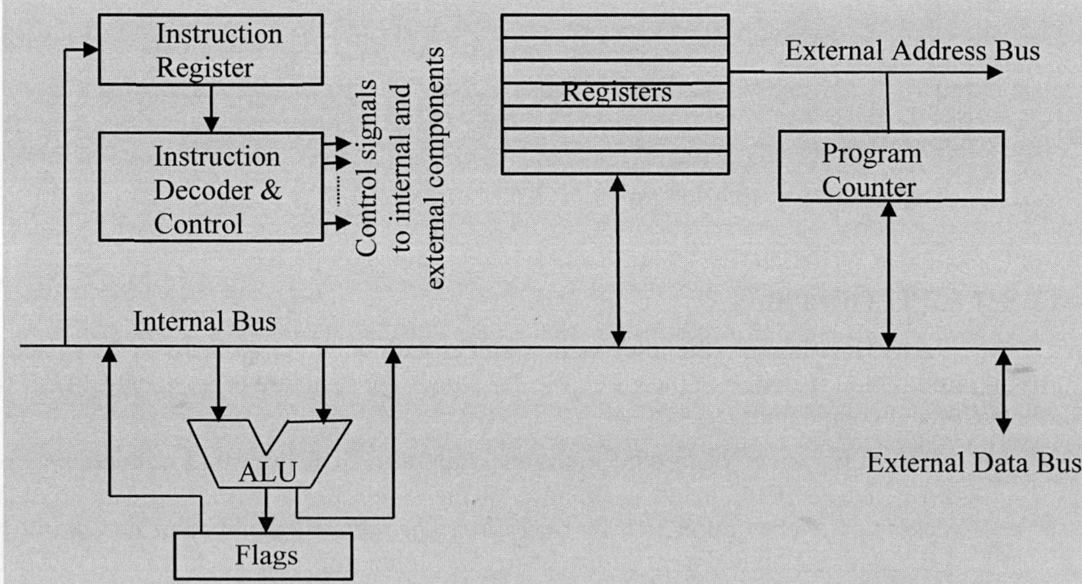

Fig 1.7: Structure of a typical CPU

   c. *Instruction Register* (*IR*): This register holds the instruction as it is fetched from the memory. Each instruction is stored in memory in a coded form. Once it reaches the IR, the *Instruction Decoder* is used to decode it. Based on the instruction, the controller generates the control signals over successive time frames to accomplish the intended task of the instruction.

1.2.5 Operation of CPU

CPU executes the instructions one-by-one starting with the instruction at memory location pointed to by the PC. It typically follows the sequence of operations "Fetch → Decode → Execute" for each instruction. The operations continue till the processor executes a HALT instruction, or as long as the processor is powered. The sequence of operations has been enumerated in Table 1.1.

Table 1.1: Steps in instruction execution

Fetch	1. Address of next instruction pointed to by PC is put on the address bus. 2. RD signal activated. 3. Next instruction from memory reaches Instruction Register. 4. PC incremented to point to the next instruction.
Decode	5. Decoder decodes the instruction and decides the sequence in which various control signals are to be activated to accomplish the instruction.
Execute	6. Operands for the instruction brought from memory and/or registers. 7. Operation carried out in ALU, Flags updated. 8. Result stored back in register/memory.

Example 1.4: Next we shall look into instruction execution by a hypothetical CPU shown in Fig 1.8.

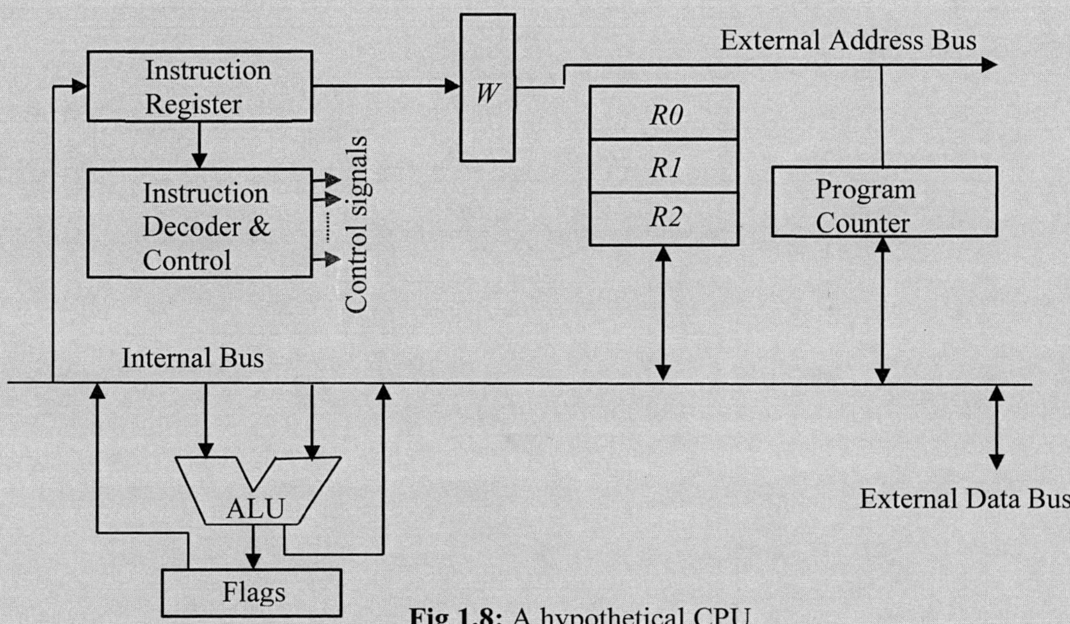

Fig 1.8: A hypothetical CPU

The CPU has three registers *R0*, *R1* and *R2* in it. Apart from that, there is a special register *W* that can hold an address. The address field present in an instruction may be copied from *IR* to it and made available to the address bus to access memory locations. To understand the control signals generated over the time-steps, we assume that each register has got two signals associated with it – *load* and *enable*. When the *load* signal is activated, the content from the bus it is connected to, is copied into it. When the *enable* signal is activated, content of the corresponding register is put onto the bus. For example, to copy the content of register *R0* to register *R1*, the signals to be activated are *enable_R0* and *load_R1*. Similarly, ALU has control signals to perform different arithmetic and logic operations. We shall consider the following three instructions.

- LOAD *R0*, 1000 ; Load the content of *Memory*[1000] into *R0*
- ADD *R0*, *R1*, *R2* ; *R2* ← *R0* + *R1*
- STORE *R2*, 3000 ; Store the content of *R2* at *Memory*[3000]

Control signals activated at different time steps to execute these instructions have been shown in Table 1.2.

Table 1.2: Control signals activated for different instructions

Instruction	*Time Step*	*Control Signals*
LOAD *R0*, 1000	t_1	*Enable_PC, RD*
	t_2	*Load_IR*
	t_3	*Decode, Increment_PC*
	t_4	*Load_W, Enable_IR*
	t_5	*Enable_W, RD, Load_R0*
ADD R0, R1, R2	t_1	*Enable_PC, RD*
	t_2	*Load_IR*
	t_3	*Decode, Increment_PC*
	t_4	*Enable_R0, Enable_R1, Add_ALU, Load_R2*
STORE *R2*, 3000	t_1	*Enable_PC, RD*
	t_2	*Load_IR*
	t_3	*Decode, Increment_PC*
	t_4	*Load_W, Enable_IR*
	t_5	*Enable_W, WR, Enable_R2*

It may be noted that the time steps t_1 and t_2 correspond to *Fetch* stage, t_3 corresponds to *Decode* phase and the rest of the time steps constitute the *Execute* phase of operation. *Fetch* and *Decode* stages (that is, time steps t_1 to t_3) are same for all instructions, *Execute* phase depends upon the instruction being carried out.

1.3 8085: An 8-bit Microprocessor

A microprocessor is a single silicon chip that includes all the components of a processor, such as, ALU, registers, controller etc. to form a CPU. From our knowledge of digital design, it is understood that the components inside a CPU (as discussed in Section 1.2.4) can be realized using discrete electronic circuit elements, such as, logic gates and flip-flops. This strategy of processor design was followed in the late 1960s. However, the devices used to be quite large and too slow. In the early 1970s, with the advancement in semiconductor chip manufacturing process, entire CPU logic could be fabricated on a single silicon chip, leading to the invention of microprocessors. The size of the processor was almost several thousand times smaller and speed several hundred times higher. This has been possible as in semiconductor technology, on-chip communication is much faster than off-chip.

The first microprocessor was Intel's 4004, introduced in 1971. It has been a 4-bit processor with 10-bit address bus and 4-bit data bus, operating at 108 kHz. It was quickly succeeded by 8008 (8-bit data bus), 8080 and 8085. The microprocessor 8085, introduced in 1976, is a processor with 8-bit data bus, 16-bit address bus, operating at 3 MHz clock.

Was there a miniprocessor?

Answer is "no". From discrete component based design, the processors evolved into microprocessors. However, compared to today's complex processors, the microprocessors designed at the beginning were too simple.

1.3.1 The 8085 Chip

The 8085 CPU comes as a 40-pin chip with a supply voltage requirement of +5V. It can operate with a single-phase clock frequency 3 MHz, though some advanced versions (8085A-2) can operate upto 5 MHz. The pin layout of the chip has been shown in Fig 1.9(a). The pins can be grouped as per their functionality. The grouping of pins has been shown in Fig 1.9(b).

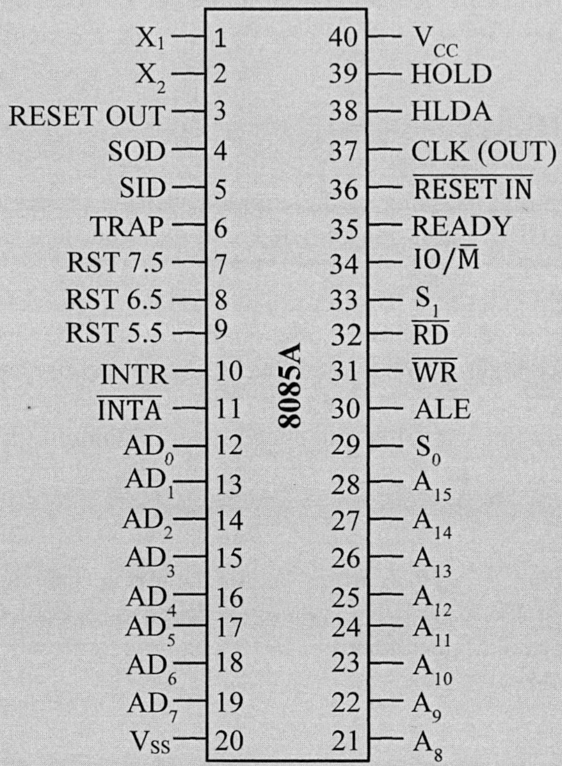

Fig 1.9(a): 8085A pin diagram

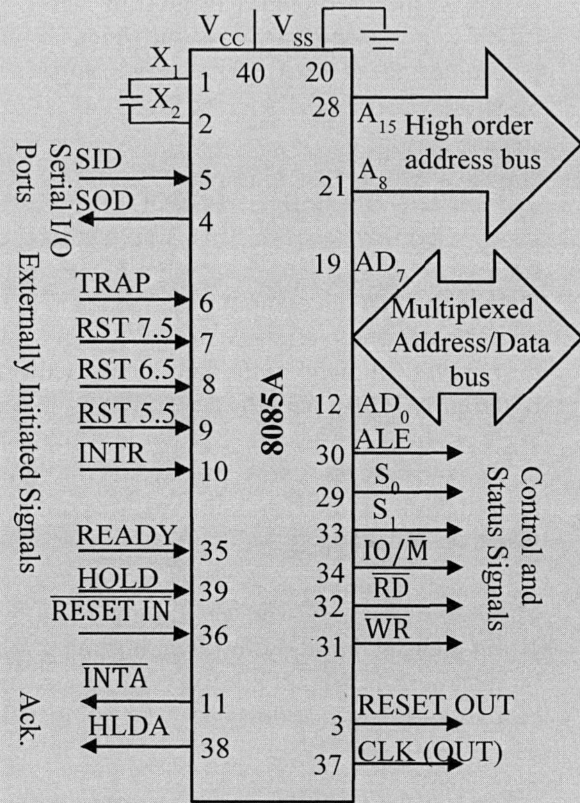

Fig 1.9(b): Grouping of 8085A pins

Address and Data Bus: The 8085 CPU has 16-bit address bus A_{15}-A_0 and 8-bit data bus D_7-D_0. To reduce the overall pin count, the lower order address bus A_7-A_0 has been multiplexed with data bus lines D_7-D_0. For memory access, corresponding to the 16-bit address, the higher order address bits A_{15}-A_8 are held continuously at higher order address bus. However, the lower order address bits, A_7-A_0 are held on the lines AD_7-AD_0 only for some initial time. After that, the data corresponding to the access is available on the lines AD_7-AD_0. A special control signal, ALE (*Address Latch Enable*) is kept high for the duration in which the address bits

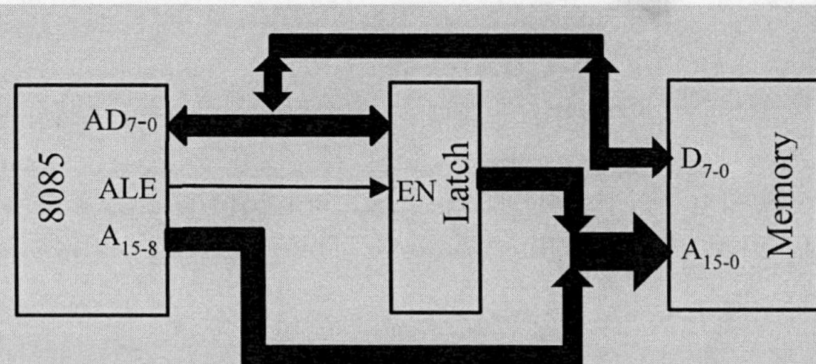

Fig 1.10: Address bus demultiplexing

are available in AD_7-AD_0. ALE signal could be used to demultiplex the address and data lines by using an external latch, as shown in Fig 1.10.

X_1, X_2, CLK (OUT): A crystal is connected between X_1 and X_2 to generate clock signal for 8085. Internally, the crystal frequency is divided by 2. Thus, to make the processor work at 3 MHz, the crystal frequency should be 6 MHz. The processor clock is also available at CLK (OUT) pin to connect to other peripherals that may need synchronization with the processor clock.

Externally Initiated Signals: There are several pins in this category. Out of them, INTR, TRAP, RST 7.5, RST 6.5 and RST 5.5 are known as interrupt lines. An activation on these lines will cause the 8085 CPU to suspend its current work and diverge to some special routine, which may be for serving some special device etc. For example, if a keyboard has been interfaced to 8085 via some interrupt line, a key press may cause an interrupt to the processor. The processor now diverges to a special routine to read the key value. Once the service is over, the processor will resume its suspended work. The line $\overline{\text{INTA}}$ is to acknowledge an INTR input. The signals HOLD and HLDA are used for interfacing other bus masters to the system. A bus master may be responsible for bulk data transfer from memory. On getting signal in the HOLD line, the 8085 relinquishes its control over address, data and control lines. It is acknowledged in the HLDA pin. The bus control is regained via interrupt when the secondary bus master no more needs the bus. On getting a low in the $\overline{\text{RESET IN}}$ line, the processor resets with its program counter becoming zero and activating the RESET OUT pin to inform the interfaced devices.

Serial I/O Ports: The lines SID (Serial Input Data) and SOD (Serial Output Data) can be used for serial I/O operations, one bit at a time.

Status Signals: Signals like $\overline{\text{RD}}$, $\overline{\text{WR}}$ are used for memory interfaces. The lines S_0, S_1 and IO/$\overline{\text{M}}$ indicates the operation that the 8085 is currently doing, such as, memory read, memory write, I/O read, I/O write, fetch, interrupt etc.

1.3.2 Internal Architecture of 8085

Fig 1.11 shows the internal architecture of 8085A CPU. This is also known as the *Processor Programming Model*, since it depicts the programming resources of the CPU, available to the user/programmer. For the 8085A CPU, it consists of a set of general purpose and a few special purpose registers.

General Purpose Registers (GPRs): There are six general purpose registers to store 8-bit data inside the CPU. These are named as B, C, D, E, H and L. The registers can be paired into three 16-

bit registers – BC, DE and HL. The registers can hold operands for different operations. The 16-bit pairs can also be used to provide address to operand stored in memory.

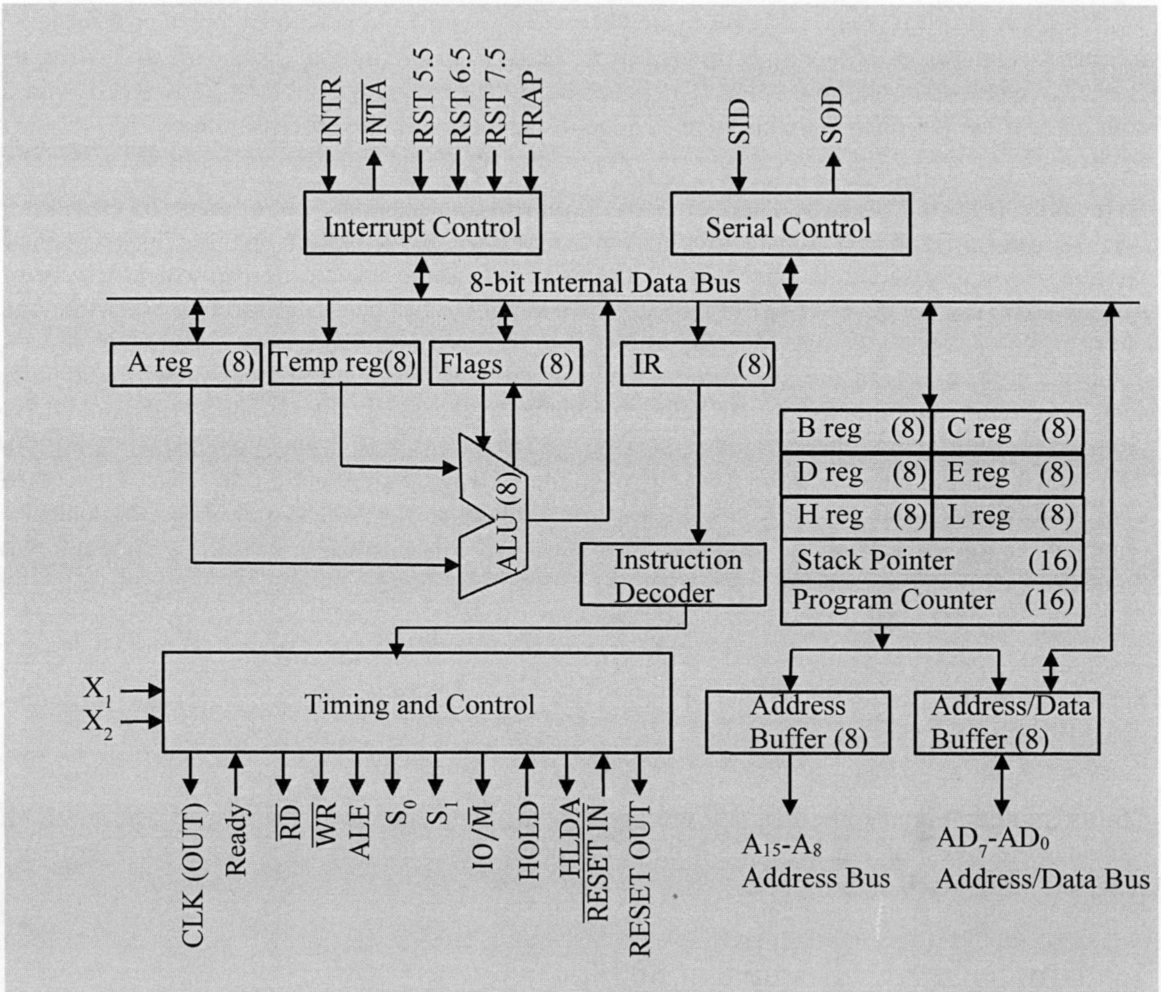

Fig 1.11: Internal Architecture of 8085A

Special Purpose Registers: There are several special purpose registers, as noted next.

1. **Accumulator (A register):** This is an 8-bit register, acting as one of the source operands and the destination for all ALU operations. ALU can perform 8-bit arithmetic and logic operations. While carrying out the ALU operation, a temporary register (marked as Temp in Fig 1.11) holds the second operand for two-operand operations.

2. **Flags:** This is an 8-bit register, though only 5 bits of it are used to contain status information corresponding to the last ALU operation. The flag bits are Zero (Z), Carry (CY), Sign (S), Parity (P) and Auxiliary Carry (AC).
3. **Program Counter (PC):** A 16-bit register that contains the address of the memory location corresponding to the next instruction to be executed.
4. **Stack Pointer (SP):** A 16-bit register that is used to point to a RAM location corresponding to "stack". The "stack" is a part of RAM that is used in the context of subprogram call or an interrupt. For both these situations, processor saves the return address in stack, before jumping to the subprogram. So that, when the subprogram/service routine is over, the PC could be reloaded with the value saved in stack, and thus resume the suspended operation. Availability of stack aids in realizing nested subprograms as well.

1.3.3 Instruction Set of 8085

The instructions supported by the 8085 CPU can be classified into five groups, as detailed in Table 1.3. A complete discussion on the same is beyond the scope of the book. Readers may consult the references mentioned at the end of the unit for the same.

Table 1.3: Classification of 8085 instructions

Type	*Purpose*	*Examples*

Data Transfer	Transfer data from source to destination. The source may be a register, a memory location or an immediate value. Destination may be a register or a memory location. Both operands cannot be memory.	MOV C, A ; A register copied to register C
		MVI B, 4FH ; B register gets 4FH
		MOV A, M ; A gets Memory[address in HL]
		LXI H, 125AH ; H gets 12H, L gets 5AH

Arithmetic Operations	Several arithmetic operations are supported – addition, subtraction, increment, decrement.	ADD B ; A gets A + B SUB C ; A gets A – C INR L ; L gets L + 1
Logical Operations	Logical operations, such as, AND, OR, XOR, Rotate, Compare, Complement are supported.	ANA B ; A gets A AND B CMP C ; Compare A with C, flags affected RLC ; Rotate accumulator left
Branching	Jump conditionally or unconditionally, call subprogram, return from subprogram	JMP 1000H ; PC loaded with 1000H JC 1000H ; PC loaded with 1000H is CY=1 CALL 1000H ; Subprogram call RET ; Return from subroutine

Machine Control	Special instructions affecting the operation of the CPU	HLT ; Halt the CPU operation RST ; Software interrupt NOP ; Do nothing

Example 1.5: The following is a 8085 code fragment that can find the maximum of a set of numbers stored from the memory location 3000H. The number of numbers in the set is stored at location 3000H, the numbers start from 3001H. The largest number will be stored at location 5000H.

```
    LXI H, 3000H     ; Set HL-pair to the address of the array
    MOV C, M         ; Get number of numbers in C
    INX H            ; Make HL-pair to point to the first number
    MOV A, M         ; Get first number in A, assume it to be the largest
    DCR C            ; Decrement count
L1: INX H            ; Make HL-pair point to the next number
    CMP M            ; Compare current largest in A with next number
    JNC L2           ; If CY=0, it means A is still the largest, no action
    MOV A, M         ; Update new largest in A
L2: DCR C            ; Decrement count
    JNZ L1           ; Goto L1, if some numbers left
    STA 5000H        ; Store the largest at memory location 5000H
```

1.4 8086: A 16-bit Microprocessor

The processor 8086 was introduced in 1978 with 20-bit address bus and 16-bit data bus. However, as many of the existing microprocessor based systems were developed around 8085 processor with 8-bit data bus. In the year 1979, a variant 8088 was introduced with internal architecture same as 8086 but having 8-bit external data bus. Both 8086 and 8088 are 40-pin chips. Over 8085 or other 8-bit processor and many of the interfaced devices had 8-bit data bus only, necessity was felt to have a processors, 16-bit 8086/88 processor enjoys advantages like increased memory addressing (1 mega, compared to 64 kilo), increased speed (upto 10 MHz), powerful instruction set, possibility of working in a multiprocessor environment. The 8086 chip can operate in two modes – the *minimum* mode and the *maximum* mode. The minimum mode is very close in operation as 8085. Details of signals in the minimum mode has been shown in Fig 1.12. The $MN/\overline{MX}$ pin set to '1' forces the minimum mode, while setting the input to '0' enables the maximum mode operation. For the maximum mode operation, a bus controller (such as, 8288) is employed to generate the necessary control signals. Pins of 8086 change their functionality slightly to give inputs to the bus controller. For example, the pins S0, S1 and S2 are introduced instead of $\overline{DEN}$, $DT/\overline{R}$ and $M/\overline{IO}$ respectively. Another control LOCK is used to prevent other processors from getting control of the bus.

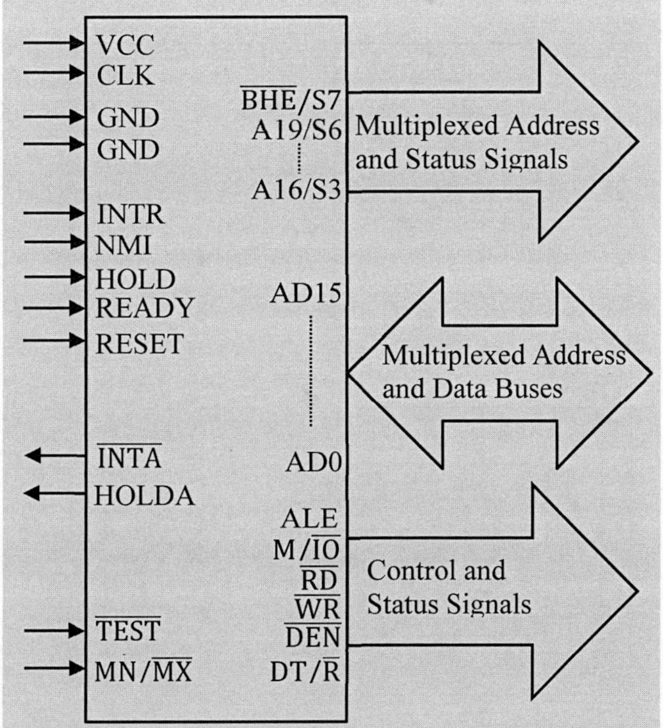

Fig 1.12: The 8086 in Minimum Mode

1.4.1 Internal Architecture of 8086

The internal architecture of 8086 CPU has been shown in Fig 1.13. It can be logically divided into two internal units – the *Bus Interface Unit* (*BIU*) and the *Execution Unit* (*EU*). BIU is responsible for fetching instructions, read/write data from/to memory locations and I/O ports. EU is entrusted with the job of executing the instructions fetched by the BIU.

Bus Interface Unit (BIU): The BIU interfaces the 8086 with external memory and I/O devices. The 8086 has 20-bit address bus and a 16-bit data bus. Thus, it can access a total of 1 mega memory locations of size 16-bit each. A 20-bit address produced by the 8086 processor consists of two parts – *segment* and *offset*, each of 16-bit width. An address is computed by left shifting the 16-bit segment value by 4 bits, creating a 20-bit value and then adding the 16-bit offset to it. That is,

$$address = 16 \times segment\ value + offset$$

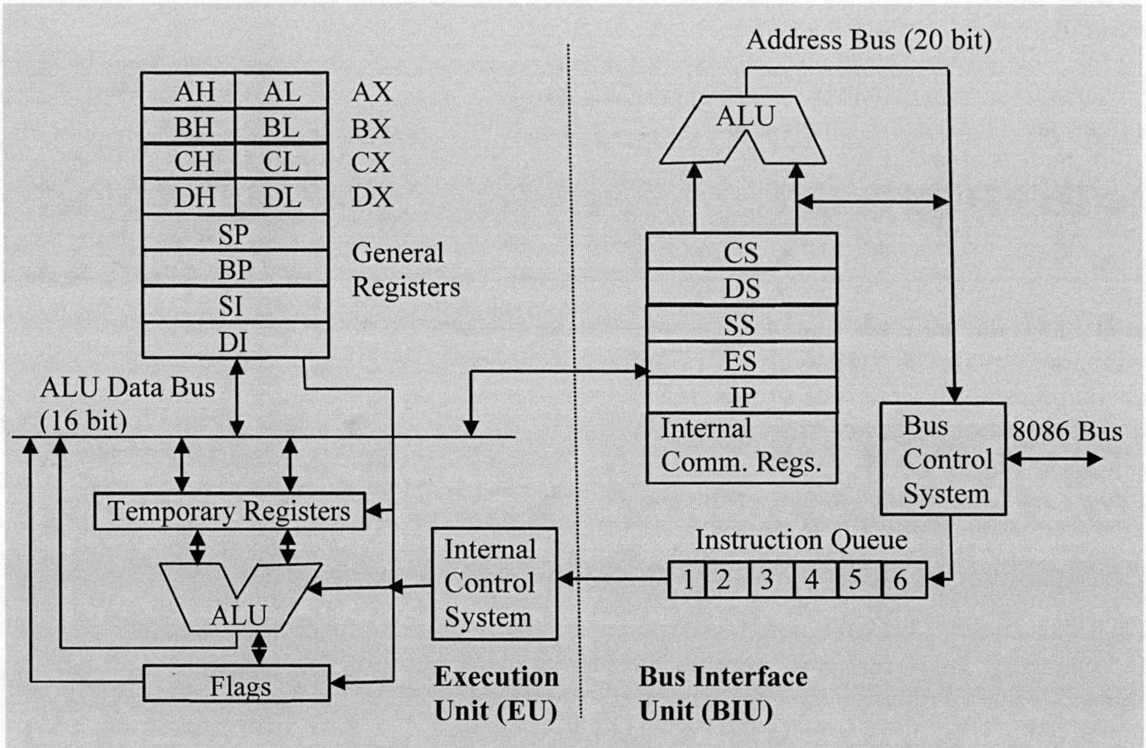

Fig 1.13: Internal Architecture of 8086

To specify the segment part, the 8086/88 CPU uses four segment registers, each of 16-bit width – *Code Segment* register (CS), *Data Segment* register (DS), *Stack Segment* register (SS) and *Extra Segment* register (ES). The processor allows four active segments for any program, at a time. The code segment of a program is supposed to contain the program code. The data and stack segments are to contain the data part and the stack part of the program, respectively. An additional segment is allowed that is typically used as an extra data segment. When a program is loaded into the memory, the segment registers CS, DS, ES and SS are initialized suitably to point to the base of those segments. It may be noted that each segment can be of size upto 64 k, thus the amount of active part of a program, at any point of time is $4 \times 64\ k = 256\ k$. Of course, the segment registers can be reloaded with some other values to refer to program fragments (code, data etc.) beyond 256 k size limit.

To perform program fetch, another 16-bit register, *Instruction Pointer* (IP) is used. IP is equivalent to PC on 8085. To get the next instruction from memory, the register pair CS:IP is used to generate the 20-bit address, $16 \times CS + IP$ using the 20-bit ALU present in the BIU. Successive bytes are fetched into an *Instruction Queue* (6 bytes in 8086, 4 in 8088). Presence of this instruction queue enables fetch-execute overlap in 8086/88. When the current instruction is being executed by the EU, BIU may bring in successive instructions, upto 6 bytes, into the queue.

Execution Unit (EU): The EU is responsible for decoding and executing individual instructions. It has a 16-bit ALU for performing arithmetic and logic operations. Apart from a few temporary registers (not available to the user), there are three sets of registers, as noted next.

- *General Purpose Registers*: There are four, 16-bit general purpose registers – AX, BX, CX and DX. Each of them can also be used to behave as two 8-bit registers. AX is composed of 8-bit registers AH and AL, BX containing BH and BL, CX containing CH and CL and DX being composed of DH and DL. The register AX also behaves as accumulator, as in 8085.
- *Pointer Registers*: Stack Pointer (SP) and Base Pointer (BP) are the two 16-bit registers, used to access data in the stack segment. SP is incremented/decremented automatically during stack operations. Memory access via SP and BP uses SS as the segment register, the address being computed as, $16 \times SS + SP$ (or BP).
- *Index Registers*: The 16-bit Source Index (SI) and Destination Index (DI) registers are used primarily for indexed memory access. By default, the access via SI uses DS as the segment register (address = $16 \times DS + SI$) and via DI uses ES as the segment register (address = $16 \times ES + DI$). They are also used in single-byte instruction MOVSB to transfer the content from a source block (pointed to by DS:SI) to a destination block (pointed to by ES:DI) with CX register holding the number of bytes to be transferred.

The instruction set of 8086/88 processor can be grouped into the following categories.

- Data Transfer Instructions – MOV, XCHG, PUSH, POP etc.
- Arithmetic Instructions – ADD, SUB, MUL, DIV etc.
- Logical Instructions – AND, OR etc.
- String Manipulation Instructions – MOVS, LODS, STOS, REP etc.
- Process Control Instructions – STC, STD, NOP, HALT, WAIT, LOCK etc.
- Control Transfer Instructions – JMP, JE, JC, CALL, RET etc.

A detailed discussion on the instructions is beyond the scope of this book and can be found in the references noted at the end of the Unit.

1.5 Microcomputer Systems

Computing systems built around microprocessors are commonly known as microcomputers. They have got applications in almost all domains of scientific and business computations. Apart from the processor, such systems typically contain components, such as, RAM, ROM, General Purpose Input-Output (GPIO) interfaces, Communication interface, Timers, Counters, Analog Interfaces (such as, Analog-to-Digital and Digital-to-Analog Converters (ADCs and DACs) etc.

The generic components in a microcomputer system has been shown in Fig 1.14. The microcomputer systems available today can be broadly classified into the following categories.

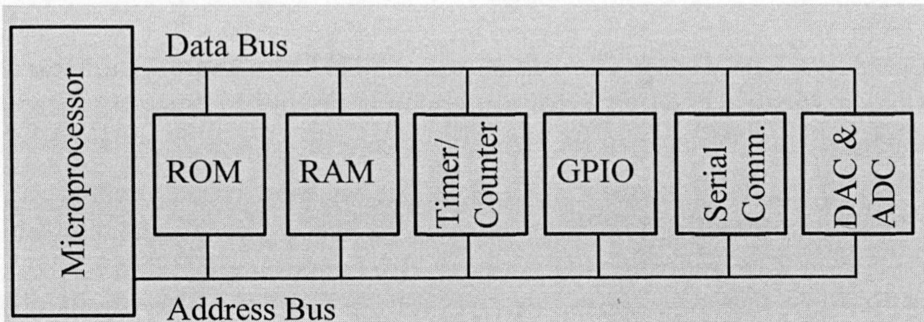

Fig 1.14: Generic Microcomputer System

1. *Personal Computer (PC)/Desktop*: These are mostly single-user systems with applications, such as, office automation, finance, internet access, limited computation etc. They often contain large number of system and application software.
2. *Workstation*: These are high performance desktop systems that specialize in executing certain engineering/scientific applications efficiently. Typical examples of such applications are Computer-Aided Design (CAD), Computer-Aided Engineering (CAE) and Computer-Aided Manufacturing (CAM). The workstations generally possess high-end microprocessors, large memory (both primary and secondary) and often a high-resolution screen, specialized I/O devices etc.
3. *Single-Board Computers*: These are computers housed on a single *Printed Circuit Board* (*PCB*) and is often used for educational and training purposes. Apart from the microprocessor, the board contains limited amount of ROM, RAM, chips to realize timer/counter operations and interfaces for very simple I/O devices (like matrix keyboard, seven-segment LED, LCD modules, switches for digital inputs, etc.). The ROM contains a simple *monitor* program, responsible for monitoring the system resources and aiding in executing user programs.
4. *Single-Chip Microcomputers* (*Microcontrollers*): In this category, the entire microcomputer system is fabricated onto a single silicon chip. Such systems are typically used in different controller applications.

1.6 8-Bit Microcontroller Architecture

Fig 1.15 shows the block diagram of a typical microcontroller. On a single chip, it integrates a processor along with its interrupt logic, oscillator to generate clock, memory (ROM and RAM), Analog-to-Digital and Digital-to-Analog Converters, Parallel and Serial I/O Interfaces, one or more Timers/Counters etc. However, to keep the area and power consumption within a reasonable limit, the processor is often made much simpler than powerful microprocessors, ROM and RAM space is limited to hold small application programs only. Microcontrollers are most widely used in dedicated applications, known as *Embedded Systems*, such as, mobile phones, digital camera, security alarm, plant control etc. to name a few. Some microcontrollers, particularly those used in embedded applications have specialized interfaces like Serial Peripheral Interface (SPI), Inter Integrated Circuits (IIC/I2C) etc.

Intel introduced the 8-bit microcontroller 8051 in 1981 with 128-byte RAM, 4kB ROM, two timers, one serial port and four 8-bit parallel ports. After its initial success, Intel allowed other manufacturers to produce different variants of 8051. Accordingly, variants like 8031, 8052 etc. came. Some other 8-bit microcontrollers that came into existence are Zylog's Z8, Microchip 16C74 and 16F874 from PIC. Table 1.4 shows a comparison between the most commonly available 8-bit microcontrollers.

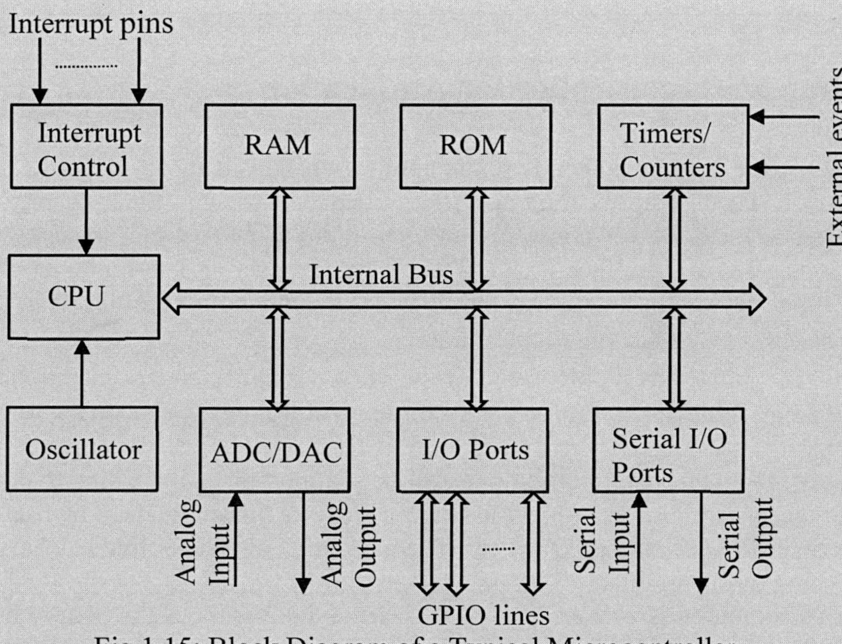

Fig 1.15: Block Diagram of a Typical Microcontroller

Table 1.4: Comparison between 8-bit Microcontrollers

Microcontroller	*RAM (Bytes)*	*ROM (kB)*	*Speed MHz*	*No. of Timers / Counters*
8031	128	0	12	2
8051	128	4	12	2
8052	256	8	12	3
8751	256	8 EPROM	12	3

87C58	256	32 EPROM	12-24	3
87C51GB	256	8 EPROM	12-16	3
89C61x2	1024	64 Flash	20-33	3
AT89S8252	256	8 Flash, 2 EPROM	24	3
PIC16C74	192	4	20	3
AVRATTINY10	32	1	12	1
Z8	1024	8	20	2

1.6.1 Selecting Microcontroller for Application

With many different microcontrollers available from various vendors, it is extremely important to choose the most suitable one for an application. This is more due to the fact that these devices are broadly used in application-specific embedded systems. Such systems have many concerns in terms of size, power consumption, cost, time-to-market etc. to name a few. Each microcontroller has its own architecture, unique instruction set and in-built peripherals. Thus, choosing the proper device for an application becomes a challenge. The following are the major concerns in selecting a candidate microcontroller.

1. Whether the highest available speed of the device is sufficient for the application or not. As shown in Table 1.4, even for the 8-bit microcontrollers, speed varies from 12 MHz to 33 MHz.
2. The size of the microcontroller chip is also very important as it is going to decide the PCB size for the system. For example, the chip may have a 40-pin dual-inline packaging (DIP), 40-pin quad-flat packaging (QFP) etc. The packaging also determines the assembling and prototyping of the product.
3. Power consumption is also an important issue, as it determines the battery life for battery operated applications. With increasing power consumption, heat generation also increases which may necessitate cooling arrangements.
4. Amount of on-chip RAM/ROM space available should ideally be able to hold the entire program for the application. Otherwise, external memory is needed to be interfaced, subject to the availability of such facility with the microcontroller. It may be noted that access to on-chip memory may be 10-100 times faster than the off-chip external memory access.
5. Availability of other on-chip resources, such as, number of I/O pins, number of timers and their sizes, availability of ADCs and DACs along with the number of channels and resolution etc. These must cater to the requirements of the application.
6. Cost of a single microcontroller chip becomes a deciding factor in the overall cost of the system.
7. Ease of upgradation to higher performance and/or lower power consumption variants.

8. Availability of good development platform. Though Table 1.4 has listed a number of microcontrollers, each one has its own instruction set. Mastering all of them is very difficult, if not impossible, for any system designer. To solve this problem, the vendors of these chips normally come up with a set of software to help in programming the microcontroller. It is often the case that the development platform allows the program to be written in some high-level language, such as C. Microcontroller-specific compiler and assembler translate the program to machine language. User-friendliness of such development platform often bias the selection of microcontroller by the designer.
9. Availability of microcontroller chip in the market is another guiding factor. For easy availability, the original designers of microcontrollers often license other companies to manufacture their chips. For example, the widely popular 8051 chip is produced by companies like Intel, Atmel, Infineon, Dallas, Philips (NXP) etc. Many of the microcontrollers are now available as *Intellectual Property Core* (*IP Core*) to be integrated in single chip *System-on-Chip* (*SoC*) designs. With the advancement in VLSI design, this has become a possibility.

1.7 Lower and Higher Level Languages

The CPU of a microcontroller understands the instructions coded in binary form only. Thus, any program to be executed by the processor, must be in this format. A program in binary form is called a *machine language* program. Though easily understood by the processor, it is too cumbersome for the system designer to write a program in machine language. At the same time, the system designer may wish to work close to the actual CPU hardware (in terms of CPU registers, ALU operations etc.) to have a much optimized version of his/her program. To enable it, processor designers have created an intermediary language for the valid instruction set of a processor. This is called the *assembly language* of the processor. For every instruction supported by the processor, the designer has a fixed, binary coded instruction in the machine language. Typical example may be the assembly language statement "ADD B" of 8085, which has a fixed machine language code 87H. A user may write the program in assembly language in a text file. It will be converted to a machine level binary file by a tool (often provided by the processor designer), called *assembler*. This has been shown in Fig 1.16. Programs written in assembly language interacts directly with CPU registers and other system resources. Thus, the size of the program and the time needed for its execution can be determined by the programmer easily by consulting the user manual of the processor.

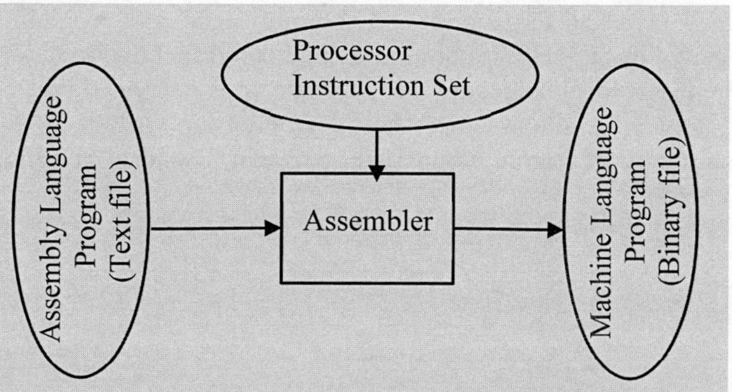

Fig 1.16: Assembly Language vs. Machine Language

Thus, machine language is the lowest level at which a program may be written for a processor. Assembly language constitutes the next higher level. However, for a program of medium to high complexity, writing it directly in assembly language is also difficult. In the absence of programming constructs like *loop*, *if-then-else*, *switch-case* etc., it is too tedious to express the program logic elegantly in assembly language. Also, the maintainability, debugging and upgradation of assembly language program become important issues. Even with a moderate degree of documentation of program code, it is very difficult for a third person to understand an assembly language program. In contrast, programs written in languages like C/C++ allow all the programming facilities. Such languages are known as *higher-level languages*. A program written in a high-level language is converted to machine level by means of tools known as *compilers*. Compilers use the assembler of a processor to target the final code to a specific processor. Program updating, migrating to other processors also become very easy. The compiler may be asked to generate the assembly language program also, as a by-product. This has been shown in Fig 1.17. It should be understood that due to automated translation of programs written in higher level languages, the machine code generated by a compiler may not be highly optimized, compared to the assembly language program written by an experienced system programmer. A summary of feature comparison between low-level and high-level languages has been shown in Table 1.5.

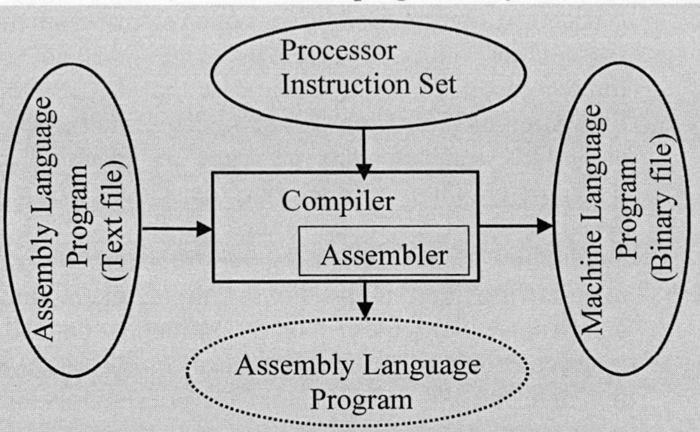

Fig 1.17: High-Level Language Compilation

Table 1.5: Feature comparison between low-level and high-level languages

Feature	*Low-level Language*	*High-level Language*
Programmer friendly	No	Yes
Machine friendly	Yes	No
Debugging	Difficult	Easy
Maintenance	Difficult	Easy
Compiler/Interpreter	Not needed	Needed
Porting across platforms	Not portable	Can be ported
Library functions	Not available	Available

1.8 Integrated Development Environment

From the discussion in the last section, to realize a program written in some high-level language, using a particular microcontroller requires a set of tools (such as, compilers) specific to that processor. To make such system design, development and debugging easy, the vendors often come up with an integrated environment that aids in the entire development cycle. Such an environment, called an *Integrated Development Environment* (*IDE*) contains all the tools necessary for microcontroller based system design. An IDE typically contains a code editor, a compiler and a debugger. A *Graphical User Interface* (*GUI*) is also provided. Apart from the domain of microcontrollers, IDEs are also available in other areas. For example, *Microsoft Visual Studio* provides an environment for developing computer programs, supporting various programming languages.

For an IDE targeted to microcontroller based system design, the tools included in the IDE are as follows.

1. *Editor*: This is possibly the first tool in the chain leading to system development. The program code, in some high-level language, is written using the editor. The code is also often called the *source code.*
2. *Compiler*: Once the source code is ready, the compiler is used to translate it into machine code, also called *object code*. It should be understood that the IDE may be running on a PC with Pentium processor, whereas, the compiler in IDE is producing code for some other microcontroller, say 8051. Here, 8051 is the *target processor*. Such a compiler running on a system and producing code for some other target processor is called a *Cross Compiler*.
3. *Assembler*: The source code may also be written in the assembly language of the processor. An assembler will be used to translate the same to machine language. The assembler is also included as a step in the compilation process.
4. *Linker*: A linker may combine a number of object code files into a single executable. This facilitates a number of designers developing parts of the program and combine into one module later. Apart from the modules developed by the designers, an IDE may contain predesigned libraries to be included

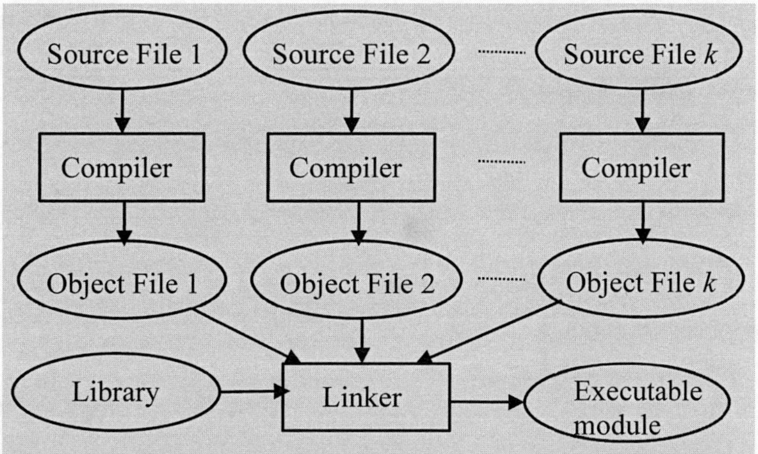

Fig 1.18: Linking multiple source and library modules

in the executable. For example, there may be library modules to glow an LED or reading some sensor values, available as library routines readily integratable with the system developed. Fig 1.18 shows the details.

5. *Debugger*: A debugger is a software running inside the IDE that can be used to diagnose logical errors in the code. The debugging can be done by the help of a *simulator* or an *emulator*.
    a. *Simulator*: A simulator for the microcontroller tries to model the entire behaviour of the microcontroller in software. However, it should be understood that a simulator cannot match the speed of a real microcontroller. Simulating the external events (such as, inputs from sensors arriving at desired time) is also very difficult. Thus, a simulator may not be able to truly mimic the behaviour of the overall system. Simulator is best suited to test algorithms that run completely within the microcontroller.
    b. *Emulator*: This is a piece of hardware that behaves exactly as the microcontroller chip. The functionality of the microcontroller is emulated in real-time. In real microcontroller, the program code is placed in ROM/EPROM which makes it difficult to modify. On the other hand, an emulator stores the program in RAM which behaves as the program memory. The RAM code can be modified quickly to aid in the debugging process. Once the designer is satisfied with the performance of the system in the emulator, the program may be downloaded into ROM/EPROM of the microcontroller. Some microcontrollers (such as, 8051) allows external program and data memory to be interfaced with them. For such chips, the emulator may utilize the microcontroller itself for the purpose of emulation, with program stored in external RAM instead of on-chip ROM.

Some of the well-known IDEs for microcontrollers include *MPLAB* for PIC microcontrollers, *Arduino* for Arduino microcontrollers and *Keil* for range of microcontrollers like 8051, ARM7, C16x/ST10 etc.

Example 1.16: Fig 1.19 shows the structure and essential components of *Keil μVision* IDE. It has full featured source code editor, device database for configuring the tools, integrated compiler, assembler and linker, source- and assembler-level debugger with peripheral simulator, debugging on target hardware and flash programming to download final code into the flash ROM of the microcontroller.

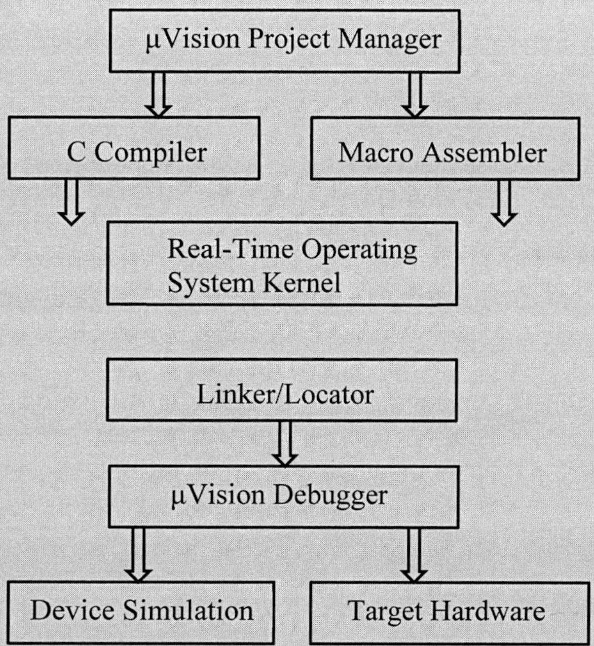

Fig 1.19: Components in Keil μVision IDE

UNIT SUMMARY

Microprocessors and microcontrollers are heart of any computing system – it may be a microcomputer or any other electronic system targeted to a dedicated application. Microprocessors constitute the CPU of a microcomputer. It contains a dedicated set of registers, one or more ALU, decoding logic and controller for operation. Memory chips and peripherals are interfaced with the CPU via address-, data- and control buses. Program instructions are fetched to the CPU, decoded and executed over time steps, using control signals generated by the controller. The 8085 is an eight-bit microprocessor with relatively simple internal architecture and instruction set. This is one of the very widely used microprocessors, primarily before the introduction of 16-bit microprocessor 8086/88 and its advanced successors. When an entire microcomputer is put into a single chip, it is called a microcontroller. With memory and other commonly used peripherals put into a single chip, it has found wide applications in electronic system design. One of the most popular and well known 8-bit microcontroller is 8051. With several microcontrollers available in the market, choice of the one to be used for an application is often guided by its internal resources, speed, cost etc. Availability of good design environment translating the required functionality specified in high-level language to final machine code of the microcontroller, aiding in debugging and correction, also guides the selection process.

EXERCISES

Multiple Choice Questions

MQ1. The sequence of phases of processor execution is
(A) Fetch-Decode-Execute (B) Decode-Fetch-Execute
(C) Execute-Fetch-Decode (D) Execute-Decode-Fetch

MQ2.The second phase of instruction execution is
(A) Fetch (B) Decode (C) Execute (D) None of the other options

MQ3. The item which is definitely not part of microprocessor
(A) ALU (B) Register (C) Bus (D) None of the other options

MQ4. The operand present in all arithmetic/logic operations in 8085 is
(A) A (B) Immediate value (C) B (D) HL

MQ5. Destination in all arithmetic/logic operations in 8085 is
(A) A (B) Immediate value (C) B (D) HL

MQ6. Serial input of 8085 is
(A) SID (B) SOD (C) SLD (D) None of the other options

MQ7. In 8085, compared to crystal frequency, processor frequency is
(A) Same (B) Half (C) Double (D) None of the other options

MQ8. To get control of address and data buses from 8085, the line to be used is
(A) HOLD (B) HLDA (C) RESET (D) None of the other options

MQ9. In 8085, the active state values of INTR and INTA signals are
(A) Both high (B) INTR high, INTA low
(C) INTR low, INTA high (D) Both low

MQ10. In 8086 and 8088 instruction queues are of size (in bytes)
(A) 6, 6 (B) 4, 6 (C) 6, 4 (D) 4, 4

MQ11. In 8086, data access by which register uses SS as the default segment register
(A) SP (B) BP (C) Both SP and BP (D)DI

MQ12. In 8086, for MOVS instruction, the source block is pointed to by
(A) CS:DI (B) DS:SI (C) ES:DI (D) SS:SI

MQ13. In 8086, width of physical address, width of offset and segment part are
(A) 16 bits each (B) 20 bits each
(C) 20, 16, 16 bits (D)16, 20, 20 bits

MQ14. The maximum number of active segments at a time in an 8086 program is
(A) 1 (B) 2 (C) 3 (D) 4

MQ15. Number of segment registers in 8086 is
(A) One (B) Two (C) Three (D) Four

MQ16. Which of the following is NOT a criterion in choosing a microcontroller?
(A) Number of pins (B) On-chip debugging
(C) Easy availability (D) None of the options mentioned

MQ17. Microcontrollers do not have

(A) Registers (B) Timers
(C) DAC, ADC (D) None of the other options

MQ18. In microcontrollers, access to registers is
(A) Faster than on-chip RAM (B) Slower than on-chip RAM
(C) Same speed as on-chip RAM (D) None of the other options

MQ19. In microcontrollers memory access is generally faster than microprocessors because
(A) Memory is on-chip (B) Length of buses small
(C) Data access is less (D) None of the other options

MQ20. A low-level language is friendly to
(A) Programmer (B) Processor
(C) Both Programmer and Processor (D) None of the other options

MQ21. Porting of programs across microcontrollers will be easy if the program is written in
(A) Machine language (B) Assembly language
(C) High-level language (D) None of the other options

MQ22. Simulator and emulator are
(A) Both software (B) Software and hardware respectively
(C) Hardware and Software respectively (D) Both hardware

MQ23. The first tool in IDE tool flow is
(A) Editor (B) Compiler (C) Assembler (D) Debugger

MQ24. Executable code is produced by
(A) Editor (B) Compiler (C) Linker (D) Debugger

MQ25. The tool that can give more confidence on the correctness of the design is
(A) Simulator (B) Emulator (C) Compiler (D) Linker

Answers of Multiple Choice Questions

1:A, 2:B, 3:D, 4:A, 5:A, 6:A, 7:B, 8:A, 9:B, 10:C, 11:C, 12:B, 13:C, 14:D, 15:D, 16:D, 17:D, 18:C, 19:A, 20:B, 21:C, 22:B, 23: A, 24: C, 25: B

Short Answer Type Questions

SQ1. Enumerate the CPU signal lines to be connected to memory for interfacing.

SQ2. With respect to Example 1.4, list down the control signals to be activated at different time steps to execute the instruction "SUB R0, R1, R2" that computes R2 $\leftarrow$ R0 – R1.

SQ3. How is the ALE signal used in demultiplexing of AD_7-AD_0 in 8085?

SQ4. How does the ALU in BIU differ from the ALU in EU of 8086?

SQ5. How does the physical address get computed in 8086?

SQ6. How does a microcomputer system differ from a general computer system?

SQ7. Identify the typical components of a microcontroller.

SQ8. How does a microcontroller differ from a microprocessor?

SQ9. Compare the features of low- and high-level languages.

SQ10. Identify the components of an IDE.

Long Answer Type Questions

LQ1. A hypothetical CPU has 15-bit address bus and 8-bit data bus. Draw a diagram depicting the interfacing of 8kB RAM and 4kB ROM with it using memory chips of size 2k×4-bits each. Show all control line connections as well.

LQ2. Compare between the operations of 8085 with 8088.

LQ3. Enumerate the criteria guiding the selection of a microcontroller for an application.

LQ4. Compare the features of high-level language C with the assembly language of 8085.

LQ5. How does the operation of a compiler differ from that of linker?

Numerical Problems

NQ1. A hypothetical CPU has 10-bit address bus. Assuming the system to have a 512 byte memory chip interfaced with it, compute the maximum number of peripheral devices that could be accessed by the processor.

NQ2. Suppose the content of registers A and B of the 8085 CPU are 139 and 125. Compute the content of A register after executing the instruction "ADD B".

NQ3. Compute the address put onto the address bus of 8086 processor if the contents of CS and IP registers are 20E0H and 0231H.

NQ4. Compute the frequency at which 8085 processor will work if the crystal has a frequency of 6.2 MHz.

NQ5. The 8051 CPU has 128 byte RAM and 4kB ROM space. Determine the number of address lines sufficient to access the program and data memory respectively.

Answers of Numerical Problems

1: 512, 2: 8, 3: 21031H, 4: 3.1 MHz, 5: 7, 12

KNOW MORE

Going back to the history of development of microcontrollers, during 1970s, *Gary Boone* of *Texas Instruments* discovered a single integrated circuit chip that could hold all the essential circuit components to make a calculator. With this chip, only a keypad and a display unit are to be added to make a complete calculator. The chip with around 5000 transistors provided 3000 bits of program memory and 128 bits of data memory. The invention was named as *TMS1802NC*. Looking into the broad range of requirements from users, TI continued to improve upon the chip. By 1974, the microcontroller *TMS1000* was commercially available. On the other hand, Intel produced their first microcontroller 8048 in 1976 and introduced the hugely successful 8051 in 1980. In the 1990s, electrically erasable flash memories came. As a result, a number of microcontrollers from Microchip and Atmel use this flash memory technologies. Further developments include advanced microcontrollers, like ARM. These devices are being used in almost every domain of human life, starting from automobiles, lighting, communication, low-power hand-held devices (such as, smart phones) to even tooth brushes and toys.

REFERENCES AND SUGGESTED READINGS

[1] S. Chattopadhyay, SWAYAM/NPTEL course on "Microprocessors and Microcontrollers", https://onlinecourses.nptel.ac.in/noc20_ee42/preview.

[2] R. Gaonkar, "Microprocessor Architecture, Programming and Applications with the 8085", Prentice Hall.

[3] M.A. Mazidi, R.D. McKinlay, J.G. Mazidi, "The 8051 Microcontroller: A Systems Approach", Pearson.

Dynamic QR Code for Further Reading

S. Chattopadhyay, SWAYAM/NPTEL course on "Microprocessors and Microcontrollers".

2 The 8051 Architecture

UNIT SPECIFICS

Through this unit, the following concepts have been elaborated:

- *Features of different commonly available 8051 variants;*
- *Functionality of its pins along with their function-wise grouping;*
- *The internal architecture of the 8051 chip, in terms of its CPU, memory, I/O ports and timers;*
- *The clock and reset circuitry for the 8051;*
- *Usage of parts of memory as stack;*
- *Hardware structure of I/O port pins;*
- *Interfacing of external program and data memory chips;*
- *Concepts of timing diagrams and instruction execution cycles;*
- *A classification summary of the instructions of 8051;*
- *Assembly language program structure for the 8051.*

The overall discussion in the unit is to give the details of the 8051 architecture, starting with the pin diagram of the chip and the internal block diagram. It has been assumed that the reader has gone through the Unit-1 of this book and has got an initial grasp on the general processor structure, memory interfacing and instruction execution process. A basic understanding of programming will be helpful for this unit, as well, particularly to follow the overview of assembly language programming part. A good number of examples have been included to explain the concepts, wherever needed.

A large number of multiple choice questions, relevant for the topics discussed in this unit, have been provided with their answers. Apart from that, subjective questions of short and long answer type have been included. A few numerical problems with answers have been provided. A list of references and suggested readings have been given, so that, one can go through them for more details. The section "Know More" has been carefully designed so that the supplementary information provided in this part becomes beneficial for the users of the book. This section mainly highlights the initial activity, the history of the development of 8051 and some features of the 8051 chip that have been carried forward to many advanced processors.

RATIONALE

This unit on the 8051 architecture illustrates the internal organization and working of the 8051 chip. Starting with the identification of the features of the 8051 variants, it next looks into the pin-level detail of the chip. The unit discusses about the internal blocks of the 8051 chip, the distribution of on-chip RAM into different portions, such as, register banks, bit- and byte-addressable locations, the special registers etc. and I/O ports. The clock circuitry explains the clock input alternatives, while the reset circuit provides mechanism to reset the chip. The unit discusses how to set up a stack in the RAM. The I/O pins of the 8051 are of special type, providing pin-level control over the I/O operations. The input operation needs a special activity to enable the pins for reading. The on-chip memory of the 8051 is very limited. To go for any medium to large size program, it is necessary to interface external memory modules. This is done by providing the address and data lines through the ports. To understand the operating procedure of the CPU, it is necessary to view the activation of various signals over the time. This can be captured best by the timing diagrams spanning over the clock cycles. The 8051 chip supports a set of instructions of different types – data transfer, arithmetic and logic operations, bit manipulation, program branching etc. In order to write a correct assembly language program, familiarity of operation of the assembler, its input-output formats are required. This unit makes the reader to have a basic understanding of the assembly language program structure and its input/output files. Thus, the unit gives a good understanding of the structure and operation of the 8051 chip.

PRE-REQUISITES

Electronics: Unit 1 of the book

Programming: Basic Computer Programming

UNIT OUTCOMES

List of outcomes of this unit is as follows:

U2-O1: State the functionality of pins of the 8051

U2-O2: Draw block-level diagram of internal architecture of the 8051

U2-O3: Enumerate the registers and their functionalities

U2-O4: State the operation of clock and reset circuitry of the 8051

U2-O5: Draw the structure of I/O pins

U2-O6: Interface external program and data memories to the 8051

U2-O7: Draw timing diagrams for external memory access

U2-O8: List instruction types of the 8051

U2-O9: State the structure of assembly language programs

Unit-2 Outcomes	*EXPECTED MAPPING WITH COURSE OUTCOMES* (1- Weak Correlation; 2- Medium correlation; 3- Strong Correlation)					
	CO-1	*CO-2*	*CO-3*	*CO-4*	*CO-5*	*CO-6*
U2-O1	2	3	1	-	-	-
U2-O2	1	3	-	-	-	-
U2-O3	2	3	-	-	-	-
U2-O4	2	2	-	-	-	-
U2-O5	1	3	-	2	-	-
U2-O6	2	3	-	3	-	-
U2-O7	2	3	-	1	-	-
U2-O8	2	3	1	-	-	-
U2-O9	2	-	1	-	-	-

2.1 Introduction

The microcontroller 8051 is the first one in the MCS-51 family introduced by the Intel Corporation in 1981. It has the resources in it, as noted in Table 2.1. There are two more members in the MCS-51 family. The first one, the 8031 processor, has zero on-chip ROM with other features same as 8051. The second one, the 8052 processor, has several augmented features, compared to 8051. For example, the 8052 has 8kB on-chip ROM, 256 bytes RAM, 3 timers and 8 interrupt sources. Among the 8051 microcontrollers also there are several variants. This has happened as 8051 is fabricated by different manufacturers under different part numbers. The products mainly differ in the memory technology used to realize the ROM. In the following some such variants have been enumerated.

Table 2.1: Features of 8051 Processor

CPU	8 bit
ROM (on-chip)	4 kB
RAM (on-chip)	128 bytes
Timer/Counter	2, 16-bit
Digital I/O	32 pins
Serial Port	1
Interrupts	6
Program memory address space	64 kB
Data memory address space	64 kB

- *8751*: It uses UV-EPROM to realize the on-chip ROM. For programming, PROM burner is needed. It needs a UV-EPROM eraser to erase the content to aid in reprogramming. The erasing takes time upto 20 minutes.
- *AT89C51*: It uses flash memory for on-chip ROM. Thus, the microcontroller needs a ROM burner, however, eraser is not needed. It saves reprogramming time.
- *DS89C4x0*: This constitutes a family of microcontrollers (*x* varying from 2 to 5) with flash ROM. The chips have on-chip loader that can be interfaced to a PC via serial COM ports.
- *OTP versions*: The *one-time-programmable* (OTP) versions of 8051 are available with cheaper unit price, compared to flash versions. These are often used in mass production of systems, once the program logic has been debugged and finalized using the flash versions.

2.2 Pin Distribution

Fig 2.1(a) shows the pin layout of the 8051 chip which is a 40-pin DIP organization. Fig 2.1(b) shows the grouping of pins. In the following, the functionality of each pin has been discussed in brief.

- **V_{CC}** (Pin 40) and **V_{SS}** (Pin 20): These constitute the single power-supply needed by the 8051 chip. VCC is +5V with a current rating of 125mA and the maximum power dissipation 1W.
- **XTAL2** (Pin 18) and **XTAL1/CLKIN** (Pin 19): A crystal of 12 MHz (recommended) is connected between the pins with two 30 pF disc capacitors, as shown in Fig 2.1(b). Alternately, external clock source can be directly connected to XTAL1, with XTAL2 left unconnected.
- **RST** (Pin 9)**:** This is an active high reset input for the 8051. The power-on reset circuitry for the 8051 has been shown in Fig 2.1(b). The circuit consists of a 10μF capacitor and a 8.2kΩ resistor. A push-button switch may be connected in parallel to the capacitor to act

as asynchronous reset input to the 8051. The switch must be closed for at least two *machine cycles* (discussed later) of the processor to give a proper reset pulse.

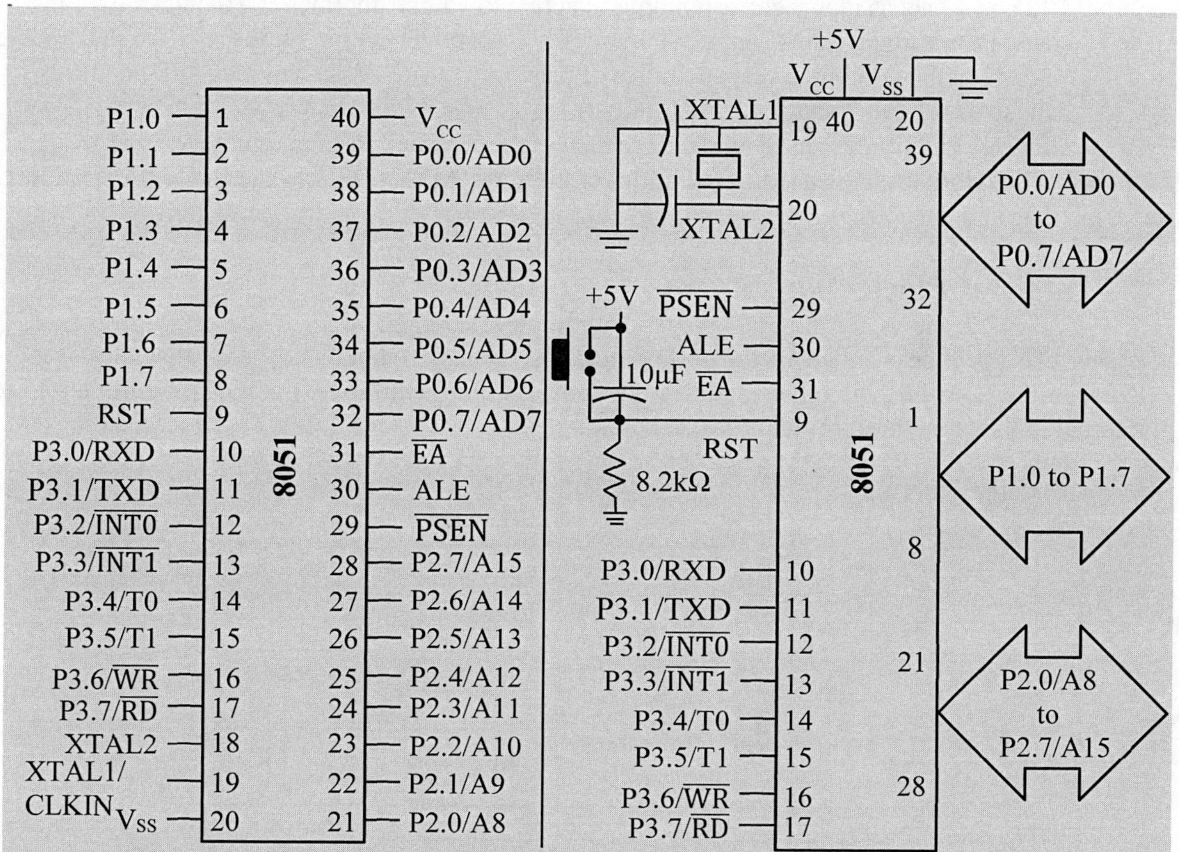

Fig 2.1(a): 8051 pin diagram

Fig 2.1(b): Grouping of 8051 pins

- $\overline{\textbf{EA}}$ (Pin 31): The pin indicates *external access* by the 8051. When set to high, the 8051 uses internal ROM for instructions. When the line is set low, the external memory is accessed.
- **Port 0** (Pins 32 to 39): These pins act as an 8-bit I/O port. The pins are also used to provide multiplexed address-data bus lines AD7-AD0. The port bit lines are open-drain and thus need external pull-up resistors to be connected for their proper operation.
- **Port 1** (Pins 1 to 8): This is an 8-bit I/O port and is the only port whose lines are not assigned additional functions.
- **Port 2** (Pins 21 to 28): The port bit lines are assigned the additional role to provide higher order address lines A8-A15 for external memory access.

- **Port 3** (Pins 10 to 17): The port bits can be used for I/O purposes. However, each pin has got some alternate function assigned to it. The pins 10 and 11 are used for serial I/O. Pins 12 and 13 act as inputs corresponding to active low interrupt lines $\overline{INT0}$ and $\overline{INT1}$. Pins 14 and 15 are timer control inputs T0 and T1, respectively. Finally, the pins 16 and 17 are assigned the additional responsibility of providing write ($\overline{WR}$) and read ($\overline{RD}$) controls for the external data memory access.
- $\overline{\textbf{PSEN}}$ (Pin 29): It is used as strobe to access the external program memory.
- **ALE** (Pin 30): It is used to demultiplex the lines AD7-AD0 into the lower order address bus and data bus.

2.3 Internal Block Diagram

Fig 2.2 shows the internal block diagram level organization of the 8051 processor. It consists of the blocks noted in the following subsections. It should be noted that all accesses between the CPU and the other modules (such as, on-chip memories, timers, I/O ports etc.) are internal to the chip, thus providing fast access.

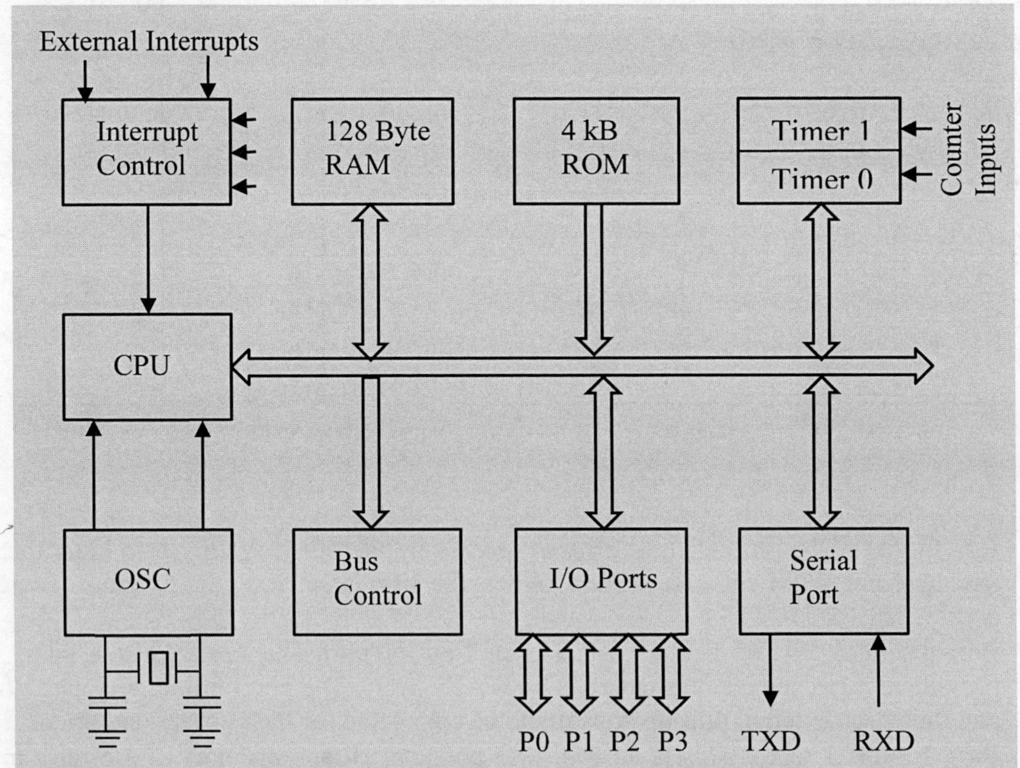

Fig 2.2: Internal Block Diagram of the 8051

2.3.1 CPU

The CPU consists of an *Arithmetic Logic Unit* (*ALU*), *Instruction Decoder and Control* and a number of *registers*. The ALU is a 8-bit one, capable of performing several types of arithmetic and logic operations. Like other CPUs, the instruction from program memory with location pointed to by the *Program Counter* (*PC*) is fetched into an *Instruction Register*. The instruction is decoded by the *Instruction Decoder* to generate relevant sequence of control signals. Apart from PC, the CPU contains a set of general- and special-purpose registers. As the CPU registers are mapped onto RAM locations, details of the registers will be discussed in conjunction with the RAM.

2.3.2 Memory

The 8051 chip has 4kB on-chip program memory implemented using EPROM/flash technology. It also has 128 byte data memory (RAM). Thus, the RAM location addresses range over 00H to 7FH. However, beyond 7FH (and till 0FFH), some RAM addresses are defined to correspond to some special function registers. It may be noted that only few of the address locations between 80H and 0FFH are used for this purpose, rest of the locations are not usable. The internal RAM organization has been shown in Fig 2.3. It consists of the following components.

Address								
FF–80	Special Function Registers							
7F–30	General Purpose RAM							
2F	7F	7E	7D	7C	7B	7A	79	78
2E	77	76	75	74	73	72	71	70
2D	6F	6E	6D	6C	6B	6A	69	68
2C	67	66	65	64	63	62	61	60
2B	5F	5E	5D	5C	5B	5A	59	58
2A	57	56	55	54	53	52	51	50
29	4F	4E	4D	4C	4B	4A	49	48
28	47	46	45	44	43	42	41	40
27	3F	3E	3D	3C	3B	3A	39	38
26	37	36	35	34	33	32	31	30
25	2F	2E	2D	2C	2B	2A	29	28
24	27	26	25	24	23	22	21	20
23	1F	1E	1D	1C	1B	1A	19	18
22	17	16	15	14	13	12	11	10
21	0F	0E	0D	0C	0B	0A	09	08
20	07	06	05	04	03	02	01	00
1F–18	Register Bank 3							
17–10	Register Bank 2							
0F–08	Register Bank 1							
07–00	Register Bank 0							

Fig 2.3: Internal RAM Locations

1. **Register Banks (00H to 1FH):** These are the lowest 32 bytes of RAM space grouped into 4 banks of 8 locations each. Each bank consists of registers R0, R1, R2, R3, R4, R5, R6 and R7. At a time, only one bank of registers is active that can be used by the instruction being executed. Activation of banks is controlled by two status bits in the Processor Status Word (PSW) register. Instructions can use the name of a register or a memory address to refer to an operand. For example, the RAM address 04H and register R4 in Bank-0 refer to the same memory location.

2. **Bit-Addressable RAM (20H to 2FH):** These are 16 memory locations of which individual bits can be referred to by the bit-manipulating instructions. Such instructions can set/clear a bit, complement it or check the value. Some of the *Special Function Registers* (*SFR*s), noted later, are also bit-addressable.
3. **General Purpose RAM (30H to 7FH):** These 80 bytes of RAM locations could be used as general purpose storage space by the programs. It may be noted that for most of the applications, a stack space is needed for subprograms and interrupt handlers. The stack is also sometimes implemented in this region. As a result, the remaining usable space may be quite small.
4. **Special Function Registers (SFRs):** Several addresses in the range of 80H to 0FFH are dedicated for SFRs. Out of the total 128 locations available in this range, only 21 have been used and the remaining addresses are undefined. A user program should not try to access those addresses, as the result may be unpredictable. The used registers are noted next.
   - **Accumulator (0E0H):** Also referred to as *A* register in the instructions, the accumulator is used in all arithmetic and logic instructions. It holds one of the source operands and also acts as destination for such instructions. It is a 8-bit bit-addressable register.
   - **B Register (0F0H):** This is another general purpose 8-bit register, which is also bit-addressable. The primary use of *B* register is as an operand and a destination of multiplication and division instructions.
   - **Stack Pointer (81H):** It points to the top of the stack. The stack is implemented in the on-chip RAM. On reset, the 8-bit stack pointer is initialized with 07H. It is not bit-addressable.
   - **Data Pointer (82H – 83H):** This is a 16-bit register consisting of two 8-bit parts – *Data Pointer High* (*DPH*) with RAM address 83H and *Data Pointer Low* (*DPL*) with memory address 82H. The DPTR register can be used to access on-chip ROM or an externally connected RAM. The register is not bit-addressable.
   - **Interrupt Related:** Two registers *Interrupt Enable Control* (*IE*) and *Interrupt Priority Control* (*IP*) are available at RAM addresses 0A8H and 0B8H respectively, both being bit-addressable. The IE register is used for enabling/disabling certain interrupts while the IP is used to define the relative priorities between the enabled interrupts.
   - **Timer/Counter Related:** The current values of timers/counters are held in a few 8-bit registers. For *timer-0*, the lower byte is stored in register *TL0* (memory address 8AH), higher byte in *TH0* (8CH). For *timer-1*, the corresponding registers are *TL1* (8BH) and *TH1* (8DH). Apart from that, *TCON* register at 88H controls the operation of the timers/counters. Mode set register *TMOD* at 89H configures the modes of the timers/counters. Out of all these, only the TCON register is bit-addressable.
   - **Serial I/O Related:** A bit-addressable register *SCON* at RAM address 98H controls the serial I/O operations. The *SBUF* register at 99H contains the data received/transmitted serially.

- **Power Control:** The PCON register at RAM address 87H sets the power control to be applied. The register is not bit-addressable.
- **Processor Status Word (0D0H):** This 8-bit PSW register contains 4 bits corresponding to the status of the last ALU operation. Two more bits in it control the register bank to be used by the instructions, one bit is available to the user for programming, while one bit is kept undefined. Table 2.2 shows the bit usages of PSW register.

Table 2.2: Bits of PSW Register

Bit	Functionality
0 (PSW.0)	Parity. Set/cleared to indicate odd/even number of 1s in the accumulator.
1 (PSW.1)	Undefined.
2 (PSW.2)	Overflow. Detects overflow in signed arithmetic operations, that is, result is beyond -128 to +127.
4 (PSW.4), 3 (PSW.3)	Also called RS1 and RS0, used to select the register bank. *RS1* *RS0* *Bank selected* *Address range* 1 1 3 00H-07H 1 0 2 08H-0FH 0 1 1 10H-17H 0 0 0 18H-1FH
5 (PSW.5)	Termed as *Flag 0* (*F0*), the bit is available to the user.
6 (PSW.6)	Auxiliary Carry. Set if there is a carry from bit-3 to bit-4 in addition or a borrow from bit-4 to bit-3 in subtraction.
7 (PSW.7)	Carry. Set if there is a carry/borrow in 8-bit addition/subtraction.

2.3.3 Digital I/O Ports, Timers/Counters

There are four 8-bit parallel ports, called Port 0, Port 1, Port 2 and Port 3. The port bits can be programmed individually to act as input or output. Apart from acting as I/O ports, Port 0 and Port 2 also provide the address and data lines for external memory access. Some bits of Port 3 provide the read/write control signals. Port 1 is the only port having I/O activities alone. Apart from parallel I/O, serial communication block provides facilities for serial transmission of data.

There are two timers in the 8051 microcontroller – *Timer-0* and *Timer-1*. The timers can also be used as counters to count external events occurring on pins *T0* and *T1*, respectively. The timers can be configured into 16-bit, 13-bit and 8-bit modules.

2.4 Clock Circuit

The 8051 chip possesses two alternatives to provide clock to it – (i) using crystal (ii) direct clock input.

(i) **Using crystal to generate clock:** A crystal of suitable frequency is to be connected between the pins XTAL1 and XTAL2. The 8051 chips produced by different manufacturers support upto certain maximum clock frequencies for the crystal. For example, a 12 MHz microcontroller must have a crystal with frequency 12 MHz or less connected to it, while for a 20 MHz chip, the crystal connected may be of frequency upto 20 MHz. Fig 2.4(a) shows the connection diagram for the circuit. Two 30 pF capacitors are also needed in it.

(ii) **Direct clock input:** As an alternate to crystal oscillator based clock generation, any other frequency source (such as, a TTL controller) can be connected to XTAL1 with XTAL2 left unconnected. It has been shown in Fig 2.4(b).

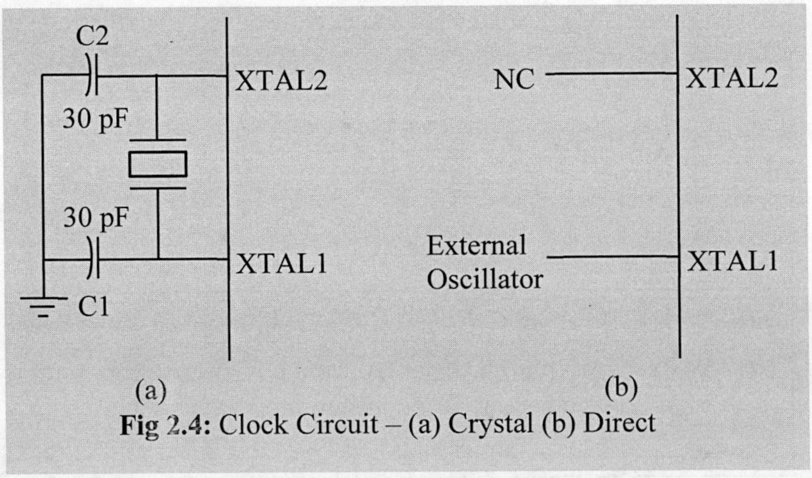

Fig 2.4: Clock Circuit – (a) Crystal (b) Direct

Machine Cycle: A machine cycle refers to the time for a group of related activities, such as, accessing the memory. One *machine cycle* for the 8051 chip consists of a number of clock cycles. The original 8051 was designed to have 12 clock cycles per machine cycle. Thus, depending upon the frequency of the crystal connected to it, duration of a machine cycle may vary even for this original version of the 8051. A certain number of machine cycles are needed to execute a complete instruction. The data sheet of the 8051 chip lists the number of machine cycles needed for each instruction. As noted earlier, there are many different manufacturers of 8051. With the advancement in VLSI technology, these variants support different maximum clock frequencies. The number of clock cycles per machine cycle and the number of machine cycles needed for an instruction, also vary across these implementations. For example, a MOV instruction in the original 8051 chip needs 1 machine cycle with 12 clock cycles in the machine cycle. On the other hand, the same MOV instruction needs 2 machine cycles in DS89C4x0, each machine cycle requiring just one clock cycle.

Example 2.1: Assuming the crystal frequency to be 11.0592 MHz, let us compute the time needed to execute (i) MOV (ii) MUL instructions, for 8051 and DS89C4x0 chips. First, the duration of a clock cycle is 1/11.0592 = 0.0904 μS. Hence, duration of a machine cycle for 8051 is 12×0.0904 = 1.0848 μS. For DS89C4x0, machine cycle duration is 1×0.0904 = 0.0904 μS. From the data sheet, it can be found that the number of machine cycles for MOV in 8051 is 1 and for DS89C4x0, it is 2. Thus, the time needed to execute a MOV instruction in 8051 is 1.0848 μS, while for DS89C4x0 it is 2×0.0904 = 0.1808 μS. For MUL, 4 machine cycles are needed for 8051 and 9 for DS89C4x0. Thus, the time required for a MUL instruction in the 8051 is 4×1.0848 = 4.3392 μS. For DS89C4x0, the corresponding time is 9×0.0904 = 0.8136 μS.

2.5 Reset Circuit

The 8051 chip has an active high RESET input (marked as RST, Pin 9). The input line should be held low during normal operation of the chip. To reset the chip, a high pulse of duration equal to at least two machine cycles be applied to RST. As noted previously, different 8051 variants

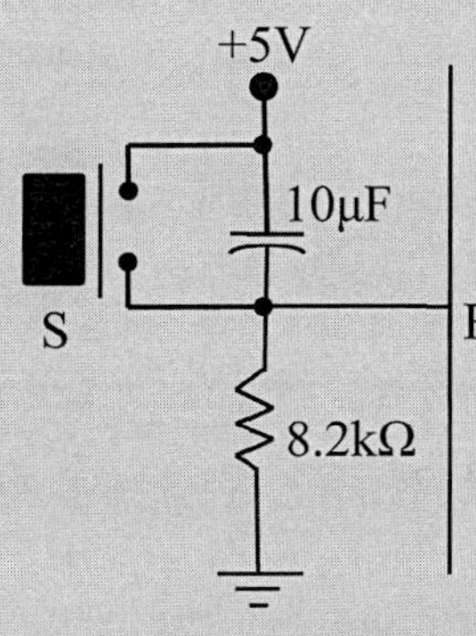

Fig 2.5: Reset Circuit

Table 2.3: Register values on reset

Register	Value (Hex)
Accumulator	00
B	00
PC	0000
DPTR	0000
PSW	00
SP	07
Ports P0-P3	0FF

have different durations for a machine cycle. Thus, the duration of high pulse to reset will also vary accordingly. There are two ways to reset the 8051 chip – (i) Power-on Reset and (ii) Reset Switch. Fig 2.5 shows how the two resets may be actuated. When the power is turned on, the circuit holds the RST pin high for an amount of time dependent on the value of the capacitor and the charging rate. These values be such that after power-on, the oscillator in the clock circuitry starts working and that the RST pin is high for at least two machine cycles. Typically, a capacitor of 10 μF and a resistor of 8.2 kΩ serve the purpose, for most of the 8051 variants. For asynchronous reset, a Reset Switch *S* may be connected in parallel to the capacitor. Closing of S takes the logic value of RST to high. The switch should be kept pressed for at least two machine cycles to cause a reset. On reset, the contents of important registers in the 8051 chip are as shown in Table 2.3.

2.6 Stack and Stack Pointer

In any computer system, stack is a portion of RAM that is used by the CPU to store some temporary information. It is typically used to save the return address of a subprogram call. The 8051 CPU saves the content of PC register while executing a CALL instruction to branch to a subprogram. At the end of the subprogram, there should be a return instruction, RET, that retrieves the value from stack and put it into PC to return to the calling point of the main program. Same is the case for interrupt handlers. Apart from address, some other register contents could also be saved in stack and retrieved back. These are done by the PUSH and POP instructions, respectively.

To keep track of the stack, the 8051 CPU has a special register, called the SP (stack pointer). This is an 8-bit register. On reset, the SP register is initialized to 07H. Thus, the stack in the 8051 commences from the RAM location 08H. RAM locations from 08H to 1FH could be used as stack, as the RAM locations 20H-2FH are reserved for bit-addressable memory. Thus, the stack can be of size 24 bytes. In case a stack of size more than 24 bytes is needed, the RAM locations 30H to 7FH could be used with the SP initialized accordingly.

Another important point to note is that the default stack locations 08H onwards clash with the portion of RAM used by the registers R0-R7 in Bank-1, as well. The programmer needs to take care of this, while writing the code. If the program intends to use the registers in Bank 1, as well as stack, the SP register should be reassigned beforehand to create stack in some different area, for example 30H onwards.

Example 2.2: Consider that the 8051 is going to execute a subprogram call instruction "CALL 0800H" stored at memory location 0200H. Thus, the PC content at this point is 0200H. From the data sheet of 8051, size of the CALL instruction is 3 bytes. The next instruction will be at location 0203H. Before branching to the subprogram, this return address will be saved in the stack. Assuming that the present content of SP is 0AH, the values 03H and 02H will be saved into the stack and the stack pointer will be incremented to 0CH. PC will be loaded with 0800H to start executing the subprogram. At the end of the subprogram, there will be a "RET" instruction. Upon executing the RET, contents from the stack locations pointed to by SP will be restored in the PC. Thus, PC gets loaded with 0203H and SP gets decremented by two to 0AH. Execution of the main program resumes from location 0203H.

2.7 Input-Output Ports

The 8051 has four ports for I/O operations, named as Port 0, Port 1, Port 2 and Port 3. Each port has 8 bidirectional I/O pins. For any port, the pins can be programmed individually to act as input or as output. Each I/O pin has an associated D-latch that can hold the value at the corresponding pin. As discussed in Section 2.2, out of the four ports, only the Port1 can be considered as assigned the pure I/O responsibilities. Port 0 pins have the task of acting as multiplexed lower-order address and data bus. Port 2 provides higher order address. Port 3 bits have the additional responsibilities, as noted in Table 2.4.

Table 2.4: Alternate Functions of Port 1

Bit No.	Alternate function
0	RxD
1	TxD
2	$\overline{\text{INT0}}$
3	$\overline{\text{INT1}}$
4	T0
5	T1
6	$\overline{\text{WR}}$
7	$\overline{\text{RD}}$

2.7.1 Hardware Structure of I/O Pin

The generic hardware structure of an I/O pin in 8051 has been shown in Fig 2.6. This corresponds more to the pins of Port 1, as those are not assigned any additional functionality. The overall structure consists of the following components.

- **Connection to data bus:** Each port bit is connected to one of the data bus lines. The data transfer takes place between the 8-bit data bus lines and the port bits.
- **D-latch:** One D-latch is used to hold the value that is output from the CPU to the pin. For this, the *Latch_Enable* signal be made high.
- **Tristate buffers:** Two tristate buffers control the flow of information from the port to the data bus line. Tristate buffer TB1 controls the availability of pin input to the CPU bus line. TB2 controls the latch output reaching the CPU bus. TB1 has the control input *Read_Pin*, while TB2 has *Read_Latch*. Naturally, the two control signals should not be activated simultaneously. The 8051 has different groups of instructions for the two categories of operations.

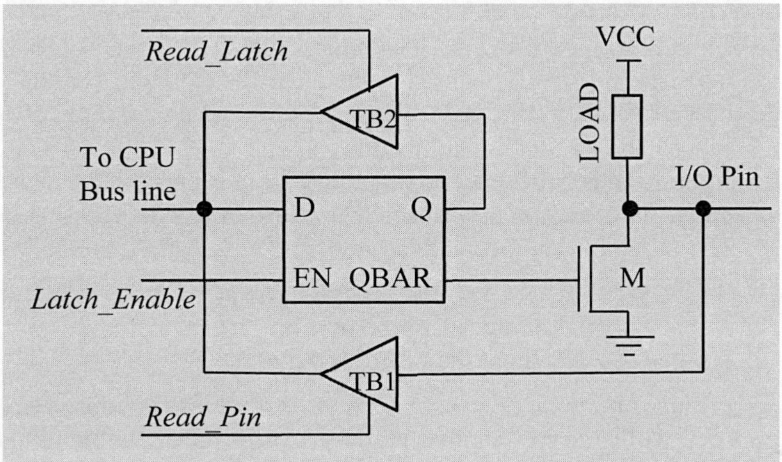

Fig 2.6: Hardware Structure of I/O Pin

- **Gate transistor:** Enabling and disabling the gate control input to the nMOS transistor turns it on or off. Accordingly, the port pin logic level becomes high (with transistor M being off) or low (with M on).

Write Operation: To write a high (1) to the I/O pin, that is for an output operation, the CPU bus bit has to be turned high and the *Latch_Enable* signal activated. This will set Q to 1 and QBAR to 0. The transistor M gets turned off. As a result, the port pin gets charged to 1 through the Load. Similarly, for a 0 output, the bus bit is set to 0. QBAR becomes 1, turning on the transistor M. The port pin line discharges through M, going to logic 0.

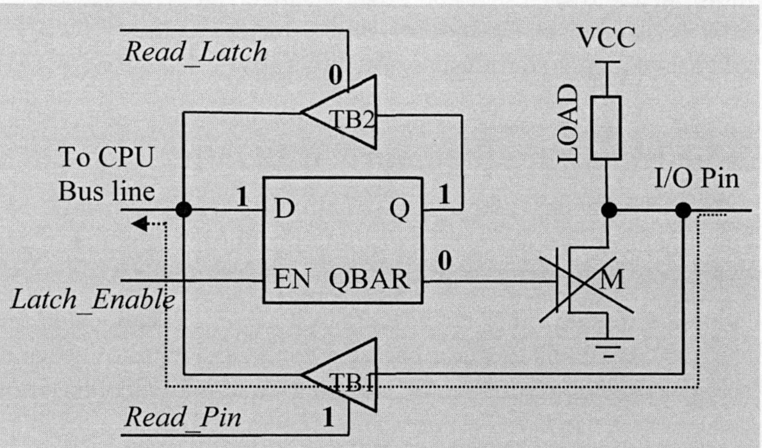

Fig 2.7: Hardware Structure of I/O Pin

Read Operation: As noted earlier, there are two types of I/O read (input) operations supported in 8051. The first one reads the content of the D-latch. This is implemented by activating the *Read_Latch* and deactivating *Read_Pin*. The other category reads the value given as input at the port pin. For this, *Read_Pin* is activated, while *Read_Latch* is deactivated. However, there is an issue with this input operation. Consider that the D-latch has been set previously with the value Q = 0, that is, QBAR = 1. As QBAR is 1, it turns on the transistor M. Now, with M turned on, the port pin cannot stay at logic high, as it will get discharged via M, in that case. Thus, though reading a 0 input at port pin can be error-free, to read a 1, it is necessary that D-latch is set to Q = 1, QBAR = 0. This can be ensured by outputting a 1 to the port bit. Thus, whenever an input operation is needed, to ensure correct result, it is required that an "output 1" operation is performed at the port bit. This will set QBAR to 0, disabling the transistor M. The situation has been illustrated in Fig 2.7 after the following two operations have been performed in sequence.

1. Output 1 to the port bit
2. Input the bit from the port

As a result, any input operation consists of two instructions. The first instruction writes a 1 to the port pin, while the second instruction performs the actual input operation.

2.7.2 Port 0 Structure

Structure of Port 0 pins is a bit different, compared to the other ports. A typical Port 0 pin structure has been shown in Fig 2.8. Compared to Fig 2.6, in a Port 0 pin, there is no internal pull-up resistance connected. Thus, the port bits are *open-drain*. Writing a 1 to the D-latch turns off the transistor M, which causes the pin to float. It does not create problem in the port acting as multiplexed address/data bus. However, while using it for I/O purposes, an external pull-up resistance must be connected to source current to the pin. For address/data multiplexing, the port bit is connected to some latch (for example, 74LS373), thus external pull-up is not needed in that case. Due to its open-drain configuration, the Port 0 can drive more number of fanouts, compared to other ports. While the ports Port 1, Port 2 and Port 3 can drive upto 4 TTL inputs, Port 0 can drive upto 8 TTL inputs.

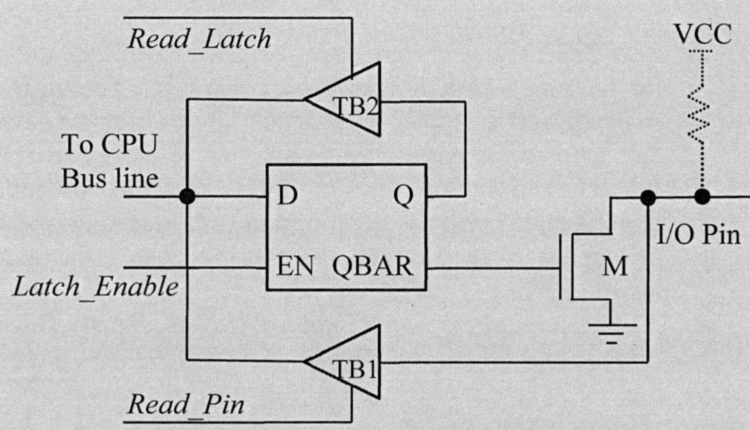

Fig 2.8: Hardware Structure Port 0 Pin

2.8 Memory Organization

The basic 8051 chip has 4kB ROM and 128 byte RAM in it. These are on-chip storage, providing the fastest access from the CPU. Out of the 4kB ROM space, certain part may be used by the system designer to have the core routines to support the devices that are needed for the system, keeping little space for further user routines to be integrated with it. Depending upon the complexity of the system being developed, the on-chip ROM space may not be sufficient also. The situation is more acute with the RAM space. As noted previously, out of the 128 byte RAM space, only the locations 30H-7Fh are earmarked for general-purpose usage, commonly known as *scratch-pad*. Among these 80 bytes also, sometimes the stack has to be accommodated. Scarcity of RAM space often necessitates interfacing external RAM for keeping data values. With the support of external memory chips integrated, the program memory and the data memory can be upto 64kB each. The instructions and the control pins of the 8051, responsible for external program memory access are totally different from those used for data memory access. This enables having each of the program and the data memory to be 64kB in size. This is a marked difference from many processors, such as 8085, where the 16-bit address bus allows connecting upto 64kB memory, without any distinction between the program and the data.

The important signal lines of the 8051 chip that are used for interfacing external memory, have been noted in the following.

1. **Port 0:** The signal lines of Port 0 provide the 8-bit data bus (D0-D7) and the lower-order 8-bits of the address bus (A0-A7) in a multiplexed fashion. The port bits have been given the alternate name AD0-AD7 to reflect their functionality. Similar to 8085, this multiplexing helps in saving the number of pins for the chip.
2. **Port 2:** The lines of Port 2 are also used to provide the higher order address lines A8-A15 for memory access. The *program counter* (*PC*) being 16-bit wide, higher-order byte is sent to Port 2 and the lower-order byte to Port 0, for the external program memory access. For data memory access, generally another 16-bit register DPTR is used.
3. **EA:** The pin *External Access* (*EA*) is an active low input signal. If the signal line is kept high, the 8051 will use the program code stored in its on-chip ROM. On the other hand, if the signal is set to low, the 8051 accesses the external program memory to fetch instructions.
4. **ALE:** The *Address Latch Enable* (*ALE*) is an active high output signal of the 8051 chip. It is made high whenever the lower-order address byte is put on AD0-AD7 (that is, Port 0). Similar to the 8085 processor, an external 8-bit latch is needed to hold the address lines steady, even after the ALE has been withdrawn. Generally, the ALE signal is activated for two clock cycles. The address-data bus demultiplexing process has been shown in Fig 2.9.

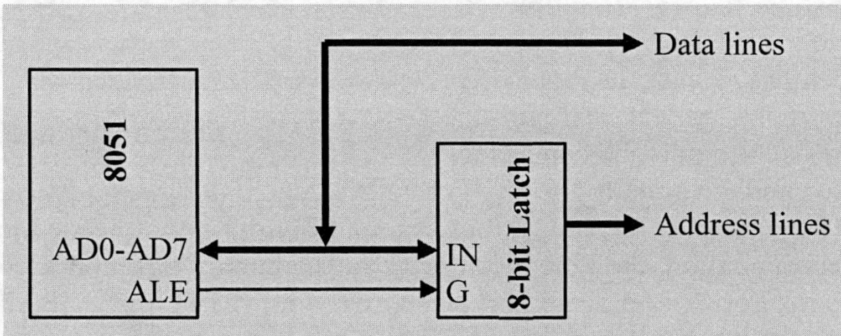

Fig 2.9: Demultiplexing of Address and Data Lines

5. **PSEN:** The signal, *Program Strobe Enable* (*PSEN*) is an active low output signal of 8051. It is used to access the external program memory. The external program memory is generally implemented via ROM having an *Output Enable* (*OE*) pin. The PSEN line is connected to OE.
6. **RD:** The *Read* (*RD*) is an active low output signal of 8051, used to read data from the external data memory. The data memory can be upto 64kB in size with address provided by the DPTR register.
7. **WR:** The Write (WR) is also an active low output signal, used for writing data onto the external data memory.

2.8.1 External Program Memory Interface

Fig 2.10 shows the access rules to the program memory interfaced, based upon the EA input setting. As shown in Fig 2.10(a), when the EA pin is grounded, the 8051 uses the external program memory only, for its entire address range. However, with EA = 1, the 8051 uses both the on-chip and the external program memories. The on-chip memory is size-restricted to 4kB. Thus, for program addresses generated by the CPU in the range 0000H to 0FFFH, the on-chip ROM is accessed. For addresses in the range 1000H to 0FFFFH, the external ROM is accessed. This has been shown in Fig 2.10(b).

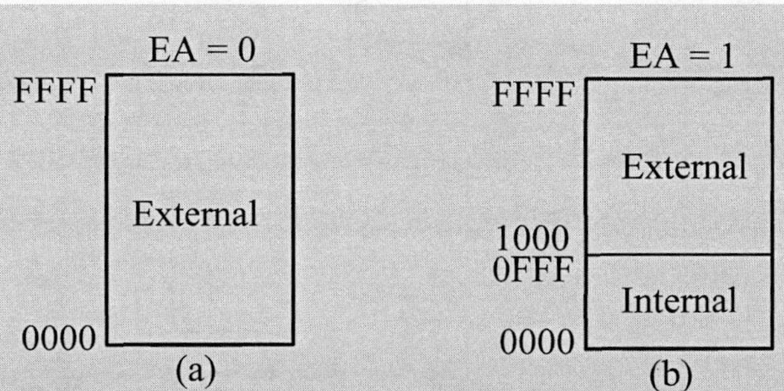

Fig 2.10: External Program Memory with (a) EA = 0, (b) EA = 1

Fig 2.11 shows the connection of signal lines onto the 8051 side to access external program memory. The EA pin may be set to high or low, as discussed. Port 2 provides the higher order address bus lines. The lower-order address lines are extracted from the Port 0 lines AD0-AD7 through demultiplexing, using 8-bit latch. The PSEN line is available for connecting to the OE line of the external ROM.

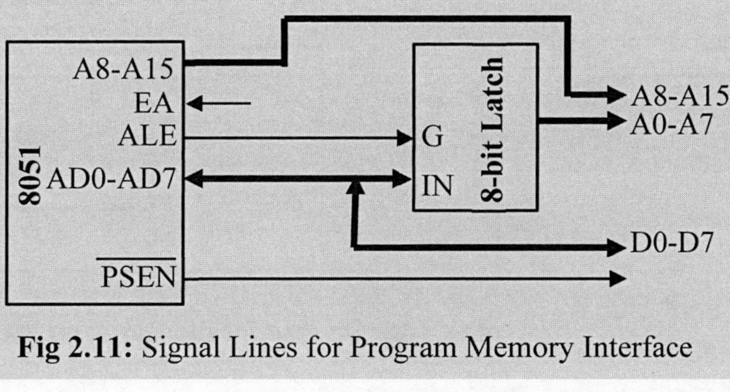

Fig 2.11: Signal Lines for Program Memory Interface

Example 2.2:

Consider the interfacing of 64kB external program memory to the 8051 chip. It is assumed that the on-chip ROM space will not be used by the system and that the 64kB space will be arranged with ROM chips of 16 kB each. Thus four such chips are needed. The interface has been shown in Fig 2.12.

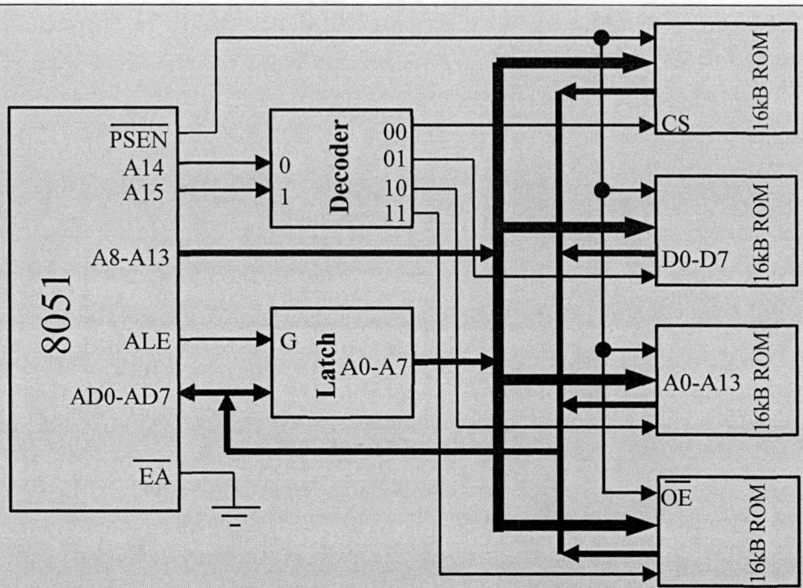

Fig 2.12: Example Program Memory Interface

2.8.2 External Data Memory Interface

The 8051 provides facility to interface upto 64 kB of external data memory. Fig 2.13 shows the signal lines of the 8051 that need to be used for this interfacing. Compared to the program memory access lines, the differences are as follows.

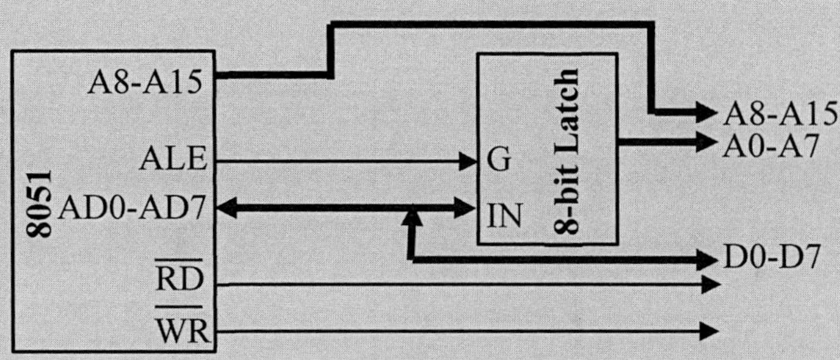

Fig 2.13: Signal Lines for Program Memory Interface

- No dependency on EA line.
- PSEN connection is not required.
- Port 0 and Port 2 lines are used to provide 16-bit address- and 8-bit data-bus lines.
- Read (RD) and Write (WR) signals from Port 3 are used for read and write operations.

Example 2.3: Fig 2.14 shows an example external data memory interface with the 8051 chip. The system realizes 64 kB external data memory space. Each RAM chip is assumed to be of size 16 kB. Four such memory chips have been integrated here. The address- and data-bus connections are similar to that for Example 2.2. However, the PSEN and EA lines do not have any role. Instead of them, RD and WR controls have been connected with individual RAM chips.

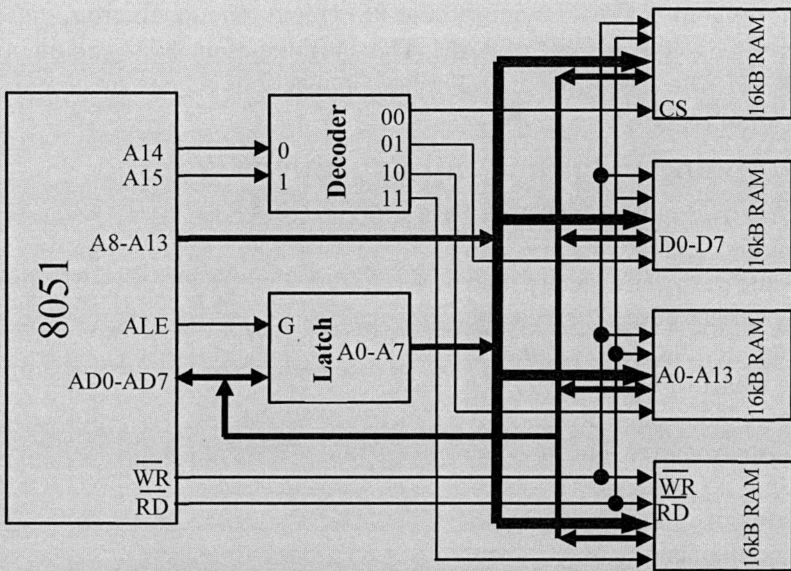

Fig 2.14: Example Data Memory Interface

2.8.3 Combined External Program and Data Memory

From our discussions, it can be observed that the 8051 supports a total of 128 kB external memory. Out of this, 64 kB is for program (often realized using ROM) and 64 kB is for data (realized using RAM). The RAM, as a memory can also be used to hold program code. Thus, it can also be used as program memory. In many systems, it may be sufficient to have just 64 kB of external memory that can function both as program memory and data memory. This is particularly true in many of the trainer kits and system design facilities. As the software is being developed, it needs to undergo many changes during debugging. Thus, keeping the program in RAM is advantageous than in ROM for such an environment. To facilitate such

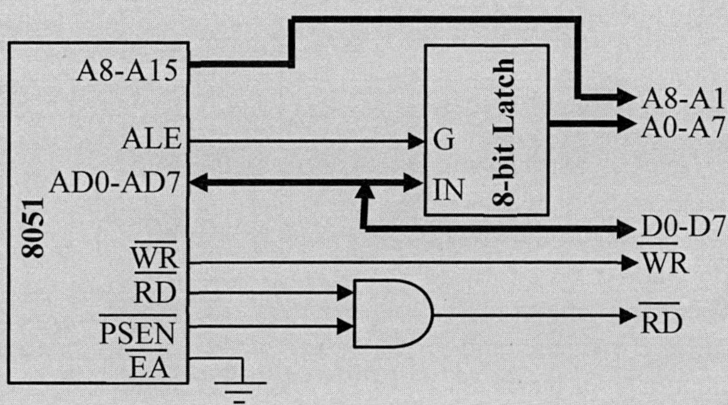

Fig 2.15: Combined Program and Data Memory

joint program and data memory, the $\overline{PSEN}$ and $\overline{RD}$ signals from the 8051 are to be AND-ed and connected to the $\overline{RD}$ line of RAM. The $\overline{WR}$ line of the 8051 should be connected to the $\overline{WR}$ input of RAM. Other address- and data-line connections remain unaltered. The configuration has been shown in Fig 2.15.

2.9 Timing Diagrams and Execution Cycles

Instruction execution by the 8051 CPU consists of several machine cycles. Number of machine cycles needed to execute a specific instruction by a variant of the 8051 can be found in the corresponding data sheet. For example, the original 8051 chip, designed by the Intel requires four machine cycles to execute a MUL instruction, 1 for a MOV instruction, and so on. As there are many available variants of the 8051, the rest of the discussions in this section have been made specific to the original Intel design. One machine cycle for this processor consists of twelve clock pulses, as shown in Fig 2.16. Also, two pulses form a *state* of the processor. A total of six states constitute a machine cycle. There are two ALE pulses per machine cycle – one between *State 1* and *State 2*, while the other one between the states 4 and 5. Each ALE pulse spans over two clock pulses.

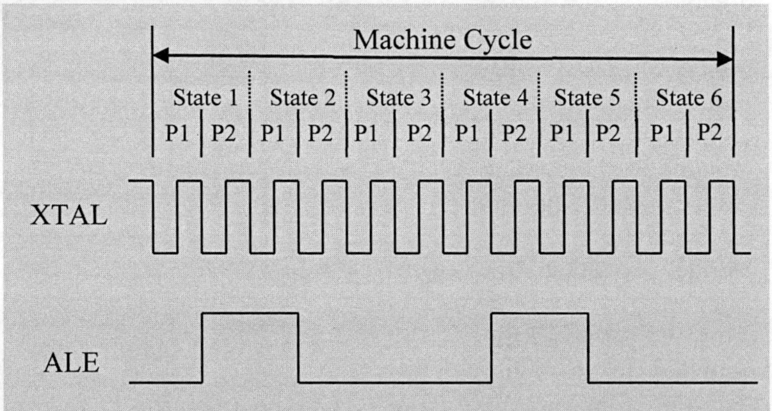

Fig 2.16: Machine Cycle of the Intel 8051 CPU

The execution of an instruction /operation by the 8051 CPU could be understood best by looking into the status of different signals and the contents of buses of it, over the clock pulses. This is often represented by timing diagrams, depicting the happenings over the

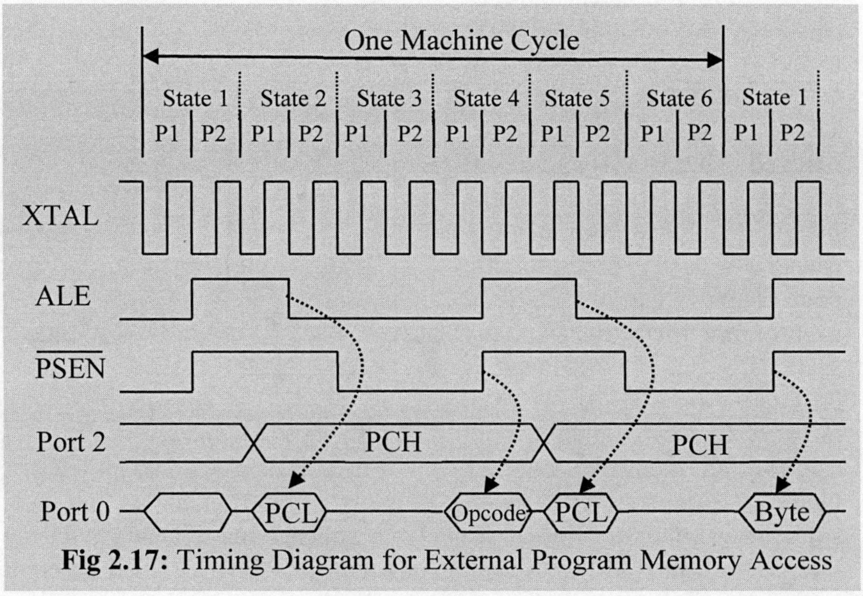

Fig 2.17: Timing Diagram for External Program Memory Access

clock pulses. As shown in Fig 2.16, in every machine cycle, the ALE signal is activated twice, indicating that the internal/external memory could be accessed twice per machine cycle. Depending upon the instruction being executed, different number of memory accesses may be necessary. Fig 2.17 shows a timing diagram corresponding to a read operation from the external program memory. It reads two bytes from the memory. The whole operation takes one machine cycle with the content of the first byte being available at pulse 2 of State 4. The other operand is available at pulse 2 of State 1 in the next machine cycle. That next machine cycle can use this data for any intended operation, such as, moving to some register. In each memory access, Port 2 holds the content of the higher-order address bus. Port 0 functions as the multiplexed address-data bus that holds the lower-order address bus content, A0-A7 at the beginning. The falling edge of the ALE signal indicates the time at which the lower-address bus content is stable and could be used to latch the address in the external latch. The line $\overline{\text{PSEN}}$ is used as strobe for the external program memory access. The rising edge of $\overline{\text{PSEN}}$ is used as strobe for the external program memory access. The rising edge indicates the time at which valid data from the external memory is available in the data bus (that is, Port 0).

The timing diagram shown in Fig 2.18 considers the situation in which a one-byte instruction is accessed from the external program memory, which in turn, instructs the CPU to read one byte from the external data memory. This is generally accomplished by the MOVX instruction,

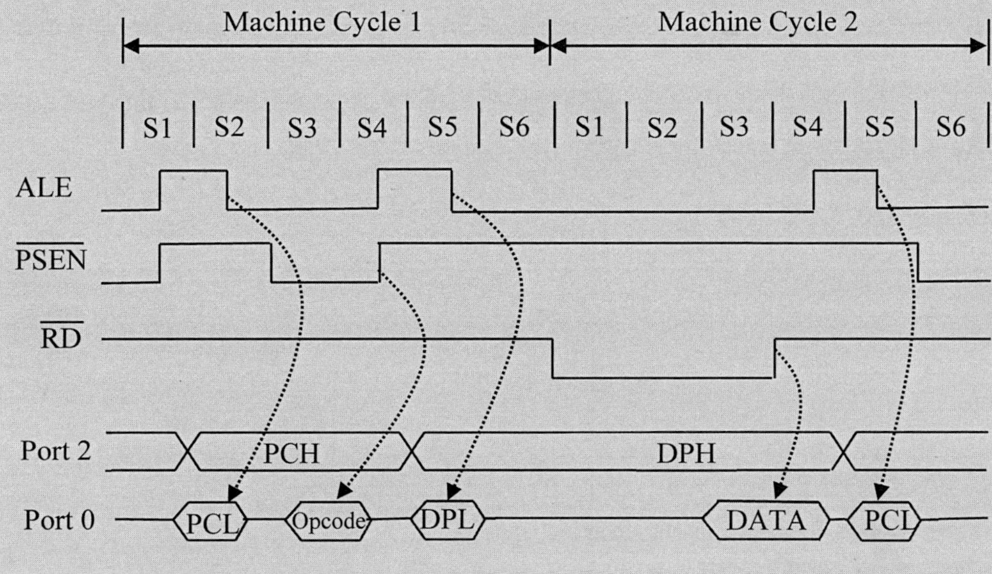

Fig 2.18: Timing Diagram with External Program and Data Memory Access

illustrated later. The whole execution spans over two machine cycles. In the first machine cycle, the external program memory is accessed, with values of PCH and PCL being put on Port 2 and

Port 0 lines respectively, to provide address. The content is read from the program memory on the rising edge of $\overline{PSEN}$. In the next machine cycle, content of DPH register is put on Port 2 and DPL on Port 0, to provide address. It may be noted that the registers DPH and DPL together constitute the 16-bit DPTR register, used for accessing external data memory. The low-to-high transition of the $\overline{RD}$ line is used as strobe for the data memory read operation.

2.10 Instruction Set Summary

In this section, we shall look into an overview of the 8051 instructions. Details of all the instructions have been presented in Unit 3. The instructions could be grouped into five categories – Data Transfer, Arithmetic Operations, Logical Operations, Bit-Manipulation Operations and Program Branching. Table 2.5 summarizes the categories along with examples.

Table 2.5: The 8051 Instruction Set Summary

Type & Mnemonics	*Operands*	*Examples*	
Data Transfer: MOV, MOVX, PUSH, POP, XCH	Register, Memory address, Pointer register, Immediate data	MOV A, R0	; A gets content of R0
		MOV R3, 5	; R3 gets RAM[5]
		MOV R5, #10H	; R5 gets 10H
		MOVX A, @DPTR	; A gets content of memory location pointed to by DPTR
		PUSH 4	; Push content of RAM[4] to stack
		POP 3	; Pop stack top to RAM[3]
		XCH A, R2	; Contents of A and R2 exchanged
Arithmetic Operations: ADD, ADDC, SUBB, INC, DEC, MUL, DIV, DA	Register, Memory address, Pointer register, Immediate data	ADD A, R1	; A gets (A + R1)
		ADD A, 5	; A gets (A + RAM[5])
		ADDC A, @R2	; A gets (A + RAM[R2] + Carry Flag)
		SUBB A, #10	; A gets (A – 10 – Carry Flag)
		INC R4	; R4 gets R4 + 1
		MUL AB	; A and B gets lower and higher bytes of A × B
		DIV AB	; A and B gets quotient and remainder of A ÷ B
		DA A	; A gets converted to BCD format
Logical Operations: ANL, ORL, XRL, CLR, CPL, RL, RLC, RR, RRC, SWAP	Register, Memory address, Pointer	ANL A, R1	; A gets (A AND R1)
		ORL A, 5	; A gets (A OR RAM[5])
		XRL A, #10H	; A gets (A XOR 10H)
		XRL A, @R2	; A gets (A XOR RAM[R2])

	register, Immediate data	CLR A CPL A RL A RRC A SWAP A	; A gets 0 ; A gets (NOT A) ; A content rotated left ; A along with Carry, rotated left ; Swap nibbles of A
Bit-Manipulation Operations: CLR, SETB, CPL, ANL, ORL, MOV	Carry Flag, Bit address	CLR C CLR PSW.3 SETB 1AH CPL 1CH ANL C, 1FH MOV C,1FH	; Carry flag gets 0 ; Clear bit 3 of PSW register ; RAM-bit 1A gets 1 ; RAM-bit 1C gets 0 ; Carry flag ANDed with bit 1FH ; Carry flag gets bit from 1FH
Program Branching – Unconditional: ACALL, LCALL, JMP, SJMP, AJMP. LJMP, RET, RETI	11-bit address, 16-bit address, 8-bit relative address	ACALL <11-bit> LJMP <16-bit> JMP @A+DPTR SJMP <8-bit> RET RETI	; PC saved in stack and PC[10:0] gets <11-bit> ; PC gets <16-bit> ; PC gets (A + DPTR) ; PC gets (PC + <8-bit>) ; Return from subroutine PC gets 2 bytes by popping stack ; Return from interrupt handler PC gets 2 bytes by popping stack
Program Branching – Conditional: JC, JNC, JB, JNB, JBC, JZ, JNZ, CJNE, DJNZ	8-bit relative address	JC <8-bit> JB 1AH, <8-bit> JNZ <8-bit> CJNE A, 5, <8-bit> DJNZ R1, <8-bit> DJNZ 5, <8-bit>	; PC gets (PC + <8-bit>) if Carry set ; PC gets (PC + <8-bit>) if 1AH set ; PC gets (PC + <8-bit>) if Zero flag not set ; PC gets (PC + <8-bit>) if A not equal to RAM[5] ; R1 gets R1 – 1. PC gets (PC + <8-bit>) if R1 is non-zero now ; RAM[5] decremented by 1. If RAM[5] non-zero, PC gets (PC + <8-bit>)
Machine Control: NOP	-	NOP	; Do nothing

2.11 Assembly Language Program Structure

Any assembly language program consists of a series of lines of assembly language instructions. Each instruction has the following components – an optional label, a mandatory mnemonic, a number of operands (depending upon the mnemonic) and an optional comment (often demarcated by a ';' character), as shown next.

[*label*:]   *mnemonic*   [*operands*]   [; *comment*]

For example, consider the following instruction.

```
HERE: MOV A, R0    ; A gets content of R0
```

HERE is a label that may be used to specify some jump target. MOV is the mnemonic, A and R0 are two operands. "MOV A, R0" is an instruction of 8051, as noted previously.

Apart from the processor instructions, an assembly language program may have some additional components that can be classified into assembler directives and storage declarations. Both of these are dependent, to a large extent, on the assembler being used to generate machine code from the assembly code. The following discussion is a generic one, which may differ to some extent in any individual assembler.

2.11.1 Assembler Directives

Most of the 8051 assemblers support the three directives – ORG (origin), EQU (equate) and END (end of source code).

1. **ORG:** It is used to indicate the starting memory address for an assembly language instruction block. It is of the form,

   ORG < *number* >

   which indicates that the code corresponding to the following instruction is meant for memory location *number*. For example, consider the following code sequence.

   ```
   ORG 1000H
   MOV A, R1
   ```

   Here, the machine code for the instruction "MOV A, R1" is to be placed at memory location 1000H. It may be noted that an assembly language program may have several ORG statements in it. Each ORG defines a new start address of its immediately following code fragment.

2. **EQU:** This defines a constant. No storage space is allotted to hold the constant value separately. A typical syntax for EQU directive of an assembler may be as follows.

   ```
   TOTAL    EQU    100
   ```

Here, TOTAL is a label. In the source code, whenever the assembler finds the label TOTAL, it is replaced by the constant 100, before translating the corresponding instruction. For example, with the previous definition of TOTAL, the assembly language statement "MOV R1, #TOTAL" is same as "MOV R1, #100".

Introduction of the EQU directive helps the programmer to write more structured programs, with the ease of modification. For example, the constant TOTAL may define the total number of numbers (100 in this case) in an array, processed by the program. The programmer may need to load several registers/memory locations with the value 100. Now, if the requirement changes and the number of numbers become 1000, all those program instructions need to change from 100 to 1000. This is an error-prone activity. On the other hand, in the presence of definition "TOTAL EQU 100" and using the constant TOTAL in all those instructions, it is very easy to effect the change from 100 to 1000 by just changing the constant definition to "TOTAL EQU 1000". All the relevant instructions get modified accordingly.

3. **END:** The END directive specifies that the assembler should not consider anything beyond this line to be part of the source code. Thus, it indicates the end of the assembly process.

2.11.2 Storage Declaration

To define the storage space to contain the data on which the source program will operate, most of the 8051 assemblers provide a pseudo-opcode *DB* (define byte). It defines one byte of storage initialized with some value. It is called a pseudo-opcode since unlike an instruction, the code generated by the assembler for this is not for execution by the CPU. Consider the following code fragment.

```
        ORG 1000H
X       DB      20H
Y       DB      30H
```

It defines two one-byte variables X and Y. The variable X is at memory address 1000H and Y at 1001H. The location 1000H is initialized for X with 20H and 1001H for Y with 30H. The DB directive can also be used to define multibyte structures, strings etc. in most of the assemblers. The following are a few examples of the same.

```
STR1    DB      "Microcontrollers and Applications"
ARR     DB      10, 20, 30, 40
```

Here, STR1 defines and initializes the storage of 33 bytes for the string "Microcontrollers and Applications". ARR defines an array of four bytes with the successive bytes initialized to 10, 20, 30 and 40 respectively.

2.11.3 Important Files

There are several files that are involved in the assembly process. First, the assembly language program is written into a text file, called the *source file*. It typically has the extension ".asm". The file is assembled to produce a binary file containing the machine code of 8051. The machine code is in a format that the IDE may download to the 8051 development kit. This binary file has the extension ".hex". The *hex file* is not understandable by the programmer writing the source code. To help the programmer in the debugging and understanding process, often the assemblers produce another text file that lists side-by-side the machine code generated and the instruction translated. This file is called the *list file* and often has the extension ".lst".

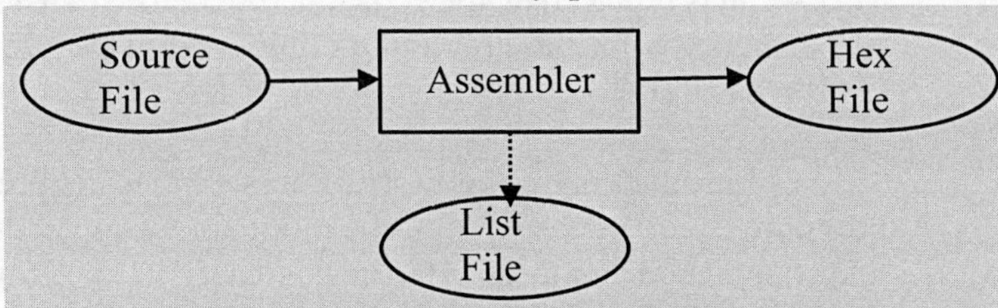

Fig 2.19: Important Files in Assembly

Example 2.4: Consider the problem of identifying the smallest number in an array of size N. The array is stored in the external data memory starting from location 2000H. The source code of the program has been listed next. Size of the array, N has been taken as a constant via the EQU declaration. Here, N has been set to 4. Comments have been attached with each line for explanation. The program is assumed to start at ROM address 0000H, identified by the ORG statement. Memory location 40H has been used to hold a temporary variable TEMP.

```
        ORG 0000H
        TEMP EQU 40H          ;   Temporary location
        N EQU 04H             ;   Size of array
        MOV R4, #N-1          ;   R4 holds a count
        MOV DPTR, #2000H      ;   DPTR points to start of array
        MOVX A, @DPTR         ;   Get first element in A
L1:     MOV R1, A             ;   Assume it smallest and copy in R1
L2:     INC DPTR              ;   DPTR points to the next element
        MOVX A, @DPTR         ;   Get next element in A
        MOV TEMP, A           ;   Save next element at TEMP
        MOV A, R1             ;   Get previous element into A
        CJNE A, TEMP, L3      ;   Compare two elements
        SJMP L4               ;   If equal, A is holding the smallest
```

```
L3:   JC L4              ;  If previous element smaller, no problem
      MOV A, TEMP        ;  If previous element larger, get smaller in A
L4:   DJNZ R4, L1        ;  Check for end of array
      END                ;  A has the smallest
```

The list file generated by the assembler will be as follows.

Line	Address	Code		Source		
1:	-	0000		ORG 0000H		
2:	-	0040		TEMP EQU 40H	;	Temporary location
3:	-	0004		N EQU 04H	;	Size of array
4:	0000	7C 03		MOV R4, #N-1	;	R4 holds a count
5:	0002	90 20 00		MOV DPTR, #2000H	;	DPTR points to start of array
6:	0005	E0		MOVX A, @DPTR	;	Get first element in A
7:	0006	F9	L1:	MOV R1, A	;	Assume it smallest and copy in R1
8:	0007	A3	L2:	INC DPTR	;	DPTR points to the next element
9:	0008	E0		MOVX A, @DPTR	;	Get next element in A
10:	0009	F5 40		MOV TEMP, A	;	Save next element at TEMP
11:	000B	E9		MOV A, R1	;	Get previous element into A
12:	000C	B5 40 02		CJNE A, TEMP, L3	;	Compare two elements
13:	000F	80 04		SJMP L4	;	If equal, A is holding the smallest
14:	0011	40 02	L3:	JC L4	;	If previous element smaller, no problem
15:	0013	E5 40		MOV A, TEMP	;	If previous element larger, get smaller in A
16:	0015	DC EF	L4:	DJNZ R4, L1	;	Check for end of array
17:				END	;	A has the smallest

UNIT SUMMARY

The 8051 is one of the most popular microcontrollers developed, studied and used in systems, over the years. Apart from the CPU, the chip contains on-chip ROM, RAM, timers and I/O ports. The on-chip RAM has several sections in it – the register banks, bit-addressable portion, scratch pad, stack space and special function registers. The basic 8051 design from the Intel has two timers and four, 8-bit I/O ports. The port bits can be configured individually as input or output. The ports can also be used to access external program- and data-memory chips, used for extending the memory capacity. Execution of instructions consists of several machine cycles, each machine cycle containing a fixed number of clock cycles. The instructions supported by the 8051 can be grouped into classes, such as, data transfer, arithmetic/logic operations, control transfer, etc. An assembly language program, apart from containing machine instructions, will generally have variable storage space, constants etc. This unit has given a detailed view of all these aspects of the 8051.

EXERCISES

Multiple Choice Questions

MQ1. If the crystal connected to the Intel 8051 chip is of frequency 10MHz, length of its machine cycle is
(A) 1.4 μs (B) 1.2 μs (C) 1.0 μs (D) 1.6 μs

MQ2. If RS0 = 0 and RS1 = 0, the register bank address range in 8051 is
(A) 00H-07H (B) 08H-0FH (C) 10H-17H (D) 18H-1FH

MQ3. If RS0 = 1 and RS1 = 0, the register bank address range of 8051 is
(A) 00H-07H (B) 08H-0FH (C) 10H-17H (D) 18H-1FH

MQ4. In 8051, to make the address range 10H-17H as the present register bank, the bits RS0 and RS1 be set to
(A) RS0 = 1, RS1 = 1 (B) RS0 = 1, RS1 = 0
(C) RS0 = 0, RS1 = 1 (D) RS0 = 0, RS1 = 0

MQ5. Bit address 42H belongs to the byte address in 8051 RAM
(A) 26H (B) 28H (C) 2AH (D) None of the other options

MQ6. Which of the following is NOT a valid status word bit in 8051?
(A) Z (B) OV (C) CY (D) AC

MQ7. Which of the following is NOT a valid status word bit in 8051?
(A) P (B) OV (C) CY (D) None of the other options

MQ8. On RESET, the value of SP in 8051 is
(A) 07H (B) 00H (C) 0FH (D) 1FH

MQ9. Which port of 8051 needs external pull-up resistances to be connected?
(A) P0 (B) P1 (C) P2 (D) P3

MQ10. For getting input from a port bit of 8051 if a '1' is not written to it, reading of which value may create problem?
(A) 0 (B) 1 (C) Both 1 and 0 (D) Neither of 0 nor 1

MQ11. Bit address 67H belongs to the byte address in 8051 RAM
(A) 2CH (B) 2DH (C) 2FH (D) None of the other options

MQ12. Bit address 42H belongs to the byte address in 8051 RAM
(A) 26H (B) 28H (C) 2AH (D) None of the other options

MQ13. IP register in 8051 controls
(A) Instruction parity (B) Interrupt parity
(C) Interrupt priority (D) None of the other options

MQ14. In a 8051 program, it is required to configure the MSB and LSB of port P0 as output. The statement for this can be
(A) MOV P0, #81H (B) MOV P0, #FFH
(C) MOV P0, #8FH (D) None of the other options

MQ15. Number of interrupt pins in 8051 is
(A) 1 (B) 2 (C) 3 (D) 4

MQ16. Flag bit in 8051 used to detect errors in signed arithmetic is
(A) P (B) OV (C) CY (D) None of the other options

MQ17. What is the meaning of the 8051 instruction “MOV A, 05H”?
(A) 05H is stored in the accumulator
(B) Fifth bit of accumulator set to 1
(C) Content of memory location 05H copied to the accumulator
(D) None of the other options

MQ18. External Access is used in 8051 to permit
(A) Peripherals (B) Power supply (C) ALE (D) Memory interfacing

MQ19. SFR address range of 8051 is
(A) 80H to 0FEH (B) 00H to 0FFH (C) 80H to 0FFH (D) 70H to 80H

MQ20. The I/O ports in 8051 that are used as address and data for external memory are
(A) P1 and P2 (B) P1 and P3 (C) P0 and P2 (D) P0 and P3

MQ21. In 8051, which bit-level operation is possible?
(A) Complement (B) Set (C) Reset (D) All the other options

MQ22. Which control signal may be generated in 8051 to access off-chip devices?
(A) ALE (B) PSEN (C) RD, WR (D) All of the other options

MQ23. Which 8051 register does not have an on-chip RAM address?
(A) Stack pointer (B) Program counter
(C) Data pointer (D) Timer

MQ24. Bit address range in 8051 on-chip RAM is
(A) 00H to 0FFH (B) 01H to 7FH
(C) 00H to 7FH (D) 80H to 0FFH

MQ25. The 8051 port bits used as external inputs for counters are
(A) P3.4, P3.5 (B) P2.4, P2.5
(C) P3.0, P3.1 (D) None of the other options

Answers of Multiple Choice Questions

1:B, 2:A, 3:B, 4:B, 5:B, 6:A, 7:D, 8:A, 9:A, 10:B, 11:A, 12:B, 13:C, 14:D, 15:B, 16:B, 17:C, 18:D, 19:C, 20:C, 21:D, 22:D, 23:B, 24:C, 25:A

Short Answer Type Questions

SQ1. Explain the operation of (a) clock circuit and (b) reset circuit of the 8051.

SQ2. Why is it necessary to write a '1' to a port bit before reading it in the 8051?

SQ3. List the signals of the 8051 necessary for external memory interfacing.

SQ4. Draw the timing diagram for external data memory access.

SQ5. Draw the timing diagram of external program memory access.

SQ6. Why is it necessary to connect external resistors to Port 0 pins?

SQ7. How to switch between the register banks in the 8051?

SQ8. What are the typical parts in an assembly language program statement?

SQ9. State the important files input and output by an assembler.

SQ10. What are the components of a list file produced by an assembler?

Long Answer Type Questions

LQ1. Enumerate the functionality of pins of the 8051.

LQ2. Draw the pin diagram and explain the operation of I/O port bits of the 8051.

LQ3. Draw the block diagram showing all control signals to interface 16kB program- and 8kB data-memory externally to the 8051.

LQ4. Explain the role of pseudo-opcodes in assembly language programs.

LQ5. List the categories of the 8051 machine instructions with examples.

Numerical Problems

NQ1. Find out the minimum time for which the reset pin be activated to reset the 8051 chip with original Intel design having a crystal of frequency 12MHz connected to it.

NQ2. Determine the maximum size of the stack of 8051 with the requirement that the stack does not interfere with the register banks.

NQ3. Consider the list file shown in Example 2.4. If the label "L3" was associated with the statement "MOV TEMP, A" at line 10, what will be value be stored at 000E to have the correct jump offset?

NQ4. A program executes the instructions

ADD A, R1

ADD A, R2

If the initial contents of A, R1 and R2 are 100, 200 and 215 in decimal, compute the content of A register after executing the two instructions.

NQ5. In NQ4 if the instruction "ADD A, R2" is modified to "ADDC A, R2", compute the content of the A register.

Answers of Numerical Problems

1: 2 μS, 2: 80 bytes, 3: 0FAH (decimal –6), 4: 3, 5: 4

KNOW MORE

The 8051 was the very first microcontroller from the Intel; the brain child of *Robert Noyce*, *Gordon Moore* and *Andy Grove*. The instruction set of the 8051 was devised by *John H. Wharton*. The 8051 is the first CPU on-a-chip that provided bit manipulation. Another very important feature of the 8051 is the usage of Register Banks, which has been followed later by many of the advanced processors, such as ARM. It helps is realizing *Context Switching*. Context Switching refers to the process of changing the executing process to another one. For this change over, all the registers of the CPU need to be saved first. After that, the CPU suspends the execution of current process and starts executing another one. This is particularly true for interrupts. Occurrence of an interrupt needs saving all registers, so that the processing can be resumed later. With the availability of register banks, if the interrupt routine uses a new set of registers, saving and restoration of registers are not necessary. This saves time in context switching.

REFERENCES AND SUGGESTED READINGS

[1] S. Chattopadhyay, SWAYAM/NPTEL course on "Microprocessors and Microcontrollers", https://onlinecourses.nptel.ac.in/noc20_ee42/preview.

[2] M.A. Mazidi, R.D. McKinlay, J.G. Mazidi, "The 8051 Microcontroller: A Systems Approach", Pearson.

[3] "MCS® 51 Microcontroller Family User's Manual", https://fdocuments.in/document/8051-manual.html".

Dynamic QR Code for Further Reading

1. S. Chattopadhyay, SWAYAM/NPTEL course on "Microprocessors and Microcontrollers".

2. "MCS® 51 Microcontroller Family User's Manual", https://fdocuments.in/document/8051-manual.html".

3 Instruction Set and Programming

UNIT SPECIFICS

Through this unit, the following concepts have been elaborated:

- *Various addressing modes and machine instructions available in the 8051;*
- *Assembly and C language programming for the 8051;*
- *Developing complete programs for the 8051;*
- *Program debugging strategies;*
- *Timers and counters for the 8051;*
- *Interrupt concepts in the 8051;*
- *Serial communication facility of the 8051.*

The discussion in the unit is to give the details of the 8051 instruction set and programming, timers, interrupts and serial communication. This is the most important unit, as far as the software development part is concerned. It highlights the ways in which the operands can be specified in the instructions. High-level programming in C language has also been introduced. It has been assumed that the reader has gone through the previous units of this book and has got an understanding of the instruction execution process. A basic background of programming is essential for this unit. A good number of examples have been included to explain the concepts, wherever needed.

A large number of multiple choice questions, relevant for the topics discussed in this unit, have been provided with their answers. Apart from that, subjective questions of short and long answer type have been included. A list of tentative practical problems has been given. A list of references and suggested readings will help the readers to get more details. The section "Know More" has been carefully designed so that the supplementary information provided in this part becomes beneficial for the users of the book. This section mainly highlights the initial activity, the history of the development of 8051 and some features of the 8051 instruction set that have been carried forward to many advanced processors.

RATIONALE

This unit on the 8051 instruction set and programming provides a detailed view of the machine instructions supported and their utilization in developing programs to solve computational and interfacing problems. The programs may be written in the assembly language or in some high-level language, like C. However, for a system designer, it is essential to understand the assembly language in order to check and debug the program logic at machine level. The unit has started with the addressing modes supported by the 8051. It specifies the ways in which an operand could be referred to in an instruction. The operand may be a constant, a register, a memory location whose address is specified directly or indirectly. The instructions of the 8051 could be classified into several categories, such as, data transfer, arithmetic and logic computations, branching etc. Each of the categories has been discussed in detail by enumerating all the instructions belonging to it, along with their applications. Complete assembly language programs have been included to enumerate the usage of instructions in program logic. The programs can also be written in high-level languages like C. However, suitable data types are needed to be included. The C programs can access the machine registers, ports etc. For problems with complex computational logic, it may be easier to write in C, rather than assembly language. To detect the logical bugs in a program, the debuggers are used. A debugger can help in executing a program line-by-line, stop at some predefined breakpoints, check/modify contents of registers and/or memory locations etc. Another important programming aspect for the 8051 is using its timers and counters. As the 8051 is used in many real-time systems, usage of hardware timers is often a requirement. The 8051 may be needed to be informed about occurrence of special events, commonly known as interrupts. The 8051 supports different types of interrupts and the programmer needs to be familiar with the development of corresponding service routines. The 8051 supports serial communication of data to devices that does not support 8-bit parallel communication, due to various reasons. Thus, this unit gives a complete view of program development techniques for the 8051, usage of its timers, interrupts and serial communication features.

PRE-REQUISITES

Electronics: Unit 1, 2 of the book

UNIT OUTCOMES

List of outcomes of this unit is as follows:

U3-O1: State the addressing modes of the 8051

U3-O2: List the operands permitted in different addressing modes

U3-O3: List the data transfer instructions

U3-O4: State the usage of arithmetic and logic instructions

U3-O5: State the branching instructions

U3-O6: Distinguish between absolute and relative branching

U3-O7: Write assembly and C programs for problems like searching, sorting, computation, I/O

U3-O8: List the features of debuggers

U3-O9: Program timers and counters of the 8051

U3-O10: Write service routines for interrupts in the 8051

U3-O11: Write program code to transmit and receive data serially in the 8051

Unit-3 Outcomes	***EXPECTED MAPPING WITH COURSE OUTCOMES*** *(1- Weak Correlation; 2- Medium correlation; 3- Strong Correlation)*					
	CO-1	***CO-2***	***CO-3***	***CO-4***	***CO-5***	***CO-6***
U3-O1	*1*	*2*	*2*	*3*	-	-
U3-O2	*1*	*1*	*3*	*3*	-	-
U3-O3	*1*	*2*	*3*	*3*	-	-
U3-O4	*2*	*2*	*3*	*3*	-	-
U3-O5	*2*	*2*	*3*	*3*	-	-
U3-O6	*2*	*1*	*2*	*3*	-	-
U3-O7	*1*	*2*	*3*	*3*	-	-
U3-O8	*2*	*2*	*3*	-	-	-
U3-O9	*1*	*3*	*3*	*2*	*1*	-
U3-O10	*1*	*3*	*3*	*2*	*1*	
U3-O11	*1*	*3*	*3*	*2*	*3*	

3.1 Introduction

The 8051 processor supports a large number of instructions. The instructions are of size 1-byte, 2-bytes or 3-bytes. Out of a total of 111 instructions supported by the 8051, 49 are single-byte instructions, while there are 45 two-byte and 17 three-byte instructions. All variants of the 8051 support the same instruction set. The instruction set is particularly optimized for 8-bit operations. Each instruction has an *opcode* part (also called the *mnemonic*) that identifies the action to be performed by the CPU. The action may necessitate zero/one/two operands to be used in the operation. Typical actions include the movement of data across the registers and memory locations, arithmetic and logical operations, controlling I/O devices via the ports, byte- and bit-level manipulations. The 8051 processor allows flexibilities in the form in which the operand addresses could be specified by the programmer. These alternatives are classified as the addressing modes for the operands. Typically, an operand may be a register, some memory location, an immediate value etc.

With the availability of compilers for high-level languages, it is possible to write programs in those languages, thus bypassing the assembly level programming altogether. However, for debugging purposes, a designer may need to check the happenings at a much deeper level, may be at the machine code level. The machine code has direct correspondence with the assembly language statements – not the high-level one. Thus, the understanding of the instruction set of the processor is essential for the microcontroller based system designers. It may be noted that most of the IDEs possess a disassembler tool that can give back the assembly language program from the machine code in program memory.

3.2 Addressing Modes

The addressing modes supported by any processor provide alternatives in which the operands of an instruction could be specified by the programmer. Likewise, the 8051 CPU provides several ways to identify the operands in an instruction. The addressing modes available with the 8051 are as follows.

- Immediate addressing
- Register addressing
- Direct addressing
- Register indirect addressing
- Bit direct addressing

As the registers of the 8051 are mapped to on-chip memory locations, it is often possible to specify the same operand in more than one ways. In the following, each of these addressing modes have been discussed in detail, with suitable examples.

3.2.1 Immediate Addressing Mode

As the name suggests, in this mode, the operand is available to the CPU as soon as the instruction has been fetched. The operand is present along with the instruction itself, no further action is needed to get it. Naturally, the operand has to be a constant value. In most of the assemblers, the constant value has to be preceded by a '#' character. The following are a few examples of the usage of immediate addressing mode.

```
MOV A, #26H            ; load 26H into the A register
MOV R7, #55H           ; load 55H into the R7 register
MOV B, #3AH            ; load 3AH into the B register
MOV P1, #59H           ; Output 59H to Port 1
MOV DPTR, #9A23H       ; load 9A23H into the register DPTR
```

It may be noted that the DPTR is a 16-bit register which can also be considered as two 8-bit registers, DPH and DPL. The last instruction "MOV DPTR, #9A23H" is equivalent to the following two instructions, taken together.

```
MOV DPH, #9AH
MOV DPL, #23H
```

3.2.2 Register Addressing Mode

The operands specified via the register addressing mode correspond to the CPU registers. The registers may be R0-R7 from the register bank, A, B or other special function registers. A few examples of instructions using the register addressing mode are as follows.

```
MOV A, R2              ; A gets a copy of R2
MOV R5, A              ; R5 gets a copy of A
ADD A, R3              ; A gets A + R3
```

It may be noted that an instruction cannot use both the registers from the register bank. For example, the instruction "MOV R2, R5" is invalid. However, this does not pose any serious problem to the programmer as the registers are mapped to memory locations and the data movement between the memory locations is permitted.

3.2.3 Direct Addressing Mode

In direct addressing mode, the instruction contains the address of the operand which is actually stored at a memory location. The mode could be used to specify the on-chip RAM locations as the operands. Following are a few such examples.

```
MOV R5, 45H        ; R5 gets the content of the RAM location 45H
MOV 55H, R2        ; RAM location 55H gets the content of R2
MOV 10H, 20H       ; RAM location 10H gets the content of RAM location 20H
```

It may be noted that the specification of the operand in direct addressing mode is similar to the immediate operand, excepting the '#' character at the beginning. This should be followed carefully by the programmer. The last example, noted above, has both the operands specified using direct addressing mode. This provides a mechanism to implement data movement between the CPU registers. For example, to move the content of the register R2 to the register R5 of Bank-0, the instruction "MOV 5, 2" could be used. As noted earlier, another probable instruction for this, "MOV R5, R2" using register addressing for both the operands, is invalid.

3.2.4 Register Indirect Addressing Mode

In this mode also, the referred operand is a RAM location. However, the address of the location is not mentioned directly in the instruction. Rather, the content of register R0 or R1 is used as the address of the memory location. It should be noted that the registers R2 to R7 could not be used in this mode. Here, the registers R0 and R1 behave like pointers in high-level languages. To mark that the register R0 (or R1) will be used as pointer in the instruction, it is preceded by a '@' character. Assuming the contents of R0 and R1 to be 40H and 50H respectively, following are a few examples of this mode of operation.

```
MOV A, @R0         ; A gets the content of memory location 40H pointed to by R0
MOV B, @R1         ; B gets the content of memory location 50H pointed to by R1
```

The registers R0 and R1 are used to index into the on-chip RAM. Similarly, to access off-chip RAM, the DPTR register can be used for indexing. For this, the MOVX instruction could be used, as shown next.

```
MOVX A, @DPTR      ; A gets the content of external RAM location pointed to by DPTR
```

3.2.5 Bit Direct Addressing Mode

This is similar to the direct addressing mode with the bit-level operands. It may be noted that the RAM locations 20H to 2FH and most of the special function registers are bit-addressable.

Each bit of these locations has a unique address (as shown in Fig 2.3, Section 2.3.2). Some examples of bit-direct addressing are as follows.

```
SETB 25H        ; Sets bit location 25H to 1
CPL 45H         ; Complements bit location 45H
```

3.3 Instructions of the 8051

The assembly/machine language instructions supported by the 8051 CPU can be grouped into four major classes – Data Transfer, Branching, Arithmetic and Logic Operations, Miscellaneous. In the following, instructions belonging to each of these categories have been discussed in detail.

3.3.1 Data Transfer Instructions

These instructions are meant for copying data from a source byte/bit to a destination byte/bit, or to exchange their contents. The opcodes coming under this category are – MOV, MOVC, MOVX, PUSH, POP, XCH and XCHD. Each of these has been elaborated next.

1. **MOV**: The instruction can be used for the movement of 1-bit, 8-bit or 16-bit data. As most of the registers and memory locations are 8-bit wide, the most common variant looks like,

   MOV *<dest-byte>*, *<source-byte>*

   Depending upon the addressing mode used to specify the destination and the source, several subvariants are possible.

   (a) *Accumulator A as destination.* Here, any of the available addressing modes can be used to specify the source, as shown in Table 3.1.

Table 3.1: MOV with A as destination

Addressing Mode	Format	Example	Meaning
Immediate	MOV A, #data	MOV A, #45H	A = 45H
Register	MOV A, Rn	MOV A, R2	A = Content of R2
Direct	MOV A, direct	MOV A, 42H	A = RAM[42H]
Indirect	MOV A, @Ri	MOV A, @R0	A = RAM[(R0)]
Note: *"MOV A, A" not allowed*			

   (b) *Accumulator A as source.* This is similar to the previous case. However, the destination operand can only be from either of the following modes – register, direct or register indirect. Some examples have been shown in Table 3.2.

Table 3.2: MOV with A as source			
Addressing Mode	**Format**	**Example**	**Meaning**
Register	MOV Rn, A	MOV R2, A	R2 = Content of A
Direct	MOV direct, A	MOV 42H, A	RAM[42H] = A
Indirect	MOV @Ri, A	MOV @R0, A	RAM[(R0)] = A

(c) *Bank register as destination.* Any of the registers R0-R7 in the current bank could be used as the destination. The source operand may be an immediate one, the Accumulator or a memory address. The cases have been shown in Table 3.3.

Table 3.3: MOV with bank register as destination			
Addressing Mode	**Format**	**Example**	**Meaning**
Register	MOV Rn, A	MOV R2, A	R2 = Content of A
Immediate	MOV Rn, #data	MOV R5, #45H	R5 = 45H
Direct	MOV Rn, direct	MOV R0, 44H	R0 = RAM[44H]

(d) *Direct memory address as destination.* With the destination operand in direct addressing mode, the source may be of any other mode including direct addressing. Table 3.4 shows the cases individually.

Table 3.4: MOV with direct memory address as destination			
Addressing Mode	**Format**	**Example**	**Meaning**
Register	MOV direct, Rn	MOV 40H, R2	R2 = RAM[40H]
Immediate	MOV direct, #data	MOV 40H, #20H	RAM[40H] = 20H
Direct	MOV direct, direct	MOV 1, 5	RAM[1] = RAM[5]
Indirect	MOV direct, @Ri	MOV 40H, @R0	RAM[40H] = RAM[(R0)]

(e) *Indirect memory address as destination.* The registers R0 and R1 could be used as pointer for the destination address of MOV instruction. Table 3.5 shows the alternatives for the source operand.

Table 3.5: MOV with indirect memory address as destination			
Addressing Mode	**Format**	**Example**	**Meaning**
Register	MOV @Ri, A	MOV @R0, A	RAM[(R0)] = Content of A
Immediate	MOV @Ri, #data	MOV @R0, #20H	RAM[(R0)] = 20H
Direct	MOV @Ri, direct	MOV @R0, 5	RAM[(R0)] = RAM[5]

(f) *Bit operands*. MOV instruction can also be used to copy one bit to another. Following are a few examples. The addressing mode of the operands is bit direct addressing.

```
MOV C, PSW.0        ; Bit-0 (Parity bit) copied to Carry bit (PSW.7)
MOV P1.5, C         ; Carry copied to Port 1, bit 5
```

(g) *16-bit data movement*. The MOV instruction works for 16-bit data as well. One of the very important 16-bit registers in the 8051 CPU is DPTR which can be used by the programmer to access external memory. The DPTR register can be initialized as follows.

```
MOV DPTR, #159AH        ; DPTR gets 159AH
```

2. **MOVC**: This instruction is used to move a code byte from on-chip ROM to the A register. The instruction is typically utilized to access on-chip lookup tables in programs. There are two variants of this instruction depending upon the 16-bit register holding the base address of the table. Either DPTR or PC can be used to hold the base value. To index into the table, the offset of the data element has to be in A. The data is copied into A.

(a) *DPTR as base register*. The corresponding instruction is

```
MOVC A, @A+DPTR
```

To use this instruction, the DPTR should be initialized to the base value.

Example 3.1: The first ten prime numbers (indexed as 0, 1, ... 9) are 2, 3, 5, 7, 11, 13, 17, 19, 23, 29. If these are stored in the ROM starting at location 200H and the register R3 contains the index of the prime we are looking for, the following code fragment using the instruction "MOVC A, @A +DPTR" could be used to get the prime in A register.

```
        MOV DPTR, #200H                      ; DPTR holds the base
        MOV A, R3                            ; A contains the index
        MOVC A, @A+DPTR                      ; A contains the prime
        ORG 200H
PRIME   DB 2, 3, 5, 7, 11, 13, 17, 19, 23, 29 ; The lookup table
```

(b) *PC as base register*. Sometimes, instead of keeping the table away from the program code, the programmer may find it more logical to keep it immediately following the code. As code is accessed via the Program Counter (PC), in such cases, it may be advantageous to use the PC as the base. The offset is as usual contained in A. The format for the instruction is "MOVC A, @A+PC".

Example 3.2: Example 3.1, when rewritten following this principle will be as follows. Here, when the CPU is executing the instruction "MOVC A, @A+PC", the PC is already pointing to the next instruction RET which is of size 1 byte. Thus, to reach the proper offset, the register A has been incremented by 1, beforehand.

```
        MOV A, R3                             ; A contains the index
        INC A                                 ; Adjust offset
        MOVC A, @A+PC                         ; A contains the prime
        RET
PRIME   DB 2, 3, 5, 7, 11, 13, 17, 19, 23, 29 ; The lookup table
```

3. **MOVX**: The instruction can be used to transfer data between the external memory and A register. Both 16- and 8-bit addresses can be mentioned for the external memory. For 16-bit address, the DPTR register is used, while the registers R0 and R1 can be used to provide 8-bit address.

   (a) *Address by DPTR*. The following instructions could be used for this purpose.

```
MOVX A, @DPTR    ; A gets the external memory byte pointed to by DPTR
MOVX @DPTR, A    ; External memory location pointed to by DPTR gets A
```

   (b) *Address by R0, R1*. The following instructions could be used to specify an 8-bit address for the external memory access.

```
MOVX A, @Ri      ; i = 0, 1. A gets the external memory byte pointed to by Ri
MOVX @Ri, A      ; i = 0, 1. External memory location pointed to by Ri gets A
```

Example 3.3: Corresponding to the program written in Example 3.1, if the primes are stored in external memory from location 2000H, the following code can be used to get the prime whose index has been specified in R3.

```
        MOV DPTR, #2000H      ; DPTR points to base
NEXT:   MOVX A, @DPTR         ; Get next prime in A
        CJNE R3, 0, L1        ; Goto L1 if not this index
        RET                   ; Got the prime, return
```

```
L1:     INC DPTR                                   ; DPTR points to next prime
        DJNZ R3, NEXT                              ; Decrement counter, get next
        ORG 2000H
PRIME   DB 2, 3, 5, 7, 11, 13, 17, 19, 23, 29     ; The lookup table
```

4. **PUSH and POP**: The PUSH instruction is used to copy one byte operand to the on-chip RAM location pointed to by the *stack pointer* (*SP*). The SP register is incremented by 1. The operand can be specified using only the direct addressing mode. Typical example of PUSH is as follows, which stores the content of A register (memory address 0E0H) to stack memory location 33H, assuming that the current value of SP is 32. The SP register is incremented to 33H.

   PUSH 0E0H

   Instructions, such as, "PUSH A", "PUSH @R0", "PUSH R2" are invalid.

   On the other hand, the POP instruction copies the content from top of stack (pointed to by SP) to the direct operand address mentioned in the instruction. For example, with SP having the value 33H, the instruction "POP 0E0H" will copy the of RAM location 33H to A register. The stack pointer SP will be decremented to 32H.

5. **XCH and XCHD**: The XCH instruction swaps the content of A register with a source byte mentioned as an operand. The generic instruction is of the format "XCH <*byte*>". The addressing modes supported for the operand along with examples have been noted in Table 3.6.

Table 3.6: XCH and XCHD instructions

Addressing Mode	Format	Example	Meaning
Register	XCH A, Rn XCHD A, Rn	XCH A, R1 XCHD A, R1	Contents of R1 and A exchanged Lower nibbles of R1 and A exchanged
Indirect	XCH A, @Ri	XCH A, @R0	Contents of RAM[(R0)] and A exchanged
Direct	XCH A, direct	XCH A, 40H	Contents of RAM[40H] and A exchanged

The XCHD (exchange digit) is similar to the XCH with the exception that only the lower nibbles (lower order 4 bits) of the source byte and A register get exchanged. The higher order nibbles remain unchanged. For example, if A = 45H and R1 = 7AH, "XCHD A, R1" will convert A to 4AH and R1 to 75H.

3.3.2 Branching Instructions

The 8051 CPU generally works by fetching the instructions serially from program memory. The next instruction to be executed is pointed to by the register PC. However, depending upon the logic of the program, this straight-line sequence often needs to be modified to create the facilities like branching to some other sequence, creating a loop structure or executing a subprogram. In the following, discussion has been carried out by grouping the relevant instructions into three categories – unconditional branching, conditional branching, subprogram call/return.

1. *Unconditional branching*. There are three instructions in this category – LJMP, AJMP and SJMP. Out of these, LJMP is a 3-byte instruction, while the other two are 2 byte wide.

- **LJMP**: The *long jump* instruction is of the following format.

  LJMP *<16-bit addresss>*

  As the address part specifies 16 bits, the branch target can be anywhere within the 64k address space of the 8051.

- **AJMP**: The absolute jump is a 2-byte instruction with the following syntax.

  AJMP *<11-bit addresss>*

  As the PC is 16-bit wide, the 11-bit address part is used to replace only the lower-order 11 bits of the PC. The higher-order 5 bits remain unaltered. Thus, the branch target must be within the 2k range of the current PC location.

- **SJMP**: The short jump is also a two-byte instruction, however, the second byte provides the distance (called offset) of the branch target from the current PC value. The format of the instruction is as follows.

  SJMP *<8-bit offset>*

  After fetching the SJMP instruction, the content of PC is equal to the address of the next memory location. To execute SJMP, the offset part is added to the PC. Now, if the offset is a positive number, it implies a forward jump. If the offset is negative, it is a backward jump. As the offset is an 8-bit value, the target must be within a distance of -128 bytes to +127 bytes. This type of limited branching is also known as *relative branch*. While translating an SJMP instruction to machine code, the assembler computes this distance and keeps as the second byte of the translated instruction. For example, consider the following code fragment.

  ...

```
L1:     MOV R1, #10
        MOV R2, #20
        NOP
        SJMP L1
```

Here the first two MOV instructions are each of 2 bytes, NOP is of 1 byte and SJMP is of 2 bytes. Thus, after the SJMP instruction has been fetched, the difference of the address location represented by L1 from the current PC value will be -7 (0F9H). It may be noted that this offset of -7 is independent of the location from which the entire program has been loaded. This type of relative addressing makes program code amenable to relocation to any part of the memory without any changes in the code itself. Apart from SJMP, all conditional branching instructions in the 8051 are also relative in nature.

2. *Conditional Branching*. These instructions modify the PC value with the jump target if the specified condition is met. All conditional branches are relative to the PC, similar to SJMP. The following are the variants available.

- **J**<*condition*>: Several instructions belong to this category in which the identification of the *condition* makes the full mnemonic. Table 3.7 shows the instructions with their meanings.

Table 3.7: J<condition> instructions

Instruction	Meaning	Example
JZ <target>	Jump if A = 0	JZ L1
JNZ <target>	Jump if A $\neq$ 0	JNZ L1
JC <target>	Jump if CY = 1	JC L2
JNC <target>	Jump if CY = 0	JNC L2
JB <bit>, <target>	Jump if <bit> = 1	JB P1.3, L1
JNB <bit>, <target>	Jump if <bit> = 0,	JNB ACC.0, L1
JBC <bit>, <target>	Jump if <bit> = 1, clear bit	JBC ACC.4, L1

Out of all the instructions noted in Table 3.7, the JBC is a special one which also clears the bit to zero.

- **CJNE**: This instruction, *compare and jump if not equal*, compares between a source byte and a destination byte. The carry flag (CY) gets set to 1 if the destination is less than the source and reset otherwise. The format of the instruction is as follows.

CJNE *<dest-byte>*, *<source-byte>*, *<target>*

Table 3.8 shows the different addressing mode combinations supported by CJNE to specify the destination and the source bytes.

Table 3.8: CJNE instructions

Addressing Mode	Format	Example	Meaning
Immediate	CJNE A, #data, target	CJNE A, #45, L1	Jump to L1 if A ≠ 45
Direct	CJNE A, direct, target	CJNE A, 42H, L1	Jump to L1 if A ≠ RAM[42H]
Register	CJNE Rn, #data, target	CJNE R1, #45, L1	Jump to L1 if R1 ≠ 45
Indirect	CJNE @Ri, #data, target	CJNE @R1, #45, L1	Jump to L1 if RAM[(R1)] ≠ 45

Example 3.4: The CJNE instruction can be used to implement some program logic that repeats a set of activities till some internal or external condition is met. For example, the following program reads continually the content of port P2. If the value read is less than 100, it is output to port P1. If the value is more than 100, it is output to port P0. If the value is exactly equal to 100, the program proceeds to the instruction labelled NEXT. It is assumed that the port P2 has been already configured as input.

```
    L0: MOV A, P2           ; Read P2 into A
        CJNE A, 100, L1     ; If A = 100, jump to NEXT
        SJMP NEXT           ;
    L1: JNC L2              ; If A > 100
        MOV P0, A           ; Output to P0
        SJMP L0             ; Read next input
    L2: MOV P1, A           ; A < 100, Output to P1
        SJMP L0             ; Read next input
  NEXT:
```

- **DJNZ**: The instruction, decrement and jump if not zero, decrements a specified byte and if the result is nonzero, control branches to the mentioned target address. A speciality of the instruction is that, none of the status flags are affected. The format of the instruction is as follows.

  DJNZ *<byte>*, *<target>*

  Table 3.9 shows the addressing mode combinations that are permissible for specifying the DJNZ instruction.

Table 3.9: DJNZ instructions

Addressing Mode	Format	Example	Meaning
Direct	DJNZ direct, target	DJNZ 42H, L1	Decrement RAM[42H], if result is nonzero, jump to L1
Register	DJNZ Rn, target	DJNZ R1, L1	Decrement R1, if result is nonzero, jump to L1

Example 3.5: The DJNZ instruction is typically used to implement loop structures in the program. Any of the general purpose registers/memory locations can be used as a counter. With each iteration of the loop-body, the counter may is decremented by 1, till the counter value becomes zero. For example, in the following code fragment, the register R3 has been assumed to contain a counter value. In the body of the loop, the input value from port P0 has been copied into the port P1 as output. It is assumed that the port P0 has been already configured as input.

```
L0:  MOV A, P0       ; Read P0 into A
     MOV P1, A       ; Output to P1
     DJNZ R3, L0     ; Decrement counter and
                     ; repeat if the counter R3 is
                     ; nonzero
```

3. *Subprogram Call/Return*. A subprogram is a part of the program code dedicated to a specific subtask. The overall computation performed by a main program may have similar subcomputations needed at different points. For example, while interfacing a display unit with successive patterns sent to the display, it is necessary to have some delay between two successive patterns. Thus, a separate delay routine may be created for this purpose as a subprogram and called from different places in the main program, as shown in Fig 3.1.

```
              Setup Pattern-1
              Output to display
              Call DELAY_RTN
              Setup Pattern-2
              Output to display
              Call DELAY_RTN
                 ...
DELAY_RTN:
              Wait for some time
              Return to main program
```

Fig 3.1: Subprogram call from main program

Similar to the unconditional branch instructions, the 8051 supports two subprogram call instructions, namely LCALL and ACALL. A basic difference between the branch and the call instructions is that unlike branch, after the subprogram has been executed, control returns to the instruction immediately following the call instruction. For this, the return address is saved onto the stack. Any subprogram ends with a RET instruction which causes the PC to be loaded with the address available at the top of the stack.

- **LCALL**: It is a three-byte instruction with the following format.

  LCALL *<16-bit address>*

  Assuming that the LCALL instruction starts at memory location 1000H, the next instruction will be at 1003H. If the SP is at 32H, the return address 1003H is stored in RAM locations 33H and 34H. The new SP value becomes 34H. The 16-bit address specified in the instruction is copied into the PC and thus the control jumps to the subprogram.

- **ACALL:** Similar to AJMP, ACALL is a two-byte instruction of the format as follows.

  ACALL *<11-bit address>*

  The 11 least-significant bits of PC is replaced with the 11-bit address to jump to the subprogram. The 16-bit return address is saved onto the stack and SP is incremented by two. As in AJMP, ACALL restricts the target to be within 2k address range from the current PC.

- **RET and RETI**: Both RET and RETI are single byte instructions, consisting of only the mnemonic. The RET instruction is used as the last instruction of a subprogram that makes the execution to be restarted from the instruction following the last LCALL/ACALL instruction. Contents from the top two bytes are popped from the stack and loaded into the PC register. The SP is decremented by two. The RETI instruction is used in the subprograms corresponding to interrupt service routines. On occurrence of an interrupt, similar to subprogram call, the control branches to a subprogram, decided beforehand. Before that, the return address is saved onto stack, similar to LCALL/ACALL. As in RET, RETI also restores the content of PC from the stack. Apart from that, RETI also restores the interrupt logic to accept any additional interrupts. If any interrupt has been pending before RETI, corresponding service routine is taken up for execution only after executing one instruction at the return address.

Example 3.6: Let us consider a program that has got some light-emitting diodes (LEDs) connected to Port P1 of the 8051. It makes all the LEDs to blink continually. For this, the program first outputs 00H to the port and then 0FFH after a certain delay. The process is repeated continually for the blinking effect. The delay is designed as a subprogram called from the main program.

```
         L1: MOV A, #00H          ; Set 00H in A
             MOV P1, A            ; Output to P1
             LCALL DELAY_RTN      ; Call Delay Routine
             MOV A, #0FFH         ; Set 0FFH in A
             MOV P1, A            ; Output to P1
             LCALL DELAY_RTN      ; Call Delay Routine
             SJMP L1              ; Repeat for ever
 DELAY_RTN: MOV R3, #0FFH         ; R3 used as counter
         L2: DJNZ R3, L2          ; Loop if R3 ≠ 0
             RET                  ; Return from subprogarm
```

3.3.3 Arithmetic and Logic Instructions

These are the core computational instructions of the 8051 CPU. The instructions could be broadly classified into the following categories – arithmetic instructions, logical instructions and rotate instructions. In the following, instructions from each category will be taken up for discussion.

1. *Arithmetic instructions*. Several arithmetic operations are supported by the 8051. These include addition (ADD, ADDC, DA), subtraction (SUBB), multiplication (MUL) and division (DIV).

    - **ADD, ADDC, DA:** These instructions work with 8-bit data. Both unsigned and signed arithmetic could be done. For the ADD instruction, the first operand and the destination are always the accumulator (A register). The second operand is a byte, as shown next.

      ADD A, *<source byte>*

      The source byte can be specified using different addressing modes. Table 3.10 shows various cases with examples.

Table 3.10: ADD with different addressing modes

Addressing Mode	Format	Example	Meaning
Register	ADD A, Rn	ADD A, R2	A = A + R2
Immediate	ADD A, #data	ADD A, #20H	A = A + 20H
Direct	ADD A, direct	ADD A, 5	A = A + RAM[5]
Indirect	ADD A, @Ri	ADD A, @R0	A = A + RAM[(R0)]

The operation affects the status flags carry (CY), auxiliary carry (AC) and overflow (OV). The addition may be a signed operation or an unsigned operation. The unsigned operation has operands and results in the range of 00H to 0FFH. For a result beyond 0FFH (255 in decimal), the CY flag becomes 1, indicating the fact. For signed operation, the valid operands and results are in the range of -128 to +127. The overflow flag (OV) indicates if the result is beyond this range.

The ADDC instruction stands for "Add with carry". The instruction is of the following format.

ADDC A, *<source byte>*

After executing the instruction, the content of A register gets modified to A + *<source byte>* + CY. The source byte may be specified using different addressing modes, similar to Table 3.10.

The DA (Decimal Adjust) instruction is used in conjunction with the addition of BCD (Binary Coded Decimal) numbers. The format of the instruction is as follows.

DA A

A decimal number when converted to the BCD format has each digit coded as a 4-bit binary number. For example, the number 45 in decimal, when converted to 8-bit binary representation will have it represented as 00101101. The same number when converted to BCD will be 01000101, with the most significant 4 bits representing the digit 4 and the least significant 4 bits representing 5. Naturally, if two BCD numbers are added using the ADD instruction of 8051, the result will need further refinement for correction. For example, addition of BCD numbers 45 (01000101) and 35 (00110101) results in the bit pattern 01111010 as the content of the accumulator. Execution of "DA A" instruction on this, results into the decimal number 80 coded into BCD as 10000000 in the accumulator.

Example 3.7: Let us consider a set of 10 numbers stored from RAM location 35H onwards. The following program will add those numbers and store the result at memory location 50H.

```
   L1: MOV R0, #35H        ; Set memory pointer in R0
       MOV R3, #10         ; Set counter in R3
       CLR A               ; Clear A
       CLR C               ; Clear CY
 NEXT: ADDC A, @R0         ; Add next number
       DJNZ R3, NEXT       ; All numbers added?
       MOV 50H, A          ; Store result at 50H
```

Example 3.8: In Example 3.7, if the numbers are in BCD format, the following program will add those numbers and store the result at memory location 50H. If the result is more than 99, location 51H will have the third most significant digit. It is assumed that the sum is less than 1000.

```
   L1: MOV R0, #35H        ; Set memory pointer in R0
       MOV R3, #10         ; Set counter in R3
       CLR A               ; Clear A
       CLR R4              ; R4 holds the 3rd digit
 NEXT: ADD A, @R0          ; Add next number
       DA  A               ; Adjust for BCD
       JNC L1              ; If CY = 0, do not change R4
       INC R4              ; Increase 3rd digit
       DJNZ R3, NEXT       ; All numbers added?
       MOV 50H, A          ; Store result at 50H
       MOV 51H, R4         ; Store result at 51H
```

- **SUBB:** This instruction is used to perform subtraction operation. The format of the instruction is as follows.

SUBB A, <*source byte*>

It subtracts the source byte and the carry flag (CY) from A register. It may be noted that there is no simple SUB instruction without carry. Thus, while doing subtraction, it is implied that the carry flag be cleared beforehand. For example, the following code fragment subtracts 29H from the accumulator.

```
CLR C
SUBB A, #29H
```

To execute the SUBB instruction, the operations carried out are as follows.

1. Take 2's complement of the source byte
2. Add it to A register
3. Invert carry flag CY

Example 3.9: Let us look into the process of subtraction followed in the 8051, considering the operation of subtracting 22H from 25H with the carry assumed to be reset.

25H	=	00100101	
22H	=	+ 11011110	(2's complement)
		1 00000011	
03H (03_{10})	=	0 00000011	(Invert carry)

On the other hand, subtraction of 25H from 22H will proceed as follows.

22H	=	00100010	
22H	=	+ 11011011	(2's complement)
		0 11111101	
FDH (-3_{10})	=	1 11111101	(Invert carry)

- **MUL:** This is the multiplication instruction. It multiplies register A with register B. Since A and B are 8-bit registers, the result is 16-bit wide. The lower-order byte of the result is put in A register, while the higher-order byte is stored in B register. The instruction is of the following format.

  ```
  MUL AB
  ```

  For example, if A $=100_{10}$ and B $= 200_{10}$, after "MUL AB", the result is 20000_{10} = 4E20H. The A register will now have 20H and B register 4EH. The MUL instruction affects the carry (CY) and the overflow (OV) flags. The CY flag is always reset and the OV flag is set to 1 if the result is more than 255.

- **DIV:** This instruction performs the operation of dividing the byte present in accumulator by the byte in B register. The instruction is of the format noted next.

DIV AB

It should be ensured that the B register content is nonzero, else the result will be undefined. After division, the quotient is made available in register A and remainder in B. For example, if A = 45_{10} and B = 7_{10}, after executing "DIV AB", the contents of A and B registers will be 6_{10} and 3_{10}, respectively. Execution of DIV clears the CY flag. The OV flag is set if the instruction attempts to divide by zero, else reset.

***Handling Overflows*:** In 8-bit signed arithmetic, the range of valid numbers is -128 to +127. If at any point of time, result of a computation is beyond this range, the result is erroneous and the 8051 indicates the error by setting the OV flag to 1. It is the responsibility of the programmer to check the OV flag after the operation, wherever necessary. The 8051 sets the OV flag in either of the two situations noted in the following.

1. *There is a carry from D6 to D7 but no carry from D7.* The carry flag is zero in this case. As there is a carry from D6 to D7, the result could not be contained in 7 bits. The carry generated at D6 position got absorbed at the D7 bit. Hence the D7 bit of both the operands must have been zero, indicating positive numbers. Whereas, in the result, the bit is 1 indicating a negative number. Hence an overflow.
2. *There is a carry from D7 but no carry from D6 to D7.* In this case, both the operands must have D7 = 1, indicating both as negative numbers. After the operation, D7 must be zero, which means a positive number. Thus, it is also a case of overflow.

2. *Logic instructions.* These instructions are useful for carrying out logical operations on the operands. The Boolean operators supported are AND, OR, XOR and complement.
   - **AND:** The AND operation is performed using the ANL (AND logical) instruction. The instruction has the following format.

ANL <*dest-byte*>, <*source-byte*>

A bit-by-bit ANDing of the *dest-byte* with the *source-byte* is performed and the result is stored in the *dest-byte*. Table 3.11 shows the usage of ANL instruction in different addressing modes.

Table 3.11: ANL with different addressing modes

Addressing Mode	Format	Example	Meaning
Register	ANL A, Rn	ANL A, R2	A = A AND R2
Immediate	ANL A, #data	ANL A, #20H	A = A AND 20H
Direct	ANL A, direct ANL direct, A ANL direct, #data	ANL A, 5 ANL 5, A ANL 35, #42H	A = A AND RAM[5] RAM[5] = RAM[5] AND A RAM[35] = RAM[35] AND 42H
Indirect	ANL A, @Ri	ANL A, @R0	A = A AND RAM[(R0)]

There is a special version of ANL instruction that works with bit operands. Here, the destination is the carry flag (CY). The instruction has the format as follows.

ANL C, *<source-bit>*

Another variant can specify the invert of source-bit as operand, as shown next.

ANL C, /*<source-bit>*

Example 3.10: The following code fragment sets the location 50H to 0FFH if the input port bits P2.2 is 1 and P2.5 is zero. Else, the location is set to 77H.

```
        MOV 50H, #0FFH      ; Set memory location 50H
        MOV C, P2.2         ; Get bit P2.2 into CY
        ANL C, /P2.5        ; AND with invert of P2.5
        JNC L1              ;
        MOV 50H, #77H       ; Set memory location 50H
L1:
```

- **OR, XOR:** Similar to AND, there are instructions to carry out the bit-by-bit operations for OR and XOR. The addressing modes supported in these instructions are similar to that for the ANL instruction. The corresponding instructions are ORL and XRL. Some such examples are noted next.

```
ORL A, R2     ;    A = A OR R2
XRL A, #20H   ;    A = A XOR 20H
```

- **CPL:** This is an instruction to complement the content of the accumulator. The 1's complement of the content is computed. The instruction is as follows.

  CPL A

  There is another variant of the instruction that works with bit operand. It complements the specified bit. The instruction is of the following format.

  CPL *<bit>*

  For example, the instruction "CPL P1.5" will complement the port 1's bit number 5.

Example 3.11: The following program fragment toggles the bits of the port P2 using the CPL instruction. The initial pattern put in port P2 sets alternate bits to 1's and 0's. After that, the bits flip continually.

```
    MOV A, #55H     ; Set A to 01010101
L1: MOV P2, A       ; Output to P2
    CPL A           ; Complement A
    SJMP L1         ; Repeat forever
```

3. *Rotate instructions*. These instructions can be used to rotate the accumulator register A towards left or right. There are four different instructions performing rotations – RR, RL, RRC and RLC. In the following, each of these has been discussed in detail.

- **RR:** The *rotate right* (RR) instruction rotates the content of accumulator right by one bit position. All bits, starting with MSB, are shifted right with the LSB fed back to the MSB. It has been shown in Fig 3.2. The format of the instruction is as follows.

Fig 3.2: RR Instruction

  RR A

- **RL:** It stands for *rotate left* (RL). The content of the accumulator is rotated left. The bits are shifted left from LSB towards MSB. The MSB is fed back to the LSB. The operation has been shown in Fig 3.3. The format of the instruction is as follows.

Fig 3.3: RL Instruction

RL A

- **RRC:** The instruction *rotate right through carry* (RRC) is similar to RR with the exception that the carry flag (CY) behaves as an extension to the least significant side of the accumulator. The bits from MSB towards the LSB are shifted to the right by one bit position. The LSB gets shifted to CY while the CY is rotated back to the MSB of A. The operation has been illustrated in Fig 3.4. The format of the instruction is as follows.

Fig 3.4: RRC Instruction

RRC A

- **RLC:** The instruction *rotate left through carry* (RLC) is just the reverse of RRC. The carry flag (CY) extends the A register in the MSB side. The execution of the instruction is as follows. The bits from LSB towards the MSB get shifted to the left, the MSB is shifted to CY, while the CY is rotated back to the LSB. The execution of RLC has been shown in Fig 3.5. The instruction has the following format.

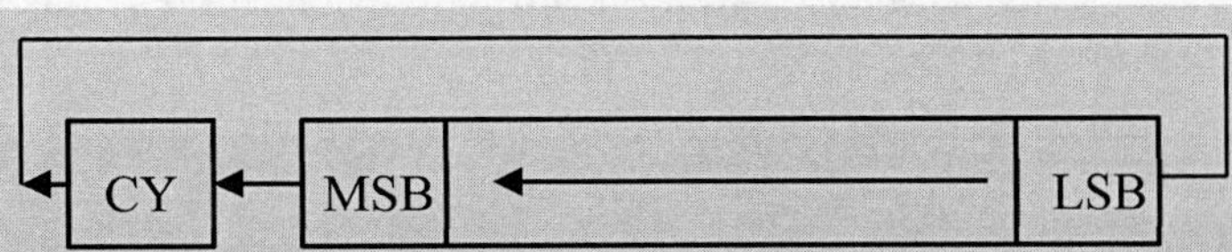

Fig 3.5: RLC Instruction

RLC A

Example 3.12: The following code fragment can be used to transfer the bits of the accumulator serially through the bit 0 of port P1.

```
        CLR C               ; Clear carry
        MOV R5, #8          ; R5 holds the count 8
NEXT:   RRC A               ; Get next bit in carry
        MOV P1.0, CY        ; Output carry to P1.0
        DJNZ R5, NEXT       ; Check if all bits transferred
```

3.3.4 Other Miscellaneous Instructions

In the last few sections, various classes of instructions have been detailed. Apart from that, there exists some more instructions in the 8051 with specific functionalities. In the following, such instructions have been discussed.

- **CLR:** The instruction can be used to clear the accumulator or a bit. There are two formats of this instruction as noted next.

```
CLR A          ; Clears the accumulator, no status flags affected
CLR <bit>      ; Clears the specified bit
```

- **INC:** This instruction increments the operand by 1. Unlike ADD instruction, it does not affect any of the status flags. There are two variants of the INC instruction. One version takes a byte as the operand, while the other one uses the 16-bit register DPTR. Different addressing modes supported by the instruction have been noted in Table 3.12.

Table 3.12: INC with different addressing modes and operands

Addressing Mode	Format	Example	Meaning
Accumulator	INC A	INC A	A = A + 1
Register	INC Rn	INC R4	R4 = R4 + 1
Direct	INC direct	INC 5	RAM[5] = RAM[5] + 1
Indirect	INC @Ri	INC @R0	RAM[(R0)] = RAM[(R0)] + 1
DPTR (16 bit)	INC DPTR	INC DPTR	DPTR = DPTR + 1

- **DEC:** This instruction decrements the operand by 1. Unlike INC, the instruction does not work for DPTR (though "DEC DPL" is supported). It also does not affect the status flags. The remaining addressing modes supported by the instruction have been noted in Table 3.13.

Table 3.13: DEC with different addressing modes

Addressing Mode	Format	Example	Meaning
Accumulator	DEC A	DEC A	A = A – 1
Register	DEC Rn	DEC R4	R4 = R4 – 1
Direct	DEC direct	DEC 5	RAM[5] = RAM[5] – 1
Indirect	DEC @Ri	DEC @R0	RAM[(R0)] = RAM[(R0)] – 1

- **NOP:** This is the *No Operation* instruction. The execution of this instruction has no effect on any of CPU registers or memory locations. Only the program counter is incremented to continue executing the next instruction. The instruction is used to introduce small delay in the execution process of the program. The instruction has the format noted next.

  NOP

- **SWAP:** This is the swap instruction that can be used to swap the nibbles of the accumulator register A. In the process, the bits D3-D0 of A gets exchanged with the bits D7-D4. Format of the instruction is as follows.

  SWAP A

  For example, the instruction "SWAP A" with A = 45H changes A to 54H.

Example 3.13: An array of N numbers have been stored in an array starting at external memory address 2000H. The following program sorts the numbers in ascending order. It uses the RAM location 40H as a temporary space for interchange operation.

```
        ORG 1000H              ;   Clear carry
        TEMP EQU 40H           ;   R5 holds the count 8
        N EQU 10               ;   Array size
        MOV R2, #N – 1         ;   Load N – 1 into R2
L1:     MOV DPTR, #2000H       ;   Set DPTR to start of array
        MOV R3, R2
L2:     MOVX A, @DPTR          ;   Get next number
        MOV R1, A              ;   Copy A into R1
        INC DPTR               ;   Point to next number
        MOVX A, @DPTR          ;   Get next number
```

```
        MOV TEMP, A         ; Copy A into TEMP
        MOV A, R1           ; Get previous number in A
        CJNE A, TEMP, L3    ; A ≠ (TEMP), goto L3
        SJMP L4             ; A = (TEMP), goto L4
L3:     JC L4               ; A < (TEMP), goto L4
        MOVX @DPTR, A       ; A > (TEMP), exchange
        MOV A, TEMP         ; two locations
        DEC DPL             ;
        MOVX @DPTR, A       ;
        INC DPL             ;
L4:     DJNZ R3, L2         ; Repeat until  R3 is zero
        DJNZ R2, L1         ; Repeat until R2 is zero
        END
```

3.4 C Language Programming for the 8051

Many electronic systems contain one/more processor(s). A majority of these systems are having dedicated functionality, such as, digital camera, mobile phone, car, refrigerator etc. Such electronic systems with dedicated functionality are commonly known as *embedded systems*. Each processor embedded into a system has an associated software. This software is commonly called, *embedded software*. With the knowledge of assembly language programming, it is possible to write such software. However, implementing complex program logic in assembly language is often very cumbersome. As a result, the programming language C is often used in these applications. The ANSI C, when augmented with the hardware oriented features, is often called the *embedded C*.

Use of C in these systems provides the following benefits.

- The C programs are generally small, compact and easier for human understanding than their assembly language counterparts. Efficient C compilers that can work across the platforms are available. Experienced C programmers provide the expert pool to develop such applications.
- C programs being at a higher level, provides better portability across systems. Changing from one microcontroller to another may just need a recompilation of the source code. Assembly code will need a complete redesign and rewriting.
- By design, C language supports constructs and data types close to the hardware.

Compared to the full C language, embedded C can be considered as a subset of it, primarily used for microcontroller based system design. The programs need to be concerned about the limited resources (memory, I/O ports etc.). Embedded C programs are generally complied using *cross-compilers* that create files to be downloaded onto the microcontroller for execution. In the following, discussion has been carried out enumerating the data types supported in embedded C along with some example code fragments.

3.4.1 Data Types

Though the C language supports different data types, for the embedded C programming targeting the 8051 processor, the following data types are most widely used.

Unsigned char: This is the most fundamental data type for an 8-bit processor like 8051. It is an 8-bit data type with supported values in the range 0 to 255.

Example 3.14: The following C language program outputs the values 00-7FH sequentially to the port P2.

```
#include <reg51.h>
void main (void)
{
        unsigned char m;
        for (m = 0; m < 0x80; m++)
              P2 = m;
}
```

Signed char: The signed character can represent values in the range –128 to +127, as it uses an 8-bit representation. This is the default data type used in Embedded C. Thus, it is necessary to be more specific in the programs in declaring variables of type "unsigned char", if the values are in the range 0 to 255.

Example 3.15: The following C language program adds 10 signed characters stored in an array a. The result is put in the variable b.

```
#include <reg51.h>
void main (void)
{
        signed char a[] = { -2, -5, 10, 20, -3, 1, -1, 45, 25, -6 };
        signed char b = 0;
        unsigned  char j;
        for (j = 0; j < 10; j++)
              b += a[ j ];
}
```

Unsigned int: The unsigned integer can represent numbers in the range 0 to 65535 (0FFFFH). The 8051 uses the 16-bit numbers for specific applications, such as, memory address, counter values etc. As all arithmetic and logic operations are performed on 8-bit data, the programmer should be careful in declaring variables of this data type. The memory locations being 8-bit wide, an unsigned integer variable will occupy two bytes. The access to those memory locations is also more complex than a byte access. As a result, the hex-file code generated by the compiler may be much larger than the same program using unsigned character variables only. It may be noted that the embedded C compilers use signed integer as default. Thus, the *unsigned* keyword is very important to be mentioned.

Example 3.16: The following C language program uses an unsigned integer variable to introduce some delay in the execution so that the bits of the port P2 are flipped continually.

```
#include <reg51.h>
void main (void)
{
      unsigned char m;
      for (; ;) {
           P2 = 0x55;
           for (m = 0; m < 65530; m++);
           P2 = 0xAA;
           for (m = 0; m < 65530; m++);
      }
}
```

Signed int: The signed integer is a 16-bit data type. Variables of this type can hold values in the range –32768 to +32767. This is the default integer data type used by the compilers.

Single bit: There are two bit data types supported by the compilers of the 8051. One of them, *bit* can refer to the bits in the bit-addressable RAM locations 20H-2FH. The other type *sbit* can be used to refer to the individual bits of *special function registers*.

Example 3.17: The following C language program flips the bit-4 of port P1 continually.

```
#include <reg51.h>
sbit BIT4 = P1^4;                    // Bit-4 of Port P1
void main (void)
{
      unsigned char m;
```

```
        for (; ;) {
            BIT4 = 0;
            for (m = 0; m < 65530; m++);
            BIT4 = 1;
            for (m = 0; m < 65530; m++);
        }
    }
```

Special function register: This is a byte type data, written as *sfr*, corresponding to the special function registers of the 8051. Unlike *sbit*, *sfr* data type corresponds to byte-size special function registers.

Example 3.18: The following C language program flips the bits of the port P2 continually using sfr data type.

```
    sfr P2 = 0xA0;
    void main (void)
    {
        unsigned char m;
        for (; ;) {
            P2 = 0x55;
            for (m = 0; m < 65530; m++);
            P2 = 0xAA;
            for (m = 0; m < 65530; m++);
        }
    }
```

Example 3.19: The following assembly language program reads the ports P0 and P1 continually, computes AND of the values read and outputs to the port P2.

```
        ORG 0000H        ;
        MOV P0, #0FFH    ; Set P0 as input
        MOV P1, #0FFH    ; Set P1 as input
    L1: MOV A, P1        ; Read next value from P1
        MOV R1, A        ; Save value read in R1
        MOV A, P0        ; Read next value from P0
        ANL A, R1        ; Perform AND operation
        MOV P2, A        ; Output result to P2
        SJMP L1          ; Continue
```

The same program written in C will be as follows.

```
#include <reg51.h>
unsigned char data1;
unsigned char data2;
unsigned char result;
void main (void)
{
    while (1) {
        data1 = P1;
        data2 = P0;
        result = data1 & data2;
        P2 = result;
    }
}
```

Example 3.20: The following assembly language program reads the port bits P0.0 and P1.4 continually, computes AND of the values read and outputs to the port P2.1.

```
        ORG 0000H           ;
        MOV P0, #0FFH       ;  Set P0 as input
        MOV P1, #0FFH       ;  Set P1 as input
    L1: MOV A, P1           ;  Read next value from P1
        RR A                ;  Rotate right A 4 times
        RR A
        RR A
        RR A
        MOV R1, A           ;  Copy content of A in R1
        MOV A, P0           ;  Read next value from P0
        ANL A, R1           ;  Perform AND operation
        RL A                ;  Rotate A left
        MOV P2, A           ;  Output result to P2.1
        SJMP L1             ;  Continue
```

The same program written in C will be as follows.

```
#include <reg51.h>
bit data1 = P0.0;
bit data2 = P1.4;
bit result = P2.1;
void main (void)
{
    while (1) {
        result = data1 & data2;
    }
}
```

3.5 Program Debugging

While the syntax errors (grammatical mistakes) in a program can be detected by compilers or assemblers, logical errors cannot be detected so easily. To detect logical errors, the programmer may go through the code manually and check for the logic flow with some representative data values. This is more commonly known as *static debugging*. The other technique involves observing the contents of the registers and memory locations after executing each (or a group of) instruction(s). This is commonly known as *dynamic debugging*. The following are some such actions permissible in a debugger.

1. **Single Step.** The technique allows executing one instruction at a time. After executing the instruction, control is given back to the user to check for values of registers and memory locations. The values could also be modified by the user before stepping into the execution of the next instruction.
2. **Breakpoint.** The debugger can make the program execution to be suspended at some specific lines of the source code. After setting a breakpoint at a source code line or a subprogram, the program execution can be initiated. If the control reaches the breakpoint, execution gets suspended and the user may check/modify the registers, memory locations etc.

Most of the *integrated development environments* (IDEs) of the 8051 support debugging at both assembly language and C program levels. The machine code is downloaded onto the development board having the 8051 chip through some cable connected via the USB or serial communication ports of the computer. The IDE executes the debugger which works by sending the commands to and receiving the data from the 8051 via some on-chip monitor routine loaded separately into the microcontroller.

3.6 Programming Timers and Counters

Timers and counters are two important components in developing systems interacting with the nature. Certain events are to be organized at some particular time instant. Accurate time delays may need to be inserted between sequences of events etc. This necessitates the availability of one/more high precision timers. Also, in many applications we need event counters. The occurrence of events may be fed as digital pulses to the 8051 which is counted by the timer/counter module.

3.6.1 Timer Programming

There are two timers in the 8051, named as *Timer 0* and *Timer 1*. Both are 16-bit timers that can be configured to work as 8-bit, 13-bit or 16-bit timers. The registers associated with the operation of timers are as follows.

1. *Timer registers*. Each timer has got two 8-bit registers, TH*x* and TL*x*, associated with it to hold the 16-bit time/ count. For Timer 0, registers are TH0 and TL0. For Timer 1, those are TH1 and TL1.

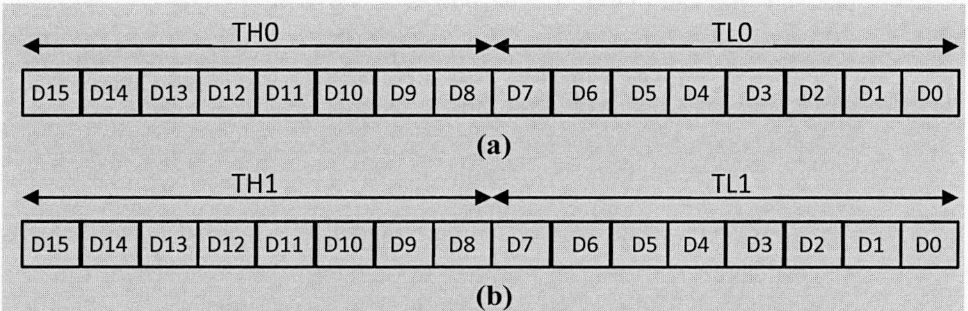

Fig 3.6: Timer registers (a) Timer 0 (b) Timer 1

The register structure has been shown in Fig 3.6. Registers can be used in conjunction with MOV instruction, similar to other registers. For example,

```
MOV TL0, #45H        ; Moves 45H to TL0
MOV R1, TH1          ; Moves TH1 to R1
```

2. *Timer mode register TMOD.* This is an 8-bit register controlling both the timers. While the bits 0 to 3 of the register control the mode of operation of Timer 0, the bits 4 to 7 are dedicated to the control of Timer 1. The structure of TMOD register has been shown in Fig 3.7. Each part has the following components.

Timer 0				Timer 1			
GATE	C/T	M1	M0	GATE	C/T	M1	M0

Fig 3.7: TMOD register structure

- **M1, M0:** These two bits determine the timer mode selection. Table 3.14 illustrates the mode settings. The modes 1 and 2 are commonly used in applications and will be explored in the following.

Table 3.14: M1, M0 bit settings

M1	M0	Mode	Operation
0	0	0	• 13-bit timer/counter • THx holds 8-bit count • TLx is a 5-bit prescalar
0	1	1	16-bit timer/counter
1	0	2	• 8-bit auto reload • THx holds reload value • TLx holds count
1	1	3	Split timer

- **C/T:** The bit selects either timer operation or counter operation. C/T = 0 implies timer operation, while C/T = 1 implies counter operation. For timer operation, the crystal is used to derive the clock source to provide clock ticks to the timer. The timer frequency is set to 1/12th of the crystal frequency, as shown in Fig 3.8. For example, if the crystal is of frequency 12 MHz, the timer will operate at a frequency of 1 MHz. For most of the 8051 based systems, the crystal is of frequency 11.0592 MHz. This is primarily to match the serial data transfer rate with the then existing IBM PC. For this crystal, the timer frequency is 921.6 kHz, resulting into the time period of 1.085 μSec. For C/T=1 (counter operation), the count pulses are fed from *T0* (P3.4) and *T1* (P3.5) for Timer 0 and Timer 1, respectively.

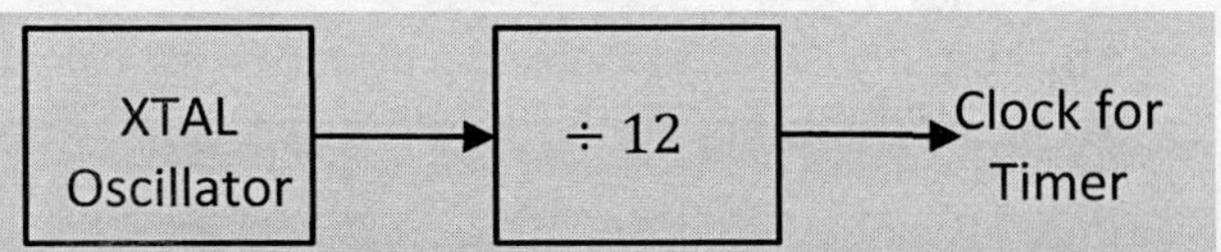

Fig 3.8: Derivation of Timer clock

- **GATE:** This bit specifies the way in which the timer will be controlled. The starting and stopping of timers can be controlled via both software and hardware means. Resetting the GATE bit (GATE = 0) will ensure only software based control to start and stop the corresponding timer. Setting the GATE bit (GATE = 1) provides combined software and hardware control to start or stop the timer.

The software control is achieved via the *TR0* and *TR1* bits in the *Timer Control* register, *TCON*. The bits TR0 and TR1 can be set or reset to serve the purpose of controlling the timers, as follows.

```
SETB TR0      ; Start Timer 0
CLR TR0       ; Stop Timer 0
SETB TR1      ; Start Timer 1
CLR TR1       ; Stop Timer 1
```

TCON register structure has been shown in Fig 3.9. The most significant four bits of TCON are to control the timers while the least significant four bits control the external interrupt lines (that will be discussed in conjunction with interrupts). The bits *TF0* and *TF1* are timer flags. The flag bit of a timer gets set when the corresponding timer rolls over from its maximum value to zero. The TF bits can also be set/reset as follows.

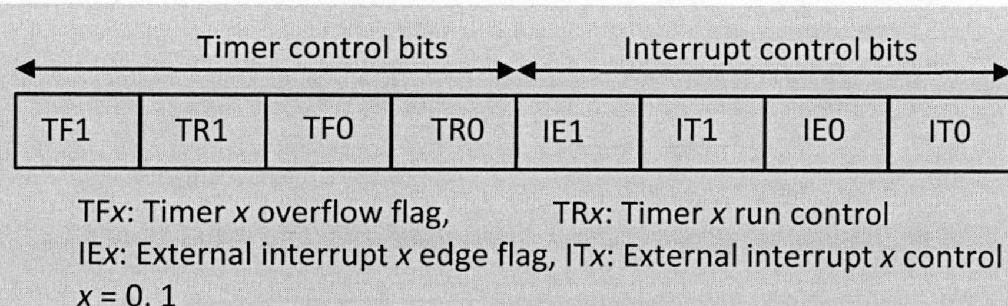

Fig 3.9: TCON register structure

```
SETB TF0      ; Set Timer 0 flag
CLR TF0       ; Clear Timer 0 flag
SETB TF1      ; Set Timer 1 flag
CLR TF1       ; Clear Timer 1 flag
```

With the setting GATE = 1, to run a timer, apart from setting the TR bit, the external interrupt pin is also required to be set high. Fig 3.10 shows the overall run control for a timer. If GATE = 0, the setting the bit TRx starts the Timer x. When GATE = 1, to run the Timer x, apart from setting the TRx bit, the INTx (multiplexed with P3.2 pin) pin should be set to 1. Thus, with

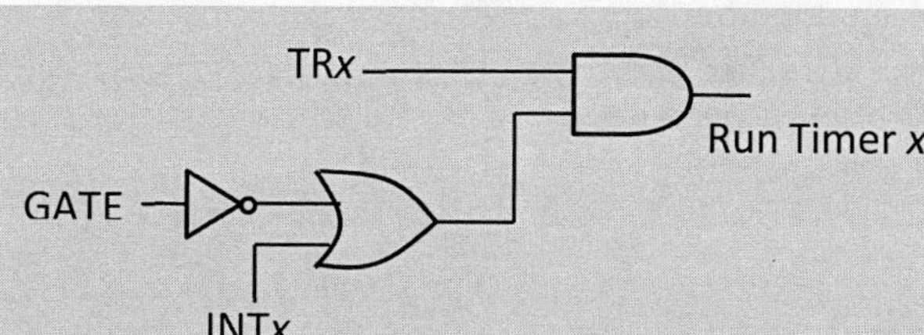

Fig 3.10: Run control for Timer

GATE = 1, the timer can be stopped by resetting the TR*x* bit via software, or by pulling the INT*x* pin low, in hardware.

As noted earlier, applications developed around the 8051 that use timer, utilize mostly mode 1 or mode 2 of operation. In the following these modes have been discussed in detail.

1. *Mode 1 timer operation*. This is a 16-bit timer operation mode. The timer may be initialized to any value between 0000H and FFFFH. The 16-bit value is loaded into the register pair TH-TL. After loading the initial value, the timer is started by executing the instruction "SETB TR0" or "SETB TR1" for Timer-0 or Timer-1, respectively. From this point onwards, the timer starts incrementing with each clock tick. After the count has reached FFFFH, at the next clock tick, the value rolls over to zero and sets the corresponding TF bit of TCON register to high. The timer operation in mode 1 has been illustrated in Fig 3.11. Assuming that the crystal frequency is 11.0592 MHz, the timer will operate at a frequency of 921.6 kHz having clock time period of 1.085 µS. Thus, if the initial value loaded in the timer is hexadecimal *XXYY*, the overflow will occur after (FFFF – *XXYY* + 1)×1.085 µS. On the other hand, to generate a time delay *D*, it is divided by 1.085 µS to get a count *n*. From this, (65536 – *n*) is computed. The resulting value is converted into a 16-bit hexadecimal value *xxyy*. The value *xx* is loaded in TH and *yy* into TL.

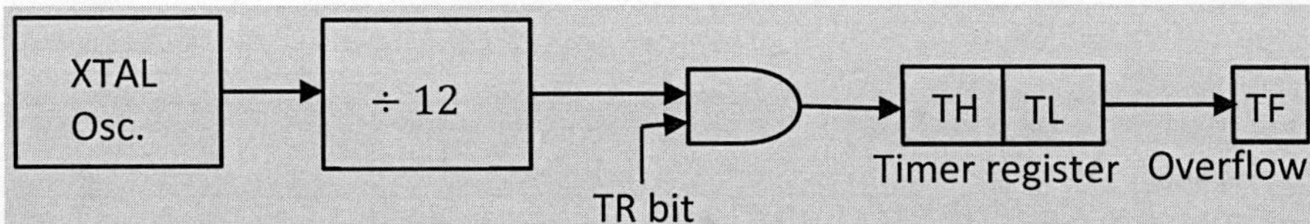

Fig 3.11: Timer in Mode 1

Example 3.21: Let us consider the problem of generating a square wave with 50% duty cycle and ON/OFF periods of 10 mS each. The time delay of 10 mS will be generated using the Timer 0 in mode 1.

As per the discussion on initializing the timer, the value of *n* should be 10 ms ÷ 1.085 µS = 9217. Thus, the initial value of the timer will be 56319 (DBFFH). Hence the TH and the TL registers should be loaded with DBH and FFH, respectively. The square wave will be generated on P2.5. The assembly language program for the same is as follows.

```
    ORG 0000H          ;
    CLR P2.5           ; Clear port bit P2.5
    MOV TMOD, #01H     ; Set Timer 0 in Mode 1
L1: MOV TL0, #0FFH     ; Load TL
    MOV TH0, #0DBH     ; Load TH
    CPL P2.5           ; Complement P2.5
```

```
            SETB TR0                ;  Start timer
        L2: JNB TF0, L2             ;  Check roll over of TF0 flag
            CLR TR0                 ;  Stop timer
            CLR TF0                 ;  Clear timer flag
            SJMP L1                 ;  Repeat
            END
```

The same program written in C will be as follows.

```
#include <reg51.h>
void Delay_Rtn (void);
sbit p2_5 = P2^5;
void main (void)
{
    while (1) {
        p2_5 = ~p2_5;               // Toggle P2.5
        Delay_Rtn();                // Call delay
    }
}
void Delay_Rtn (void)
{
    TMOD = 0x01;                    // Timer 0, Mode 1
    TL0 = 0xFF;  TH0 = 0xDB;        // Load TL0 and TH0
    TR0 = 1;                        // Start timer
    while (TF0 == 0);               // Wait for TF0 rollover
    TR0 = 0;   TF0 = 0;             // Turn off timer and clear TR0
}
```

It may be noted that the Mode 0 operation of the timer is exactly same as the Mode 1 operation, excepting that the timer is a 13-bit timer that can hold values in the range 0000H to 1FFFH in the TH-TL register pair. After the timer reaches the count 1FFFH, in the next clock tick, it rolls over to 0, raising the TF flag.

2. *Mode 2 timer operation*. This is an 8-bit timer operation with *auto-reload* facility. The TL register holds the count value and is incremented with every clock tick. After the register reaches the value FFH, in the next clock tick, it rolls back to 0 and the TF flag bit is raised. The

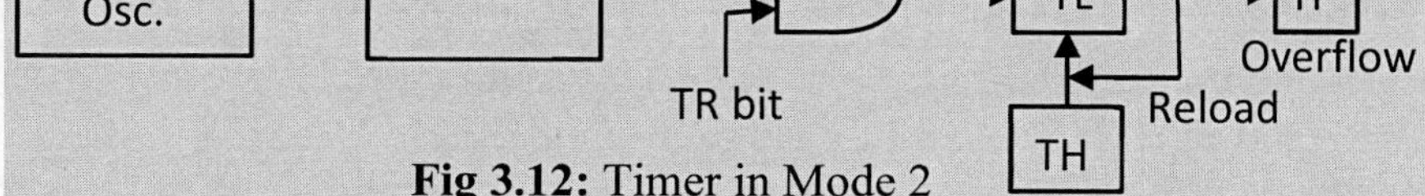

Fig 3.12: Timer in Mode 2

initial timer value is loaded into the TH register, which is copied automatically to the TL register initially, and later on at each roll over event. The programmer need not load the value to TL explicitly, only clearing the TF flag after a roll over will restart the timer. The situation has been explained in Fig 3.12, which is very much similar to Fig 3.11, excepting the reload part. However, since the maximum count value is 255, Mode 2 is not very suitable for generating large delays. In the following, *Example 3.21* has been revisited with the ON/OFF period of 20 µS.

Example 3.22: Let us consider the problem of generating a square wave with 50% duty cycle and ON/OFF periods of 20 µS each. Timer 0 in mode 2 has been used to insert appropriate delay in the waveform generation.

The value of n, in this case is should be 10 ms ÷ 1.085 µS = 19. Thus, the initial value of the timer will be 237 (EDH). Hence the TH0 register should be loaded with EDH. In mode 2, as soon as TH0 is loaded with the value, it is automatically copied into TL0. The assembly language program for the same is as follows.

```
        ORG 0000H           ;
        CLR P2.5            ; Clear port bit P2.5
        MOV TMOD, #02H      ; Set Timer 0 in Mode 2
        MOV TH0, #0EDH      ; Load TH0
L1:     CPL P2.5            ; Complement P2.5
        SETB TR0            ; Start timer
L2:     JNB TF0, L2         ; Check roll over of TF0 flag
        CLR TF0             ; Clear timer flag
        SJMP L1             ; Repeat
        END
```

The same program written in C will be as follows.

```
#include <reg51.h>
sbit p2_5 = P2^5;
void main (void)
{
    TMOD = 0x02;          // Timer 0, Mode 2
    TH0 = 0xED;           // Load TH0
    while (1) {
        p2_5 = ~p2_5;     // Toggle P2.5
        TR0 = 1;          // Start timer
        while (! TF0);    // Wait for overflow
        TF0 = 0;          // Reset timer flag
    }
}
```

3.6.2 Counter Programming

The timers available in the 8051 can be used to count external pulses also. For this, the timers need to be operated in the counter mode by setting the corresponding C/T bit of TMOD register to 1. The *T0* input pin (Pin 14) is used to feed the pulses to be counted by Counter 0, while the *T1* pin (Pin 15) is earmarked for Counter 1. The counters do upcounting on occurrence of pulses on T0 and T1. It may be noted that the pins 14 and 15 are multiplexed with Port 3 bits, P3.4 and P3.5, respectively. The operation of the counters in Mode 1 and Mode 2, counting external input pin events have been illustrated in Fig 3.13 and 3.14, respectively.

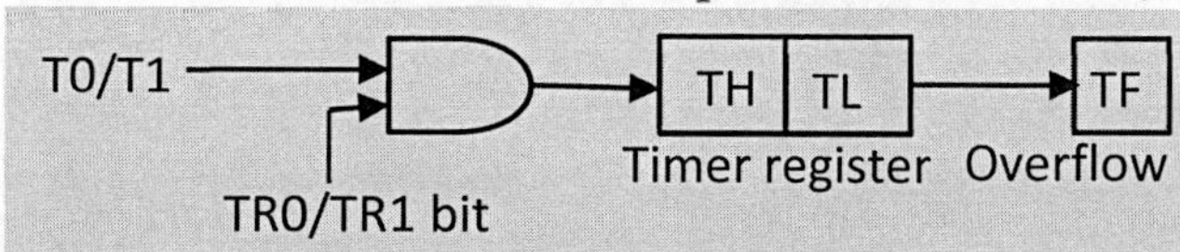

Fig 3.13: Counter in Mode 1

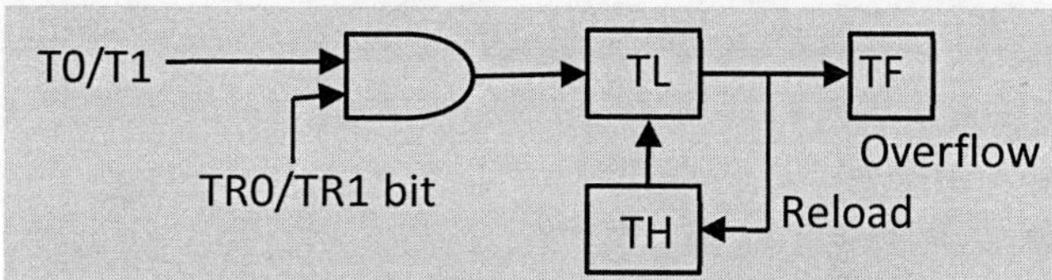

Fig 3.14: Counter in Mode 2

Example 3.23: Consider the problem of counting pulses on T0 pin using Mode 2 counter operation. The TH0 register is cleared, so that, whenever the count in TL0 exceeds 255 and it rolls over, the TL0 register will be reloaded with zero from TH0. The TF0 flag will also be set. The program outputs the current count available in TL0 to the port P1. The assembly language code for the program is as follows.

```
        ORG 0000H          ;
        MOV TMOD, #06H     ;  Set Counter 0 in Mode 2
        SETB P3.4          ;  Make T0 input line
        MOV TH0, #0        ;  Clear TH0
        SETB TR0           ;  Start counter
    L1: MOV A,TL0          ;  Get TL0 content in A
        MOV P1, A          ;  Output to Port 1
        JNB TF0, L1        ;  Continue till roll over
        CLR TF0            ;  Clear timer flag
        SJMP L1            ;  Repeat
        END
```

The same program written in C will be as follows.

```
#include <reg51.h>
sbit p3_4 = P3^4;
```

```
void main (void)
{
    TMOD = 0x06;                // Counter 0, Mode 2
    TH0 = 0;                    // Clear TH0
    p3_4 = 1;                   // Configure T0 in input mode
    TR0 = 1;                    // Start counter
    while (1) {
        P1 = TL0;               // Output TL0 count to Port 1
        if ( TF0 )  TF0 = 0;    // If roll over, reset TF0
    }
}
```

3.7 Programming Interrupts

The 8051 programming techniques discussed so far, develop program logic in which the processor controls the flow of execution. For example, if a program is supposed to do a data transfer from an input device to a memory buffer space, it has to check continually whether the device is ready for data transfer. The transfer can take place only when the device is ready. However, the processor needs to check the status in a loop. The technique is often known as *polling*. A major problem with polling is the wastage of processor time in busy wait state. The input devices are mostly electromechanical in nature and are often operated by human operators. This increases the wastage of computing power further. The situation is aggravated further if a number of devices are connected to the 8051 and the processor may check the status of those devices one by one, in a circular fashion.

A better technique for data transfer uses the concept of *interrupts*. In this, whenever a device is ready for data transfer, it informs the processor about it. The processor, busy in some other execution sequence, now suspends the current operation and branches to a special program fragment to take care of the data transfer operation. Once the data transfer is over, the processor resumes the suspended program. This avoids the wastage of processor time in busy-wait cycle.

Example 3.24: Interrupts – A Real-Life Analogy

Consider the real-life situation in which a person is reading a book in a room. The doorbell rings and the person needs to go to open the door. The visitor arriving to the house and pressing the doorbell switch generates an interrupt for the reading process by the reader. Upon hearing the doorbell, the person will first complete the line/paragraph being read, a bookmark would be kept to remember the page/line. The person will then go to open the door and interact with the visitor. Once the interaction is over, the person will come back and start reading from the point at which the reading was left. Here, going to open the door is equivalent to jumping to the routine to service the interrupt, interaction part is equivalent to the actual interrupt service and restarting the reading process is like resuming the original program being executed.

The subprogram executed by the processor, on occurrence of an interrupt is called *interrupt service routine* (*ISR*). Each interrupt supported by the processor will have its corresponding ISR. As the interrupts supported by a processor are fixed, so are the addresses of their ISRs in the memory. The addresses form the *Interrupt Vector Table* (*IVT*) for the processor. Before branching to an ISR, the return address (address of the next instruction to be executed) is saved onto stack. After completion of the ISR, the return address is taken out from the stack and loaded into the *Program Counter* (*PC*) to accomplish the return to the originally executing program.

3.7.1 Interrupts in 8051

The 8051 processor supports six interrupts, as follows. Table 3.15 summarizes the types of interrupts, the vector address, pin number etc.

1. *Reset*. This is the Pin 9 of the chip. Whenever the input is high, the 8051 gets a Reset interrupt and the control branches to ROM address 0000H.
2. *Timers*: The two timers present in the 8051 will generate interrupts – *Timer 0 interrupt* and *Timer 1 interrupt*, when the corresponding timer rolls over and the TF bit gets set. Control branches to address 000BH and 001BH, respectively for the Timer 0 and Timer 1 interrupts.
3. *INT0, INT1*: These are also called external interrupts. The corresponding pins are 12 (multiplexed with P3.2) and 13 (multiplexed with P3.3). The memory address for *INT0* is 0003H, while for *INT1*, it is 0013H.
4. *Serial Communication*: This is an interrupt activated on receiving/transmitting a character serially by the 8051.

From Table 3.15 it may be noted that for interrupts like INT0, INT1, Timers etc. the addresses are separated by just eight bytes. Thus, the corresponding service routines have space of eight bytes only. If the interrupt service routine is more than eight bytes long, an LJMP instruction can be used to jump to a memory address having an empty chunk of memory space. The situation is further tight for the Reset – only three bytes are free for its service routine that can accommodate only an LJMP instruction.

Table 3.15: Interrupts in the 8051

Interrupt	**ROM address**	**Pin No.**
Reset	0000H	9
INT0	0003H	12 (P3.2)
Timer 0 interrupt	000BH	
INT1	0013H	13 (P3.3)
Timer 1 interrupt	001BH	
Serial communication	0023H	

3.7.2 Interrupt Enable Register

By default, all interrupts are disabled on resetting the 8051. Thus, the 8051 will not respond to any of the interrupts, till those are enabled specifically via software. The enable/disable status of the 8051 is controlled by the setting of the *Interrupt Enable* (**IE**) register. The register structure has been shown in Fig 3.15. The individual bit settings are as follows.

(MSB)							(LSB)
EA	-	ET2	ES	ET1	EX1	ET0	EX0

Fig 3.15: Interrupt Enable (IE) register structure

EA: Setting EA = 0 disables all interrupts. On the other hand, if EA = 1, the status of individual interrupts are controlled by other bits of IE register as noted next.

Bit 6 is left for future extension.

ET2, ET1, ET0: Control the Timer interrupts. Out of these, ET2 is meaningful for the 8052 only, as the 8051 does not have Timer 2. ET1and ET0 correspond to enabling of Timer 1 and Timer 0 interrupts, respectively. Setting the bit to 1 enables the relevant timer, setting to 0 disables the timer.

ES: Enables or disables the serial communication interrupt.

EX1, EX0: These bits correspond to the external interrupts INT1 and INT0. Setting EX1 to 1 enables INT1, resetting to 0 disables it. Same is the case with EX0 for INT0 interrupt.

For example, for the 8051, to enable the two timer interrupts and INT0 while keeping others in a disabled mode, the IE register should be set to the bit pattern "10001011" using an instruction like,

```
MOV IE, #10001011B
```

3.7.3 Timer Interrupts

The IE register can be programmed to enable the generation of interrupts when a particular timer rolls over and the TF bit is set. Thus, after starting a timer, the 8051 need not wait checking continually the status of the TF bit. Whenever the interrupt occurs, program control gets transferred to the corresponding service routine address (000BH for Timer 0 and 001BH for Timer 1). It may be noted that the Timer Flag TF0 and TF1 will automatically reset once the control jumps to the corresponding Interrupt Service Routine.

Example 3.25: Let us consider the problem of generating a square wave with 50% duty cycle and ON/OFF periods of 20 μS each. Timer 0 in mode 2 has been used to insert appropriate delay in the waveform generation. However, compared to the previous case, the timer will generate interrupt whenever it rolls over and the corresponding service routine to complement P2.5 will get executed. The assembly language program for the same is as follows.

```
        ORG 0000H         ;
        LJMP MAIN         ;  Jump to MAIN, bypass IVT
        ORG 000BH         ;  ISR for Timer 0
        CPL P2.5          ;  Complement port bit P2.5
        RETI              ;  Return from ISR
        ORG 0030H         ;  Main routine starts here
MAIN:   MOV TMOD, #02H    ;  Set Timer 0 in Mode 2
        MOV TH0, #0EDH    ;  Load TH0
        MOV IE, #82H      ;  Enable Timer 0
        SETB TR0          ;  Start timer
L1:     SJMP L1           ;  Stay here
        END
```

The last statement of the program has been made an infinite loop to demonstrate that the 8051 need not check the TF0 flag anymore. Instead of looping here, the program may proceed to other computations also. The same program written in C will be as follows.

```
#include <reg51.h>
sbit p2_5 = P2^5;

void timer0 (void) interrupt 1
{
    p2_5 = ~p2_5;            // Complement P2.5
}

void main (void)
{
    TMOD = 0x02;             // Timer 0, Mode 2
    TH0 = 0xED;              // Load TH0
    IE = 0x82H;              // Enable Timer 0 interrupt
    while (1);               // Infinite loop
}
```

3.7.4 External Interrupts

The 8051 has two pins, called INT0 and INT1 (multiplexed with port pins P3.2 and P3.3, respectively). If these pins are activated, the operation of the 8051 gets interrupted. A generic classification of interrupt activation has been shown in Fig 3.16. An interrupt may support triggering via one of the following methods.

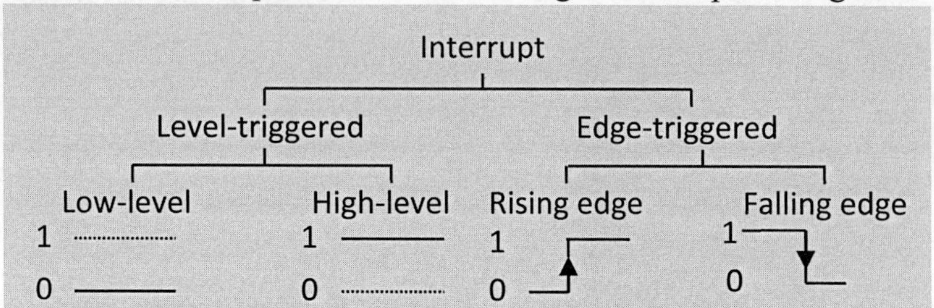

Fig 3.16: Triggering of generic interrupts

- *Low Level*: Interrupt is triggered if the corresponding pin is kept low for some time.
- *High Level*: In this case, keeping the pin high for some time triggers the interrupt.
- *Rising Edge*: Interrupt gets triggered if there is a low-to-high transition in the interrupt pin.
- *Falling Edge*: Interrupt is triggered if there is a high-to-low transition in the interrupt pin.

The 8051 interrupts, INT0 and INT1, support two triggering modes – *low-level* and *falling edge*. As noted in Fig 3.9, the lower nibble of the TCON register controls the interrupt triggering modes. The bits IT0 (TCON.0) and IT1 (TCON.1) control the interrupt type and can be set/reset by software. If the bit IT0 is set, INT0 will be triggered by a falling edge, if reset, it is low level triggered. Similar is the case in bit IT1 for the interrupt INT1. For the falling edge triggering, the occurrence of high-to-low pulse in INT0 is remembered in IE0 (TCON.1) flag bit. For IT1, it is remembered in IE1 (TCON.3). These flags are cleared upon executing the corresponding RETI instruction. However, it may be noted that the low-level of INT0 and INT1 are not remembered internally. Thus, for the low-level interrupt to be sensed properly, it must be held low till the beginning of the ISR but withdrawn before the RETI instruction in the ISR (to avoid sensing multiple interrupts on the line). As a general rule, the low-level should be maintained for around four machine cycles, but not more. For the edge-triggered interrupt sensing, the interrupt pin must be held high for one machine cycle followed by low for at least one machine cycle.

Example 3.26: Let us consider the example in which a switch has been connected to the INT0 pin and an LED to port bit P2.0. If the switch is closed, a 0 value is sent to INT0. In the service routine for the interrupt, the LED is turned ON. It remains ON for some small time, turns OFF and control returns from the service routine.

```
ORG 0000H          ;
LJMP MAIN          ; Jump to MAIN, bypass IVT
ORG 0003H          ; ISR for INT0
```

```
            SETB P2.0           ; Set port bit P2.0, LED ON
            MOV R2, #0FFH       ; R2 used as counter
      L1:   DJNZ R2, L1         ; Wait for some time
            CLR P2.0            ; LED OFF
            RETI                ; Return from ISR
            ORG 0030H           ; Main routine starts here
    MAIN:   MOV IE, #81H        ; Enable INT0
      L2:   SJMP L2             ; Wait in loop
            END
```

The same program written in C will be as follows.

```
#include <reg51.h>
sbit p2_0 = P2^0;

void external0 (void) interrupt 0
{
    p2_0 = 1;                 // Complement P2.5
    for (i = 0; i < 10000; i++);
    p2_0 = 0;
}

void main (void)
{
    IE = 0x81H;               // Enable INT0 interrupt
    while (1);                // Infinite loop
}
```

If we are looking for falling edge triggering of INT0, in the MAIN routine, IT0 (TCON.0) bit be set by executing the instruction “SETB TCON.0”.

3.7.5 Interrupt Priorities

A very pertinent question about interrupts is to determine which interrupt will get serviced first, if two or more interrupts have occurred together. Upon reset, the 8051 has the following priority setting. INT0 has the highest priority, followed by Timer 0, INT1, Timer 1, Serial Communication, in sequence. That is,

INT0 > Timer 0 > INT1 > Timer 1 > Serial Communication.

An individual interrupt can be assigned the highest priority by setting the corresponding bit in the *Interrupt Priority* (*IP*) register. The structure of the IP register has been shown in Fig 3.17. The register is bit-addressable. The two most significant bits of the register are reserved. The bit PT2 controls priority of Timer 2 interrupt in 8051, PS is for Serial interrupt, PT1 and PT0 for Timer 1 and Timer 0, PX1 and PX0 correspond to the external interrupts INT1 and INT0, respectively. For example, if the bit PT1 is set to 1 while all others are 0 in IP, Timer 1 gets the highest priority among all. If multiple bits are set in the IP register, all of them will have higher priorities than other interrupts, while within them, the priority ordering will be as per the default priority. For example, if the bits PX1 and PT0 are set to 1, the interrupts INT1 and Timer 0 will have higher priority than others, while between INT1 and Timer 0, Timer 0 interrupt will have more priority than INT1. It may be noted that if a higher priority interrupt occurs while the service routine of a lower priority interrupt is being executed, control will get transferred to the service routine of the higher priority interrupt.

(MSB)							(LSB)
-	-	PT2	PS	PT1	PX1	PT0	PX0

Fig 3.17: Interrupt Enable (IE) register structure

3.8 Serial Communication Programming

A major problem with the bus-based parallel communication between the processor and the devices is the requirement to run a large number of signal lines for connection. For applications with limited size and requiring possibly less data transfer rate, serial bit-by-bit communication may be sufficient. This reduces the pin count for the interface, as well. A serial communication takes place between a transmitter and a receiver, both of which are devices having electronic interface supporting transmission and/or reception. Serial communication can be classified into the following categories.

- *Simplex Mode*: Communication is always unidirectional between a master and a slave device.
- *Duplex Mode*: Communication is bidirectional.
- *Half-duplex Mode*: Communication is bidirectional, however, at any point of time, data is transferred in one direction only.

Serial communication can also be classified to be either *synchronous* or *asynchronous* in nature. For synchronous communication, the transmitter and the receiver need to work on the same clock signal, which may not be always feasible. If the transmitter and the receiver work on their own clock signals, it is referred to as an asynchronous transmission. Asynchronous transmission is preferable to synchronous transmission, however, needs a fixed protocol to be followed for faithful communication. For transmission, every character is put into a *frame* structure. When there are no data transmission, the line is at 1 (high). Beginning of a frame is identified by a 0-bit, called *start* bit. The start bit is followed by 8-bit ASCII code of the character being transmitted. After that, the end of frame is marked by one/two 1 (high) bit(s), called *stop* bit(s). The frame structure has been shown in Fig 3.18. Sometimes, a frame also contains a *parity* bit. The parity may be even or odd. For even parity system, the parity bit is set/reset such that the total number of 1's in the character code along with the parity bit is even. On the other hand, in odd-parity system, the total number of 1's is odd. Inclusion of parity bit in the frame may aid in detecting transmission error. During transmission, if one or any odd number of bits get modified, the recomputed parity bit at receiver will not match with the received parity bit, flagging an error. The rate of data transfer is stated as *bps* (*bits per second*). It is also called *baud rate*. For serial communication, the transmitter and the receiver must agree upon the frame format, baud rate etc.

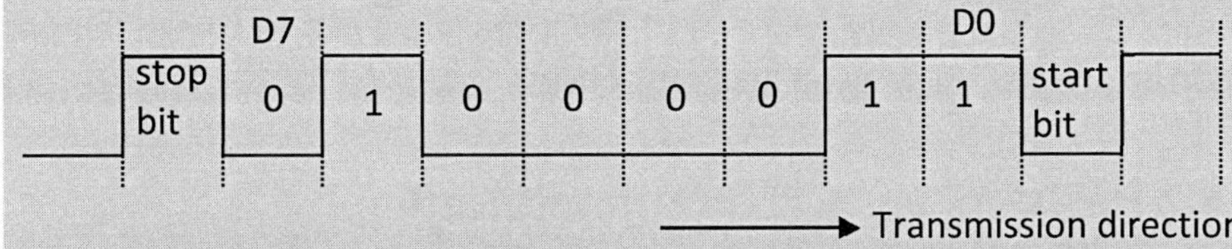

Fig 3.18: Frame structure for character 'C' (ASCII code 43H)

For serial communication, the 8051 has two pins, called *TxD* (*Transmit Data*) and *RxD* (*Receive Data*). The pins are multiplexed with the port 3 bits, P3.0 and P3.1, respectively. As a result, the voltage levels supported are +5V for a 1 and 0V for a 0. It may be noted that the serial communication standard RS232C has -3 to -25V for logic 1 and +3 to +25V for logic 0. Hence if the 8051 has to follow this standard, some additional interfacing chip (such as, MAX232) has to be used. Further discussion on this has been omitted for the sake of brevity.

3.8.1 Setting Baud Rate

Table 3.16: Typical Baud Rate Settings

Baud rate	TH1 (Hex)
9600	FD
4800	FA
2400	F4

The 8051 can be programmed to support many different baud rates. For this, the timer has to be used in Mode 2 (auto-reload). As discussed previously, for timer operation, the 8051 crystal frequency is divided by 12. To set baud rate, the serial communication circuitry within the 8051 further divides this frequency further by 32 to drive the Timer 1. Now, the TH1 register is loaded with the appropriate value, so that the timer pulses (due to roll over) could be generated at appropriate time instants. These pulses are used for bit timing. For example, assuming the crystal frequency to be 11.0592 MHz, as per the above discussion, the clock signal fed to the Timer 1 has a frequency of $((11.0592 \div 12) \div 32) = 28800$ Hz. If the TH1 register is loaded with the value 0FDH (-3 in decimal), it will take three pulses to roll over, setting the baud rate to $28800 \div 3 =$ 9600. Some typical baud rates and their corresponding TH1 register initialization values have been noted in Table 3.16. All calculations assume the crystal frequency to be 11.0592 MHz. For a different crystal frequency, the TH1 values could be determined, as explained previously.

3.8.2 Registers for Serial Communication

The 8051 has two important registers associated with serial communication – SBUF and SCON. Both the registers are 8-bit wide.

- **SBUF:** The *Serial Buffer* register is responsible for transmitting and receiving characters for the 8051. For transmitting a character serially, the character has to be written into the SBUF register. Once the character is written onto SBUF, it is put into a frame by adding the start and the stop bits. The frame transmission through TxD pin initiates immediately. Similarly, when bits are received by the 8051 via the RxD pin, the framing bits are removed and the character received is put into the SBUF register. The user program can now read the SBUF register to get the character. The SBUF register can be used in conjunction with MOV instruction as noted next.

```
MOV SBUF, # 'M'     ; Load ASCII code of 'M' into SBUF
MOV SBUF, A         ; SBUF gets content of A register
MOV A, SBUF         ; SBUF content copied to A register
```

- **SCON:** The *Serial Port Control* register is responsible for determining the framing structure and also to enable/disable transmission and reception. This is a bit-addressable register with structure as shown in Fig 3.19. The bits have the following meanings.

(MSB)							(LSB)
SM0	SM1	SM2	REN	TB8	RB8	TI	RI

Fig 3.19: Serial Port Control (SCON) register structure

SM0, SM1: These two bits determine the mode of serial transmission. Four alternative modes are supported – Mode 0, Mode 1, Mode 2 and Mode 3. Out of these, only the Mode 1 is used extensively. For Mode 1, SM0 and SM1 are set to 0 and 1, respectively. Hence, in our discussion, we shall concentrate only on this mode. Mode 1 implies 8-bit data with one start bit and one stop bit in each frame. Thus, the frame size is 10 bits. The mode also allows various baud rate settings by programming the TH1 register.

SM2: This bit is used for multiprocessor communication. For our discussion, the bit will always be set to 0 to disable multiprocessor mode.

REN: This is called the *Receive Enable* bit. By default, the 8051 only transmits data via the TxD line. If the programmer wants also to receive data serially through RxD pin, the REN bit must be set to 1. Thus, by resetting the bit, user can block the reception of serial data by the 8051.

TB8, RB8: These bits are used mostly in Mode 2 and Mode 3 of communication. Thus, in our discussion and also for most of the serial communication applications, the bits are reset to 0.

TI: The *Transmit Interrupt* bit is set to 1 by the 8051 after completing transmission of the 8-bit character available in the SBUF register. It indicates that the 8051 is ready to transfer another character. The TI flag bit is set at the beginning of sending the stop bit in the frame. The user program can check this to determine whether to copy the next character to be transmitted to SBUF.

RI: The *Receive Interrupt* bit is set when the 8051 has placed the received byte into the SBUF register. It may be noted that the 8051 receives the frame serially, removes the start and the stop bits from it and places the character into the SBUF register. The RI flag is set halfway through the reception of the stop bit. Upon detecting the RI flag set, the user program should read the character from the SBUF register, before it is lost.

3.8.3 Serial Transmission

To transmit characters serially, the 8051 first programs the Timer 1 in mode 2 (auto-reload) and loads TH1 register appropriately for the required baud rate. The SCON register is programmed in mode 1. The timer is started by setting the TR1 bit. The TI bit is cleared. To send a character, it is written into the SBUF register. The TI flag is monitored continually to check the completion of this character transmission. Once TI is found to be 1, the transfer of the character is complete. For transmitting further characters, the TI flag is cleared and the next character is copied into the SBUF register. The following example illustrates the serial transmission.

Example 3.27: Consider the problem of serially transmitting the character string "8051" at a baud rate of 9600 using the serial mode 1. The assembly language program for the problem is as follows.

```
          ORG 0000H              ;
          MOV TMOD, #20H         ; Timer 1, Mode 2
          MOV TH1, #0FDH         ; Baud rate 9600
          MOV SCON, #40H         ; Mode 1, REN disabled
          SETB TR1               ; Start Timer 1, auto-reload
          MOV A, # '8'           ; Load '8' into A
          ACALL SEND             ; Transfer '8'
          MOV A, # '0'           ; Load '0' into A
          ACALL SEND             ; Transfer '0'
          MOV A, # '5'           ; Load '5' into A
          ACALL SEND             ; Transfer '5'
          MOV A, # '1'           ; Load '1' into A
    L1:   SJMP L1                ; Loop here continually
  SEND:   MOV SBUF, A            ; Load SBUF
    L2:   JNB TI, L2             ; Wait for last bit to be sent
          CLR TI                 ; Get ready for next byte
          RET                    ; Return from subprogram
          END
```

The same program written in C will be as follows.

```
#include <reg51.h>
void Send_Ser (unsigned char);

void main (void)
{
   TMOD = 0x20;          // Timer 1, Mode 2
   TH1 = 0xFD;           // 9600 baud rate
   SCON = 0x40;          // Set SCON in Mode 1, REN disabled
   TR1 = 1;              // Start timer
   Send_Ser('8');        // Send '8'
   Send_Ser('0');        // Send '0'
   Send_Ser('5');        // Send '5'
   Send_Ser('1');        // Send '1'
   while (1);            // Wait here infinitely
}
```

```
void Send_Ser(unsigned char m)
{
    SBUF = m;                   // Copy character to SBUF
    while (TI == 0);            // Wait for last bit to be sent
    TI = 0;                     // Reset TI bit
}
```

3.8.4 Serial Reception

Similar to the case of transmission, to receive characters serially, the Timer 1 is programmed in mode 2 (auto-reload) and TH1 initialized appropriately for the required baud rate. The SCON register is programmed in mode 1 with REN enabled. The timer is started by setting the TR1 bit. The RI bit is cleared. The RI flag is now monitored continually to check the receipt of a character. When RI becomes 1, the SBUF will contain the received character. It can now be copied to some other place. The RI flag is cleared to enable reception of the next character, if any. The following example illustrates the serial reception.

Example 3.28: Consider the problem of serially receiving characters. The received characters are sent to the port P1 for display. The assembly language program for the problem is as follows.

```
          ORG 0000H            ;
          MOV TMOD, #20H       ;  Timer 1, Mode 2
          MOV TH1, #0FDH       ;  Baud rate 9600
          MOV SCON, #50H       ;  Mode 1, REN enabled
          SETB TR1             ;  Start Timer 1, auto-reload
     L1:  ACALL RECV           ;  Get next character serially
          MOV P1, A            ;  Copy A to the port P1
          SJMP L1              ;  Continue
   RECV:  JNB RI, RECV         ;  Wait for the character
          MOV A, SBUF          ;  Wait for last bit to be sent
          CLR RI               ;  Get ready for next byte
          RET                  ;  Return
          END
```

The same program written in C will be as follows.

```
#include <reg51.h>
void main (void)
{
    unsigned char my_char;
    TMOD = 0x20;                // Timer 1, Mode 2
    TH1 = 0xFD;                 // 9600 baud rate
    SCON = 0x40;                // Set SCON in Mode 1, REN disabled
    TR1 = 1;                    // Start timer
    while (1) {                 // Loop
        while (RI == 0);        // Wait for RI to become 1
        my_char = SBUF;         // Read character from SBUF
        P1 = my_char;           // Put character into port P1
        RI = 0;                 // Reset RI flag
    }
}
```

3.8.5 Serial Communication Interrupt

In Section 3.7.2 we have seen that the IE register contains ES bit which stands for enabling the serial interrupt. On the other hand, the examples noted in Section 3.8.3 and 3.8.4 contain loops that continually checks the TI and RI flags to get confirmation about transmission and reception of character, respectively. This busy wait loops can be avoided by utilizing the serial interrupt. However, in the 8051, only one interrupt has been kept for both transmission and reception. As a result, if the serial interrupt is enabled in the IE register, whenever the TI flag or the RI flag is set, it gives interrupt to the 8051. Thus, as and when a serial communication takes place, control branches to the address 0023H. In the service routine, the TI and RI flags should be checked to determine the actual source of interrupt – successful transmission or successful reception. Appropriate action can then be taken by the service routine. It has been explained in the following.

Example 3.29: Consider the system that reads port P1 and transmits the character read serially. Simultaneously, it receives characters serially and outputs it to port P2. An interrupt driven approach for the problem is as follows.

```
        ORG 0000H
        LJMP MAIN               ;  Jump to main routine
        ORG 0023H
        LJMP SERIAL             ;  Jump to Serial Int. routine
        ORG 0030H
MAIN:   MOV P1, #0FFH           ;  Make P1 input port
        MOV TMOD, #20H          ;  Timer 1, Mode 2
        MOV TH1, #0FDH          ;  Baud rate 9600
```

```
          MOV SCON, #50H          ; Mode 1, REN enabled
          MOV IE, #10010000B      ; Enable serial interrupt
          SETB TR1                ; Start Timer 1, auto-reload
     L1:  MOV A, P1               ; Read port P1
          MOV SBUF, A             ; Serially transmit
          SJMP L1                 ; Loop continually
          ORG 100H                ;
 SERIAL:  JB TI, L2               ; Jump if TI is set
          MOV A, SBUF             ; Else character received
          MOV P2, A               ; Copy to P2
          CLR RI                  ; Get ready for next byte
          RETI                    ; Return
     L2:  CLR TI                  ; Clear TI
          RETI                    ; Return
          END
```

The same program written in C will be as follows.

```
#include <reg51.h>

void serial0 () interrupt 4
{
    if (TI == 1) TI = 0;          // Clear interrupt
    else {
          P2 = SBUF;              // Put serial data onto P2
          RI = 0;                 // Clear interrupt
    }
}

void main (void)
{
    unsigned char my_char;
    P1 = 0xFF;                    // Make P1 input port
    TMOD = 0x20;                  // Timer 1, Mode 2
    TH1 = 0xFD;                   // 9600 baud rate
    SCON = 0x50;                  // Set SCON in Mode 1, REN enabled
    IE = 0x90;                    // Enable serial interrupt
    TR1 = 1;                      // Start timer
```

```
        while (1) {                  // Loop
            my_char = P1;            // Read character from port P1
            SBUF = my_char;          // Put character into SBUF
        }
    }
```

UNIT SUMMARY

The 8051 supports a large number of machine-level instructions, commonly known as assembly language instructions. Each assembly language instruction possesses a mnemonic (identifying the operation to be performed by the CPU) and a few operands (on which the operation is to be carried out). The instructions can be grouped into several categories – data transfer, arithmetic and logic operations, branching etc. On the other hand, the operands in those instructions can be a constant value, a register, a memory location etc. The 8051 supports a number of ways to specify the operands. The assembly language instructions can be used to express the program logic of a specific problem to be solved. The assembly language program is converted into the machine code with the help of assemblers. For problems with logic complexity moderate to high, it may be difficult to express the logic neatly in the assembly language. Such programs are often developed in the C language with augmentations in the data types to include signed/unsigned char/int, bits etc. Most of the IDEs of the 8051 supports program debugging by single stepping, breakpoint settings, and viewing/modifying register/memory contents etc. Timers and counters are important components of any microcontroller based system design. The 8051 contains two timers/counters which may be configured to operate in various modes. Another important feature of any processor is to inform it about events is interrupt. The 8051 supports different types of interrupt sources – timers, reset, external interrupt pins and serial communication related. Serial communication is helpful in situations where parallel communication is not possible due to pin/wire limitations. The unit provides a detailed overview of all these topics along with a good number of programming examples.

EXERCISES

Multiple Choice Questions

MQ1. Which of the following is an example of direct addressing in the 8051?
(A) MOV A, @R0 (B) MOV A, #45H
(C) MOV A, 45H (D) MOV A, R1

MQ2. Which jump instruction is a relative jump?
(A) JC (B) LJMP (C) AJMP (D) None of the other options

MQ3. The instruction "INC R5" affects the flag
(A) CY (B) AC (C) OV (D) None of the other options

MQ4. In AJMP instruction, destination is within a range of

(A) 2 kbytes (B) 4 kbytes (C) 8 kbytes (D) 16 kbytes

MQ5. Arithmetic operations supported by the 8051 can be of bit width
(A) 8 (B) 4 (C) 16 (D) All of the other options

MQ6. The "DA A" instruction works correctly for nonzero numbers upto
(A) 255 (B) 99 (C) 100 (D) None of the other options

MQ7. NOP instruction introduces
(A) Address (B) Delay (C) Memory location (D) None of the other options

MQ8. CJNE instruction sets the CY flag to 1 if
(A) destination = source (B) destination < source
(C) destination > source (D) destination ≤ source

MQ9. If R2 = 1, the instruction "DJNZ R2, L1" will take control to
(A) L1 (B) Next instruction
(C) Depends on assembler (D) None of the other options

MQ10. The instruction which will definitely clear the operand bit is
(A) JB (B) JBC (C) JNB (D) None of the other options

MQ11. The size of data moved by MOV instruction in the 8051 can be of bits
(A) 1 (B) 8 (C) 16 (D) All of the other options

MQ12. In which of the following the data to be moved be very close to the current instruction?
(A) MOVC A, @A+DPTR (B) MOVC A, @A+PC
(C) Both the cases (D) None of the cases

MQ13. MQ13. After executing MUL instruction, the CY flag is
(A) 0 (B) 1 (C) Depends on result (D) Not affected

MQ14. Which of the following is not a valid instruction in the 8051?
(A) PUSH A (B) PUSH R4 (C) POP R5 (D) All of the other options

MQ15. The minimum number of instructions executed from the interrupted program after a RETI is
(A) 1 (B) 2 (C) 0 (D) 3

MQ16. The instruction that brings LSB of A to CY is
(A) RL (B) RR (C) RLC (D) RRC

MQ17. After a SWAP instruction has been executed, bit 3 of the accumulator goes to bit
(A) 0 (B) 7 (C) 5 (D) CY

MQ18. In DIV instruction, remainder is left in
(A) A (B) B (C) R1 (D) R7

MQ19. Which of the following is not a valid 8051 instruction?
(A) INC DPTR (B) DEC DPTR
(C) INC DPL (D) DEC DPH

MQ20. The default data type for byte in Embedded C is
(A) Unsigned char (B) Signed char
(C) Unsigned byte (D) Signed byte

MQ21. In the instructions XCH and XCHD which nibble is definitely exchanged?
(A) Lower (B) Upper

(C) Both upper and lower (D) None of the other options

MQ22. The byte comparison instruction(s) in the 8051 is/are
(A) CMP (B) CJNE
(C) Both CMP and CJNE (D) None of the other options

MQ23. The BCD number 76 when converted to hexadecimal will be
(A) 76H (B) 4CH (C) 0C4H (D) None of the other options

MQ24. If the accumulator A contains 25H, after one "RR A" instruction execution, the content will become
(A) 12H (B) 4AH (C) 25H (D) None of the other options

MQ25. If the accumulator A contains 25H, after one "RL A" instruction execution, the content will become
(A) 12H (B) 4AH (C) 25H (D) None of the other options

MQ26. For timer operation, the C/T bit of the 8051 should be set to
(A) 0 (B) 1 (C) Either 0 or 1 (D) Tristate

MQ27. In the 8051 timers, for auto-reload mode, value to be loaded is stored in
(A) TH (B) TL (C) Both TH and TL (D) Neither TH nor TL

MQ28. The delay produced by the 8051 timer in Mode 1 with TH=FF and TL=00, crystal frequency 11.0592 MHz is
(A) 277.00 μS (B) 277.76 μS (C) 278.00 μS (D) 278.76 μS

MQ29. The instruction "MOV IP, #00011000B" sets priorities of interrupts as
(A) RI+TI > TF1 > INT0 > TF0 >INT1
(B) TF1 > RI+TI > INT0 > TF0 > INT1
(C) INT0 > TF0 > INT1 > TF1 > RI+TI
(D) INT0 > RI+TI > TF1 > TF0 > INT1

MQ30. The default priority of INT0 is
(A) More than INT1 (B) Less than INT1
(C) Same as INT1 (D) Double of INT1

MQ31. Timer 1 run can be controlled by
(A) TR1 (B) TF1 (C) IE1 (D) IT1

MQ32. If the GATE of TMOD register is set, the timer run can be controlled by
(A) INT (B) TR (C) Both INT and TR (D) Neither INT nor TR

MQ33. The maximum delay produced by the 8051 in Mode 1 timer with crystal frequency 12 MHz is
(A) 1 μS (B) 65536 μS (C) 65535 μS (D) None of the other options

MQ34. The number of interrupt pins in 8051 is
(A) 1 (B) 2 (C) 3 (D) 4

MQ35. For any processor, which parity scheme is better?
(A) Even (B) Odd (C) Mixed Even-Odd (D) None of the other options

Answers of Multiple Choice Questions

1:C, 2:A, 3:D, 4:A, 5:A, 6:B, 7:B, 8:B, 9:A, 10:B, 11:D, 12:B, 13:A, 14:D, 15:A, 16:D, 17:B, 18:B, 19:B, 20:B, 21:A, 22:B, 23:B, 24:A, 25:B, 26:A, 27: A, 28: B, 29: B, 30: A, 31: A, 32: C, 33: B, 34: B, 35: D

Short Answer Type Questions

SQ1. How is an immediate operand differentiated from direct operand in the 8051?

SQ2. Justify the statement – "MOV R2, R3" is not a valid instruction, however it is not a big restriction to the programmer.

SQ3. Distinguish between XCH and XCHD instructions.

SQ4. Distinguish between the usage of MOVC instruction using DPTR and PC as base register.

SQ5. Differentiate between LJMP and AJMP instructions.

SQ6. Explain how the DJNZ instruction can be used to implement a looping structure.

SQ7. Differentiate between the instructions RET and RETI.

SQ8. Why is it necessary to clear the CY bit before subtraction in the 8051?

SQ9. Write an assembly language code fragment to implement a logical NAND operation.

SQ10. What is the purpose of a NOP instruction in the 8051?

SQ11. How to calculate the initial value for timers?

SQ12. How to set the priorities of interrupts?

SQ13. How to set baud rate for serial communication?

SQ14. How to use the timers as counters?

SQ15. How to check the cause of serial communication interrupt?

Long Answer Type Questions

LQ1. Enumerate the addressing modes of the 8051.

LQ2. Explain the operations of MOVC and MOVX instructions.

LQ3. Illustrate the conditional branch instructions in the 8051.

LQ4. Explain the format and utility of different rotate instructions of the 8051.

LQ5. Enumerate the data types introduced in the C language for the 8051 programming.

LQ6. Illustrate the setting of TCON register for timer and counter operations.

LQ7. How to program the SCON register?

LQ8. Explain how to implement interrupt enable/disable operations in the 8051?

Practical Problems

PQ1. Write an assembly language program to find the minimum of an array of N numbers stored at external RAM location 2000H onwards. The minimum value be stored at external RAM location 1000H.

Hint: The code structure will be similar to the Example 3.13. Assume the first number to be the minimum and store at location 1000H. Now, read the successive numbers from the array and check if the read number is less than the value stored at 1000H. If the new number is less, update 1000H.

PQ2. Write an assembly language program to compute the square of each number in an array of N numbers stored at RAM locations 2000H onwards. Assume the resulting numbers to be within 255. Write the corresponding C program also.

Hint: Read next number from the array into A register. Copy A to B. Use "MUL AB" instruction to get the square. As the result is within 255, the result of the multiplication will be available in the A register. Copy A register back to array.

PQ3. Write an assembly language program to check if the number stored at RAM location 40H is a prime or not. If the number is a prime, store 1 at 41H, else store 0 at 41H.

Hint: To check if a number M is prime or not, it is sufficient to check if it is divisible by any other number in the range 2 to M/2. Hence, a loop may be created to check for the divisibility. If the number is not divisible by any of these, the number is prime.

PQ4. Write an assembly language program to check if all the elements in the array of N numbers starting at 2000H are same as the elements of the array starting at 1000H.

Hint: A loop may be created to check element by element, the two arrays.

PQ5. A string is said to be a palindrome if it is same when read backwards. For example, the string "MALAYALAM". Assuming that the string is stored from RAM location 40H and the number of characters in it at location 55H, check if the string is a palindrome. If the string is a palindrome, 1 is stored at 30H, else a 0 is stored there.

Hint: Two pointers R0 and R1 be set to the beginning and the end of the string. Now, the two memory locations pointed to may be compared for equality. If the two characters are same, R0 should be incremented and R1 decremented. If there is a mismatch at any point, the string is not a palindrome. The string is a palindrome if R0 crosses R1.

PQ6. Develop assembly language and C programs for generating a square wave with 25% duty cycle and time period 100 μS on port bit P2.2.

Hint: Refer to Example 3.22. However, the ON time is 25 μS and OFF time 75 μS. The delay values are to be loaded into the registers accordingly.

PQ7. Develop assembly language and C programs to count the number of pulses on the line T1 of the 8051 microcontroller. The count value should be available at port P1.

Hint: Refer to Example 3.23.

PQ8. Suppose that two switches have been connected to the INT0 and INT1 pins of the 8051. If a switch is closed, it gives a 0 value to the corresponding pin. An LED has been connected to the port bit P2.1. Develop an interrupt based program so that the LED is turned ON if the switch connected to INT0 is closed. Closing the switch connected to INT1 line turns OFF the LED.

Hint: Refer to Example 3.26.

PQ9. Develop assembly language and C programs to serially transmit the string "MICROCONTROLLER" through the 8051. The program should read P0.1 bit. Transmission of the string be repeated as long as the bit is 1.

Hint: Refer to Example 3.27.

PQ10. Develop an interrupt driven version for the problem PQ9. Moreover, instead of reading from port P0.1, the program should check a serially received byte. Transmission should stop if the received byte is character '0'.

Hint: Refer to Examplc 3.29.

KNOW MORE

One of the major applications of microcontrollers, including 8051 is in *Embedded Systems*. An embedded system is a dedicated electronic system with one/more processor(s) inside it. The system performs single or a few well defined operations only. Typical examples of such systems are digital camera, mobile phone, electronic toys, household appliances like washing machine, microwave etc., automobiles, telephone exchanges, satellites and so on. These systems often has part of it implemented in hardware and part in software to meet the system specifications. For the software part, it is mostly a microcontroller. However, other types of processors, such as, microprocessors, digital signal processors can also be used. Availability of on-chip program- and data-memory aids in the realizing such systems with smaller footprints, using the microcontrollers.

REFERENCES AND SUGGESTED READINGS

[1] S. Chattopadhyay, SWAYAM/NPTEL course on "Microprocessors and Microcontrollers", https://onlinecourses.nptel.ac.in/noc20_ee42/preview.

[2] M.A. Mazidi, R.D. McKinlay, J.G. Mazidi, "The 8051 Microcontroller: A Systems Approach", Pearson.

[3] "MCS® 51 Microcontroller Family User's Manual", https://fdocuments.in/document/8051-manual.html".

[4] S. Chattopadhyay, “Embedded System Design”, PHI Learning.

Dynamic QR Code for Further Reading

3. S. Chattopadhyay, SWAYAM/NPTEL course on “Microprocessors and Microcontrollers”.

4. “MCS® 51 Microcontroller Family User’s Manual”, https://fdocuments.in/document/8051-manual.html”.

4 I/O Interfacing

UNIT SPECIFICS

Through this unit, the following concepts have been elaborated:

- *Interfacing I/O devices to the 8051 ports;*
- *Hardware and software for the interfacings;*
- *Connecting switch, LED, keyboards, LCD, ADC, DAC with the 8051;*
- *Interfacing the 8255, the Programmable Peripheral Interface chip.*

The discussion in the unit is to illustrate the strategy to connect input-output devices with the 8051 ports. This is the most important unit, as far as interfacing is concerned. As the devices vary widely, the interfacing requirements of them also vary. Very simple devices include switch and LED for input and output, respectively. However, more complex ones include LCD, DAC, ADC etc. For each such device, the hardware and the software have been enumerated. It has been assumed that the reader has gone through the previous units of this book and has got an understanding of the assembly language and high-level programming for 8051. A basic background of digital circuit is essential for this unit. A good number of examples have been included to explain the concepts.

A large number of multiple choice questions, relevant for the topics discussed in this unit, have been provided with their answers. Apart from that, subjective questions of short and long answer type have been included. A list of tentative practical problems has been given. A list of references and suggested readings will help the readers to get more details. The section "Know More" has been carefully designed so that the supplementary information provided in this part becomes beneficial for the users of the book.

RATIONALE

This unit on I/O interfacing provides a detailed view of the hardware and software requirements to interface different types of input-output devices with the 8051. While interfacing a device, its voltage, current and timing requirements are to be kept in consideration. The interfacing programs may be written in either assembly language or in some high-level language, like C. The unit has started with the problem of interfacing simple switch and single LED to the 8051. Since the switch is a mechanical device, it is often jittery and the designer needs to take care of the same in the electronic part of the system. Glowing a number of LEDs also require the timing and brightness to be taken into consideration. This has been followed by discussion on interfacing matrix keyboard with hexadecimal digits 0 to F. Two I/O ports are used for this interfacing. To display more complex patterns, 7-segment LEDs and LCD interfacing can be used. Specifics of such interfacing have been detailed. To interface with the analog world, analog-to-digital and digital-to-analog converters are essential for most of the control applications. Interfacing different sensors are also through the analog-to-digital converters. The 8051 chip provides four I/O ports, however, the port bits are multiplexed with other functions as well. To overcome the shortage of I/O pins, often the chip 8255 is interfaced with it. The 8255 provides three dedicated I/O ports that can be used to interface with other I/O devices. Thus, the unit gives a complete overview of the interfacing strategies followed in systems developed around the 8051 microcontroller.

PRE-REQUISITES

Electronics: Units 1, 2, 3 of the book

UNIT OUTCOMES

List of outcomes of this unit is as follows:

U4-O1: Interface mechanical switches to the 8051

U4-O2: Connect LEDs to the port of 8051

U4-O3: Multiplex several 7-segment display modules with the 8051

U4-O4: Interface LCD module with the 8051

U4-O5: Connect analog-to-digital converter to the 8051

U4-O6: Connect digital-to-analog converter to the 8051

U4-O7: Extend the number of I/O ports of 8051 using the 8255

Unit-4 Outcomes	**EXPECTED MAPPING WITH COURSE OUTCOMES** (1- Weak Correlation; 2- Medium correlation; 3- Strong Correlation)					
	CO-1	**CO-2**	**CO-3**	**CO-4**	**CO-5**	**CO-6**
U4-O1	1	1	3	3	-	-
U4-O2	1	1	3	3	-	-
U4-O3	1	1	3	3	-	-
U4-O4	1	1	3	3	-	-
U4-O5	1	1	2	3	-	-
U4-O6	1	1	2	3	-	-
U4-O7	1	1	1	3	-	-

4.1 Introduction

Microcontrollers are mostly used in control applications. The controllers sense the environment/plant and actuate the devices to control it. Depending upon the activity being controlled, the type of devices connected to the microcontroller also varies. The devices can be broadly classified into two categories – the input devices (mostly sensors) and the output devices (mostly actuators). Very simple example of input device is a switch having only two positions, ON and OFF. It can be interfaced to a port bit of the 8051 to read the switch status by a program. Similarly, a single LED can be used to show the status of a port bit, which may be the outcome of some control algorithm executed by the 8051. On the other hand, many of the input-output devices may be electro-mechanical in nature. Thus, these devices are having specific requirements in terms of voltage, current, timing etc. For example, a pattern displayed on an output device should be flicker-free and steady for being interpretable by the human eyes. An input switch may be jittery in its operation that may lead to input errors. A motor which may be rotating at a certain speed, requires a finite amount of time to stop or reverse its direction. Hence, interfacing an input/output device to the 8051 requires two tasks to be carried out carefully. The first task is to design the circuit to connect the device. The hardware has to be designed in a manner, such that, the commands given by the control program through port bit settings are converted to the appropriate voltage, current or other specific requirements of the device. The second task is to design the software to be executed by the 8051 to read the input devices or write to the output devices. As the 8051 ports are limited in terms of the total number of I/O bits and their driving capacities, it may be required to interface additional chips/components to augment the same.

4.2 Simple I/O Devices

In this section, we shall look into the interfacing of very simple I/O devices with the 8051 microcontroller. Two vary basic input and output devices that one can think about are a digital switch having ON/OFF positions and a light emitting diode (LED), respectively. The digital switch can be used to provide a digital input to the 8051 while the LED can display the status of an output port bit.

4.2.1 Switch Interfacing

The simplest input device is a switch that can be turned either ON or OFF. The switch needs to be interfaced to a port pin of the 8051 to get its status read by the program. Fig 4.1 shows three different configurations in which a switch may be interfaced. Fig 4.1(a) reads in a logic 0 when the switch is closed and logic 1 when the switch is open. With switch closed, the current drawn is about 0.5 mA which the port pin can sustain. Fig 4.1(b) shows the case in which a closed switch gives logic 1 to the port pin. With the switch open, the port pin gets a logic 0. However, in this connection, if by chance the port bit is set to 0 due to an output operation from the program while the switch is also simultaneously closed, a very high current will flow to the port pin, possibly damaging the same. Similarly, Fig 4.1(c) can also lead to damage in the port pin due to a high current flow when an output operation has set the pin to 0. Thus, the configuration suggested in Fig 4.1(a) is the preferred one.

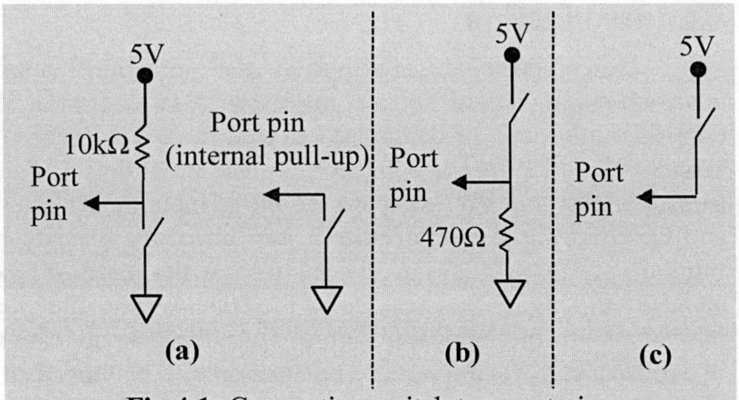

Fig 4.1: Connecting switch to a port pin

As a port of the 8051 contains 8 bits, it can be used to interface upto eight such switches together. An assembly containing such switches is called a *Dual-Inline-Package* (*DIP*) switch. Fig 4.2 shows a schematic diagram for the hardware connection of a DIP switch (with eight individual switches in it) to the port P1 of the 8051. The code fragment to read the status is as follows.

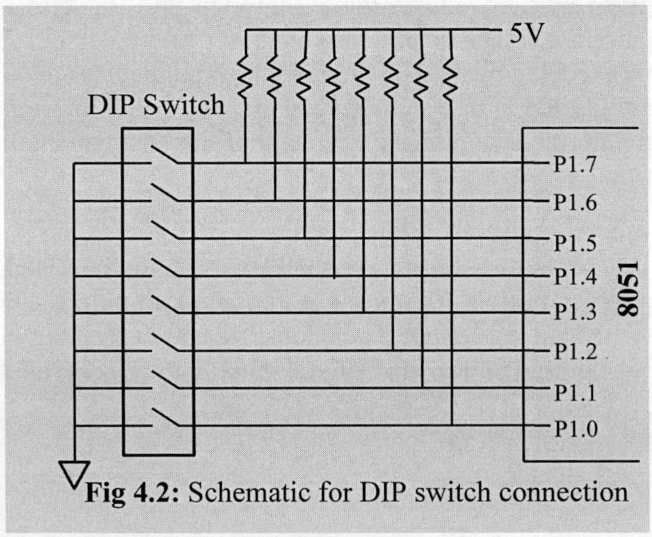

Fig 4.2: Schematic for DIP switch connection

```
MOV P1, #0FFH        ; Configure P1 in input mode
MOV A, P1            ; Read the switch status
```

Contact Debouncing

The mechanical switches, such as, push button switch, toggle switch, electromechanical relays etc. work on the principle of make-and-break contacts. The switches are normally open, leading to logic 1, as shown in Fig 4.1(a) and 4.2. However, when the switch is being closed, due to mechanical vibrations, several small pulses get created, as shown in Fig 4.3. This is known as *contact bounce* or *switch bounce*. Due to this phenomena, the 8051 may sense it as several key presses. If the switch is connected to the interrupt pin, several interrupts will get generated. Special care needs to be taken to resolve this problem. Both hardware and software based debouncing solutions have been suggested to resolve the problem of contact bouncing.

Fig 4.3: Bouncing effect in contacts/switches

- *Hardware Solution*. An RC network can be used to solve the bouncing problem. When the switch is open, the capacitor charges to a logic high level through the pull-up resistor. As a result, the output of the inverter feeding the port bit is 0. Now, if the switch is closed momentarily, the capacitor discharges quickly, making the port bit 1. Choosing the values of R and C judiciously, one can make the RC time-constant to be larger than the switch bounce time, thus preventing the possibility of the capacitor charging quickly. The structure has been shown in Fig 4.4.

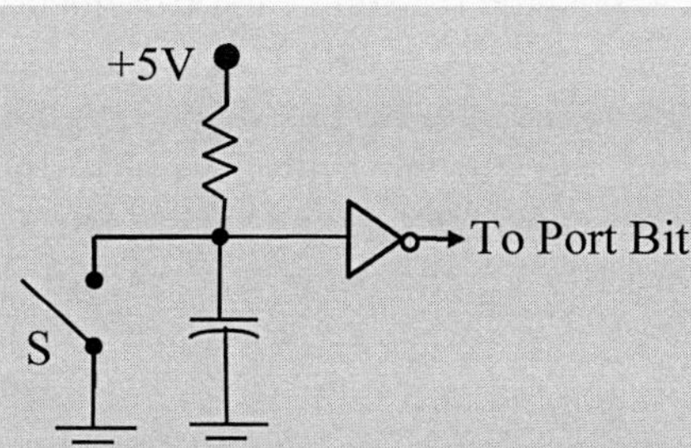

Fig 4.4: Hardware debouncing

- *Software Solution*. In the software, the switch can be read upto N times. Normally, the switch is open and the port bit is 1. If the value read from the port bit is 0, the key must have been pressed once. The program is then made to wait for an appropriate amount of delay to come over the bouncing period. Typically, the time may be 10ms. After the period, the port is read again to see if the value read is still 0, which ensures that the key

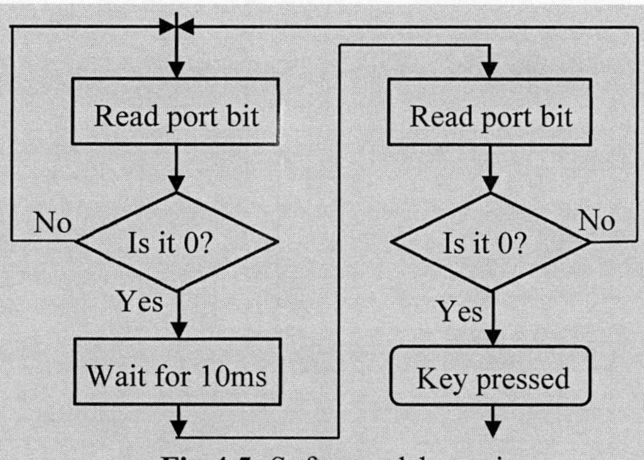

Fig 4.5: Software debouncing

has not been read as multiple presses. The whole process may be repeated a number of times to ensure confidence in operation. The flowchart for the process has been shown in Fig 4.5.

4.2.2 Light Emitting Diode (LED) Interfacing

The simplest output device that can be connected to a port pin to show the logic value at the port bit is an LED. Fig 4.6 shows three different ways in which an LED can possibly be connected to a port pin. Out of the three configurations shown, the one in Fig 4.6(a) is the safest one with good brightness of the LED. In this case, the LED is turned ON (emits light) when the port bit is 0. Most LEDs drop about 1.7 volts across it and needs about 10mA current for full glow. Thus, the resistance to be connected is about $(5 - 1.7)/10 = 330\Omega$. In the diagram, a resistance of 470Ω has been suggested, keeping the current within 10mA. In Fig 4.6(b), no current limiting resistance has been used. This may lead to failure/damage for the port and/or LED. On the other hand, the third alternative shown in Fig 4.6(c) may not get enough current from the port to have a good brightness of the LED. While for the first two cases, the LED will glow when the port bit is 0, for the third case, to glow the LED, the port bit should be 1.

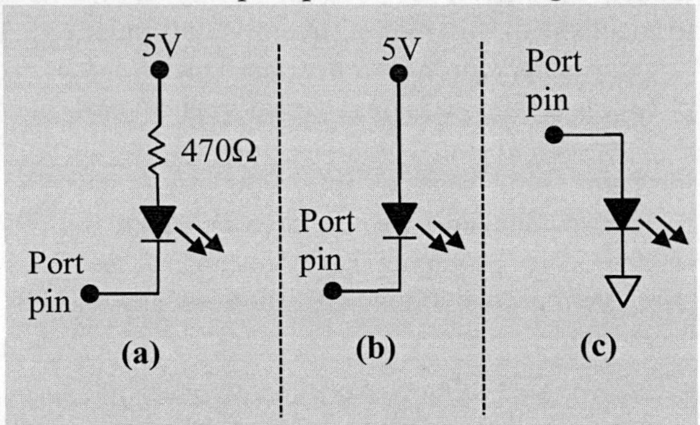

Fig 4.6: Connecting LED to a port pin

Example 4.1: The following shows an interfacing of 8 switches to Port 1 and 8 LEDs to Port 0 The value read in Port 1 is displayed in the LEDs in Port 0. The hardware connection is as shown

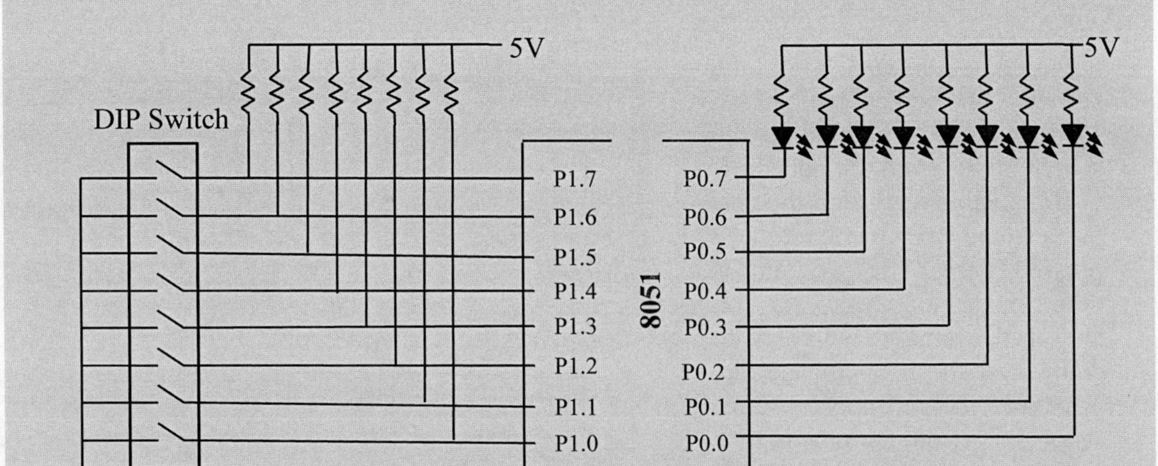

Fig 4.7: Interfacing 8 switches and 8 LEDs

in Fig 4.7. The following program reads the settings of the switches through Port 1. If a switch is pressed, the corresponding port bit will be read as a 0. The pattern read is output to Port 0. Thus, the corresponding LED will turn ON. The 8051 assembly language code for the operation is as follows. Debouncing has not been considered here since it is assumed that once a setting is done by the user, there is some delay before it is modified. This ensures that the display is stable for a particular switch setting.

```
        ORG 0
        MOV P1, #0FFH          ; Set P1 in input mode
    L1: MOV A, P1              ; Read Port P1
        MOV P0, A              ; Write to Port P0
        SJMP L1                ; Continue
        END
```

The corresponding C language program is as follows.

```
#include <reg51.h>
void main (void)
{
    while (1)  P0 = P1;
}
```

4.3 Hex Keyboard Interfacing

Fig 4.8 shows a schematic to interface a hexadecimal matrix keyboard to the 8051. A 4×4 hex keyboard has 16 keys corresponding to the hexadecimal digits 0 to F. One side of each row and column are tied to high. The other side of rows and columns are connected to the ports of the 8051. One of the ports is configured as input port, while the other one as output port. In Fig 4.8, port P1 has been used as an output port feeding the row lines, while port P2 has been configured as input to read the columns. A particular key can be identified by the row and the column it belongs to. For example, the key 6 is in row 1, column 2. Now, if the control program has made the bit P1.1 as 0 (with all other bits of P1 as 1) and the key 6 has been pressed, the bit P2.2 becomes 0. Assuming that none of the other keys 7, 5 or 4

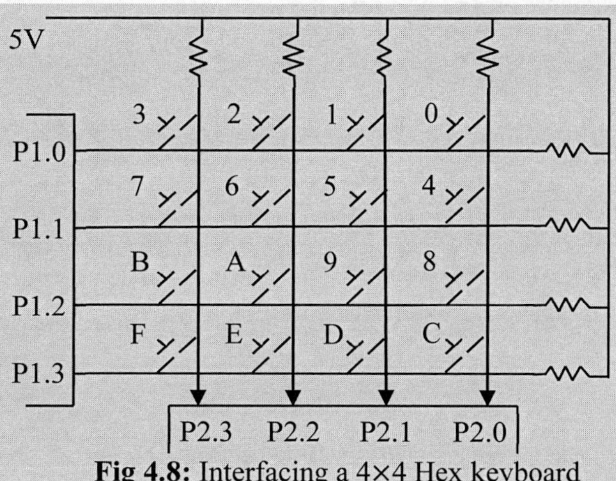

Fig 4.8: Interfacing a 4×4 Hex keyboard

has been pressed, the least significant 4 bits of the port P2 will be 1011. Thus, making the row lines 0, one at a time, and reading the column input, any key press can be uniquely identified. Some additional steps are necessary to ensure that all the keys are initially in open state. This can be checked easily by outputting an all-zero pattern to the port P1and checking that the least significant 4-bits of the port P2 are all 1's. Also, debouncing needs to be taken care of. As there is no additional capacitive circuitry connected in Fig 4.8, software debouncing is the ideal solution, in this case. Fig 4.9 shows a flowchart to elaborate the logic to be followed by the keyboard routine. After debouncing, if a key has been pressed, to detect it one row is set to 0, by turn. The columns are read and the column giving 0 to the port identifies the key. A code table may then be consulted to get the key code. For example, the co-ordinate of row-1, column-1 corresponds to the key code 5. The following is the assembly language program to scan the keyboard and get the code of the key pressed (if any) at RAM location 50H.

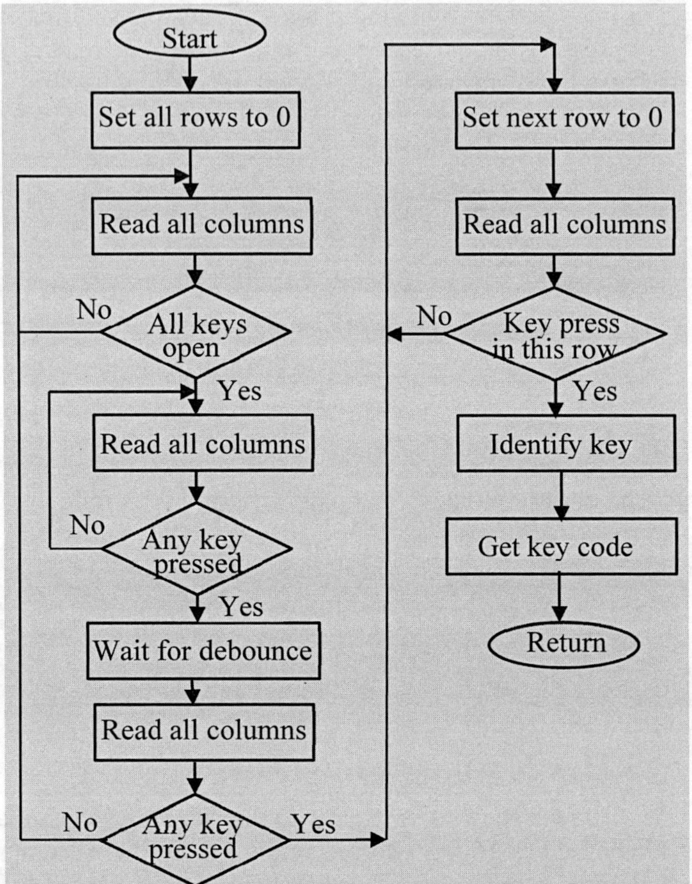

Fig 4.9: Flowchart for keyboard scan routine

```
        ORG 1000H
        MOV P2, #0FFH           ; Set P2 in input mode
L1:     MOV P1, #00H            ; Ground all rows
L2:     MOV A, P2               ; Read all columns
        ANL A, #0FH             ; Mask unused MSBs
        CJNE A, #0FH, L2        ; Check for all keys open
        ACALL DELAY             ; Some key may be pressed, wait for 20ms
        MOV A, P2               ; Read all columns
```

```
            ANL A, #0FH              ; Mask unused MSBs
            CJNE A, #0FH, L2         ; No key pressed, go back
            ACALL DELAY              ; Key pressed, wait for 20ms
            MOV P1, #0FEH            ; Ground row 0
            MOV A, P2                ; Read all columns
            ANL A, #0FH              ; Mask unused MSBs
            CJNE A, #0FH, ROW_0      ; Some key in row 0 pressed
            MOV P1, #0FDH            ; Ground row 1
            MOV A, P2                ; Read all columns
            ANL A, #0FH              ; Mask unused MSBs
            CJNE A, #0FH, ROW_1      ; Some key in row 1 pressed
            MOV P1, #0FBH            ; Ground row 2
            MOV A, P2                ; Read all columns
            ANL A, #0FH              ; Mask unused MSBs
            CJNE A, #0FH, ROW_2      ; Some key in row 2 pressed
            MOV P1, #0F7H            ; Ground row 3
            MOV A, P2                ; Read all columns
            ANL A, #0FH              ; Mask unused MSBs
            CJNE A, #0FH, ROW_3      ; Some key in row 3 pressed
            AJMP L1                  ; No key pressed, repeat scanning
     ROW_0: MOV DPTR, #KEY_ROW_0     ; DPTR = Start of Row 0
            SJMP FIND_KEY            ; Find column for the key
     ROW_1: MOV DPTR, #KEY_ROW_1     ; DPTR = Start of Row 1
            SJMP FIND_KEY            ; Find column for the key
     ROW_2: MOV DPTR, #KEY_ROW_2     ; DPTR = Start of Row 2
            SJMP FIND_KEY            ; Find column for the key
     ROW_3: MOV DPTR, #KEY_ROW_3     ; DPTR = Start of Row 3
  FIND_KEY: RRC A                    ; Rotate A and get column status to CY
            JNC MATCHED              ; Column found, if CY=0
            INC DPTR                 ; DPTR = Next column address
            SJMP FIND_KEY            ; Check for next column
```

```
MATCHED:    CLR A               ; Clear accumulator
            MOVC A, @A+DPTR     ; Get code from the table
            MOV 50H, A          ; Gct key code to RAM[50]
            AJMP L1             ; Repeat scanning

DELAY:      MOV TMOD #01        ; Timer 0, Mode 1
            MOV TL0, #0E0H      ; Load TH and TL
            MOV TH0, #0B1H      ; 0B1E0H for 20ms delay, clock 12MHz
            SETB TR0            ; Start timer
AGAIN:      JNB TF0, AGAIN      ; Monitor Timer 0
            CLR TR0             ; Stop Timer 0
            CLR TF0             ; Clear Timer 0 flag
            RET

            ORG 2000H
KEY_ROW_0:  DB '0', '1', '2', '3'   ; Row 0
KEY_ROW_1:  DB '4', '5', '6', '7'   ; Row 1
KEY_ROW_2:  DB '8', '9', 'A', 'B'   ; Row 2
KEY_ROW_3:  DB 'C', 'D', 'E', 'F'   ; Row 3
            END
```

As it could be found, the program code for the keyboard routine is quite complex and lengthy. The same can be expressed in a more compact manner using the C language for programming. In the following a C code has been given for the same function. The key code will be stored in a variable key_pressed.

```
# include <reg51.h>
# define COLUMN     P2      // P2 will read the columns
# define ROW        P1      // P1 will select rows
void delay_rtn( unsigned int del_val );
unsigned char keys[4][4] = { '0', '1', '2', '3',
                             '4', '5', '6', '7',
                             '8', '9', 'A', 'B'
                             'C', 'D', 'E', 'F' };
```

```
unsigned char key_pressed;

void main()
{
        unsigned char col_id, row_id;

        COLUMN = 0xFF;          // Configure P2 in input mode
        while (1) do {
                do {
                        ROW = 0x00;             // Ground all rows
                        col_id = COLUMN;        // Read all columns
                        col_id &= 0x0F;         // Mask unused bits
                } while ( col_id != 0x0F );     // All keys open now
                do {
                    do {
                        col_id = COLUMN;        // Read all columns
                        col_id &= 0x0F;         // Mask unused bits
                    } while ( col_id == 0x0F ); // Wait till some key pressed
                    delay_rtn( 20 );            // Wait for 20 ms
                    col_id = COLUMN;            // Read all columns
                    col_id &= 0x0F;             // Mask unused bits
                } while ( col_id == 0x0F );

                // Some key definitely pressed – identify it
                while (1) do {

                        ROW = 0xFE;             // Ground Row 0
                        col_id = COLUMN;        // Read columns
                        col_id &= 0x0F;         // Mask unused bits
                        if ( col_id != 0x0F ) {
                                row_id = 0;     // Save row index
                                break;          // Exit while-loop
                        }

                        ROW = 0xFD;             // Ground Row 1
                        col_id = COLUMN;        // Read columns
                        col_id &= 0x0F;         // Mask unused bits
                        if ( col_id != 0x0F ) {
                                row_id = 1;     // Save row index
```

```
                    break;                  // Exit while-loop
                }

                ROW = 0xFB;                 // Ground Row 1
                col_id = COLUMN;            // Read columns
                col_id &= 0x0F;             // Mask unused bits
                if ( col_id != 0x0F ) {
                    row_id = 2;             // Save row index
                    break;                  // Exit while-loop
                }

                ROW = 0xF7;                 // Ground Row 1
                col_id = COLUMN;            // Read columns
                col_id &= 0x0F;             // Mask unused bits
                if ( col_id != 0x0F ) {
                    row_id = 3;             // Save row index
                    break;                  // Exit while-loop
                }
            }

            if ( col_id == 0x0E )
                key_pressed = keys[ row_loc ][ 0 ];
            else if ( col_id == 0x0D )
                key_pressed = keys[ row_loc ][ 1 ];
            else if ( col_id == 0x0B )
                key_pressed = keys[ row_loc ][ 2 ];
            else
                key_pressed = keys[ row_loc ][ 3 ];
        }
}
void delay_rtn( unsigned int del_val )
{
        unsigned int x, y;
        for (x = 0; x < 1000; x++)
                for (y = 0; y < del_val; y++);
}
```

4.4 Seven-Segment Display Interfacing

One of the very common output devices used in the microprocessor and microcontroller based systems is a 7-segment LED display, as shown in Fig 4.10(a). In this,7 LEDs are arranged in a manner to show the digit '8'. As shown in Fig 4.10(b), different LED segments can be turned on to display the digits 0 to 9. Some other characters and symbols can also be displayed by turning on the LEDs selectively. Though it is called a 7-segment display, there are 8 LEDs in it, marked as a, b, c, d, e, f, g and dp (decimal point). One such display module can show a single digit. A number of them could be used to display multi-digit numbers. Such displays are typically used to show counters, token numbers, clock time, date etc.

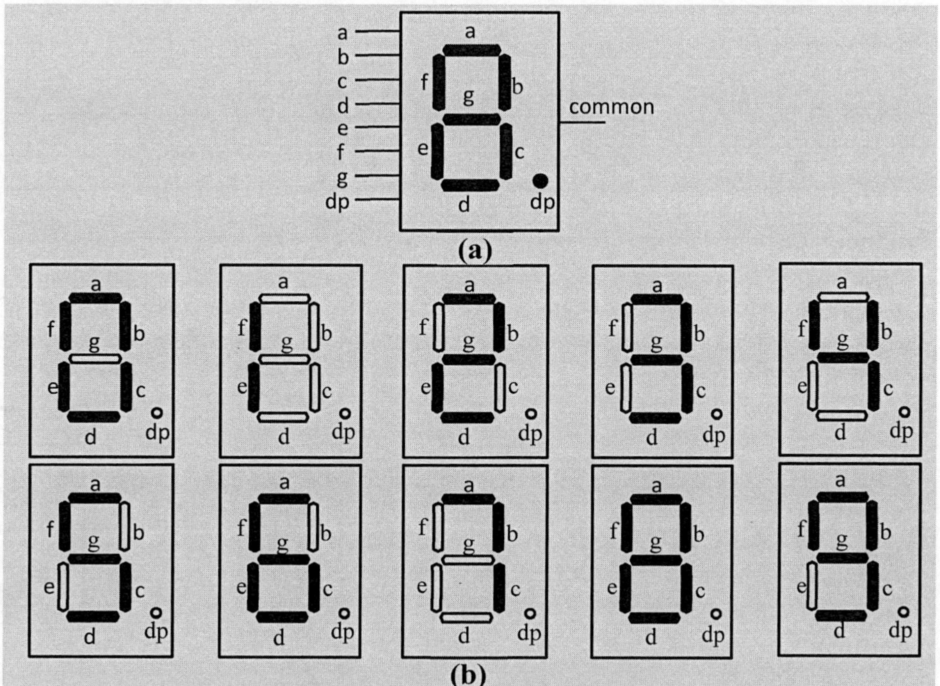

Fig 4.10: **(a)** 7-segment module **(b)** Digits

The 7-segment display modules come in two variants – *common anode* and *common cathode*. In a common anode module (shown in Fig 4.11(a)), the anode terminals of the LEDs are joined together to a common terminal. On the other hand, in a common cathode module (shown in Fig 4.11(b)), the cathode terminals are combined into a common terminal. Both have 8 LEDs in them.

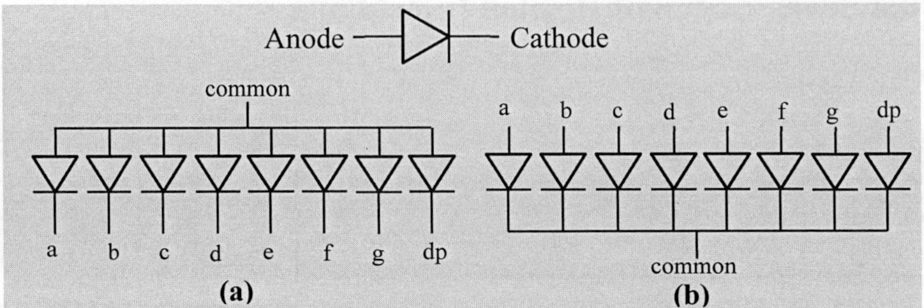

Fig 4.11: 7-segment display (a) Common anode (b) Common cathode

Out of the two configurations, common anode is the preferred one for many of the designers, as this can ensure more current through the LEDs for a brighter display. The 8051 port bits can typically sink 1.6 mA of current, compared to its source current capacity of 60 μA. Fig 4.12 shows two different ways in which the current limiting resistors can be connected in the interface.

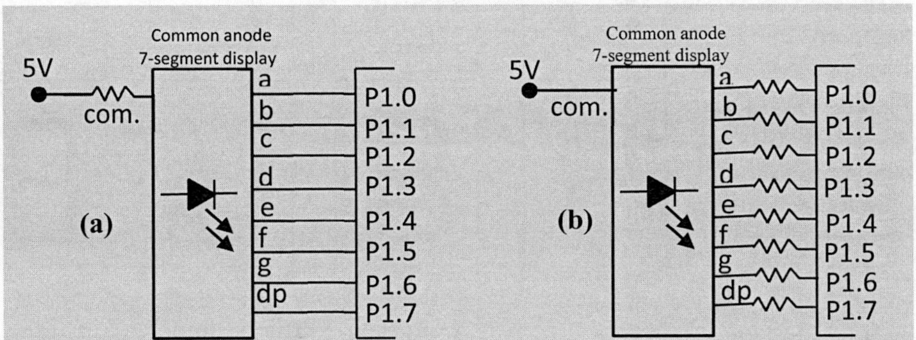

Fig 4.12: Ways to connect common anode displays

Out of these two, the structure shown in Fig 4.12(b) is preferable, as in Fig 4.12(a), brightness varies depending upon the number of LEDs turned on. For a common anode display module with inputs a to dp fed through an I/O port of the 8051, the output pattern corresponding to different digits have been shown in Table 4.1.

Table 4.1: Patterns for digits

Digit	Port Bits								Hex
	7	6	5	4	3	2	1	0	
	dp	g	f	e	d	c	b	a	
0	1	1	0	0	0	0	0	0	C0
1	1	1	0	0	1	1	1	1	CF
2	1	0	1	0	0	1	0	0	A4
3	1	0	1	1	0	0	0	0	B0
4	1	0	0	1	1	0	0	1	99
5	1	0	0	1	0	0	1	0	92
6	1	0	0	0	0	0	1	0	82
7	1	1	1	1	1	0	0	0	F8
8	1	0	0	0	0	0	0	0	80
9	1	0	0	1	0	0	0	0	90

4.4.1 Multiplexed Display

A major problem with the 7-segment display interface, shown in Fig 4.12 is that, connecting multiple such modules require large number of I/O port pins. Each module requires eight output port bits to drive the LED segments. On the other hand, most of the applications involving such LED display need a number of such modules to be integrated together.

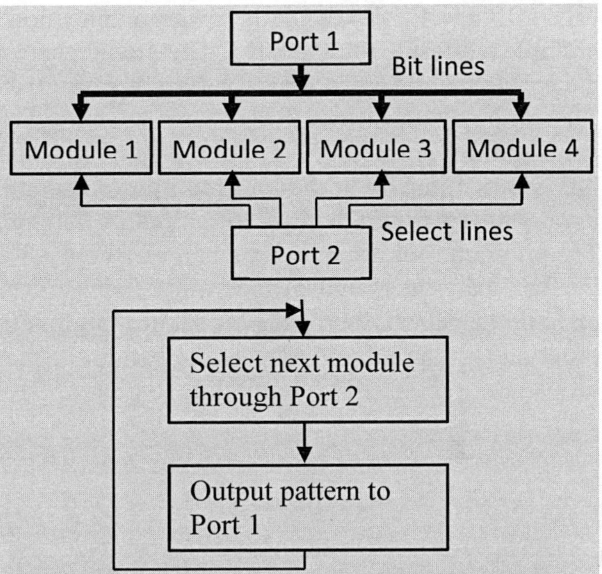

Fig 4.13: Multiplexing 7-Segment Displays

For example, a real-time clock module will need at least six such 7-segment displays (two each for the hour, minute and second parts). Interfacing such a clock display module with the 8051 is then not possible due to the I/O pin limitations. To sort out this problem, most of the interfacing solutions rely upon the *persistence* property human vision. According to it, human eye and brain retain a visual impression for about 1/30th of a second. Thus, after displaying a pattern (of sufficient brightness) if it is taken off and redisplayed within the duration of the persistence window, we shall see a steady image only. In a multiplexed display with more than one modules, the first module is selected and the pattern for it is output. Next, the second module is selected with the corresponding bit pattern sent to the port, and so on. The whole process is repeated continually, so that within 1/30 of a second, each display module gets updated with its pattern. To reduce the hardware, the port bits providing the pattern are fed to all the display modules. The selection of the module is done via appropriate port bits. Since only one module is enabled, the pattern can change the digit only in that module.

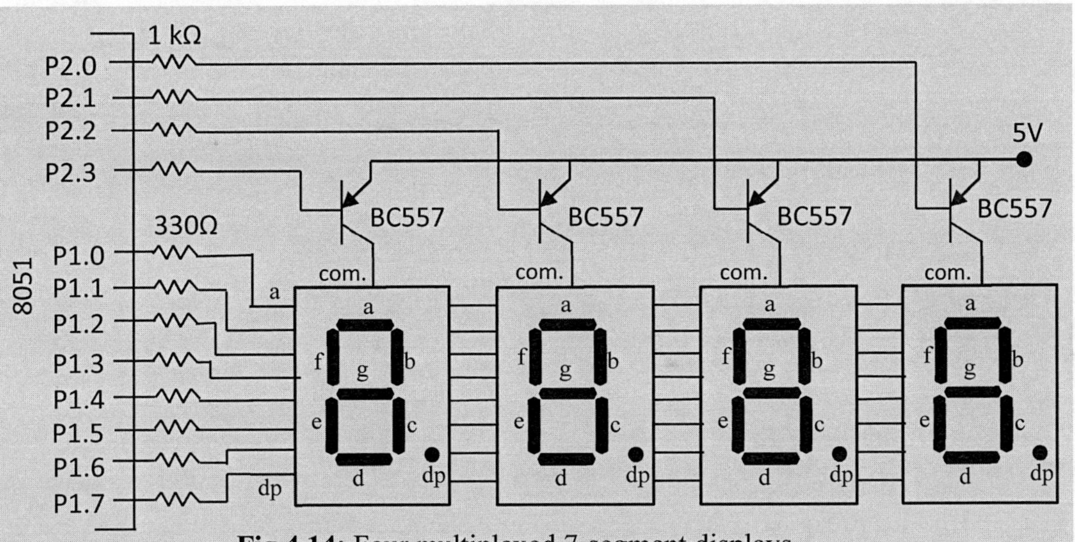

Fig 4.14: Four multiplexed 7-segment displays

Fig 4.14 shows the hardware connection for four seven-segment display modules in a multiplexed fashion to the 8051. The module selection is done via the least significant four bits of the port P2, while bit patterns for digit display are sent by the port P1. As module drives need more current, *p-n-p* transistors *BC557* have been used in the circuit. Next, we shall see how to feed bit patterns through the 8051 ports to display a numeric string of four decimal digits (for example, "1579") continually in the four multiplexed segments. The string is assumed to be stored at four bytes starting from RAM location 2000H. The program is stored from memory location 1000H. The program uses a subprogram named BIT_PATT that gets the bit pattern to be output to the port P1 for a particular digit of the string. Index of the digit is made available in register R1 before making the call. It returns the bit pattern to glow the LED segments in the register A. The display program is in an infinite loop so the pattern displayed is stable. The array DGT_PATT stores the bit pattern to be output to a module to glow the required segments for a digit (as shown in Table 4.1).

```
            ORG 1000H
DGT_PATT:   DB 0C0H, 0CFH, 0A4H,        ; Bit patterns for digits
               0B0H, 99H, 92H, 82H,
               0F8H, 80H, 90H
                                        ; Display most significant digit
      L1:   MOV R1, #0                  ; Set R1
            ACALL BIT_PATT              ; Get bit pattern in A
            MOV P1, A                   ; Send pattern to glow segments
            MOV P2, #11110111           ; Select module
            ACALL DELAY_RTN             ; Put a small delay
                                        ; Display second digit
            MOV R1, #1
            ACALL BIT_PATT
            MOV P1, A
            MOV P2, #11111011
            ACALL DELAY_RTN
                                        ; Display third digit
            MOV R1, #2
            ACALL BIT_PATT
            MOV P1, A
```

```
            MOV P2, #11111101
            ACALL DELAY_RTN
                                        ; Display fourth digit
            MOV R1, #3                  ; Read all columns
            ACALL BIT_PATT              ; Mask unused MSBs
            MOV P1, A                   ; Some key in row 2 pressed
            MOV P2, #11111110           ; Ground row 3
            ACALL DELAY_RTN
            AJMP L1                     ; Repeat display

BIT_PATT:   MOV DPTR, #STRING           ; Get start address of string
            MOV A, R1                   ; Get digit index in A
            MOVX A, @A+DPTR             ; Get the digit (character format) in A
            CLR C                       ; Clear carry bit
            SUBB A, #'0'                ; Subtract ASCII code of '0'
            MOV DPTR, #DGT_PATT         ; DPTR = Start of digit display array
            MOVX A, @A+DPTR             ; Get bit pattern into A
            RET                         ; Return

DELAY_RTN:  MOV TMOD #01                ; Timer 0, Mode 1
            MOV TL0, #0E0H              ; Load TH and TL
            MOV TH0, #0B1H              ; 0B1E0H for 20ms delay, clock 12MHz
            SETB TR0                    ; Start timer
AGAIN:      JNB TF0, AGAIN              ; Monitor Timer 0
            CLR TR0                     ; Stop Timer 0
            CLR TF0                     ; Clear Timer 0 flag
            RET

            ORG 2000H
STRING:     DB "1579"                   ; String to be displayed
            END
```

The corresponding program in C language can be as follows.

```
# include <reg51.h>
void delay_rtn( unsigned int del_val );
unsigned char DGT_PATT[10] = { 0xC0, 0xCF, 0xA4, 0xB0, 0x99,
                               0x92, 0x82, 0xF8, 0x80, 0x90 };
unsigned char STRING[4] = "1597";

void main()
{
        while (1) do {
                P1 = DGT_PATT[ STRING[ 0 ] – '0']; P2 = 0xF7; delay_rtn( 20 );
                P1 = DGT_PATT[ STRING[ 1 ] – '0']; P2 = 0xFB; delay_rtn( 20 );
                P1 = DGT_PATT[ STRING[ 2 ] – '0']; P2 = 0xFD; delay_rtn( 20 );
                P1 = DGT_PATT[ STRING[ 3 ] – '0']; P2 = 0xFE; delay_rtn( 20 );
        }
}

void delay_rtn( unsigned int del_val )
{
        unsigned int x, y;
        for (x = 0; x < 1000; x++)
                for (y = 0; y < del_val; y++);
}
```

4.5 Liquid Crystal Display (LCD) Interfacing

LCD is an electronic display device working on the principle of light modulating properties of liquid crystals, combined with polarizers. LCD can display arbitrary images, preset words, digits etc. In the recent time, LCDs have become much more preferable to the 7-segment LED displays due to the following reasons. The price of such devices have reduced significantly. As noted earlier, LCDs can display digits, characters and graphics, while the 7-segment LED displays are useful for digits and possibly a limited set of characters. Most of the LCD devices have built-in refreshing circuitry. Thus, the processor need not do anything special to keep the display stable. Programming of such devices is also very simple.

An LCD module with its pinout has been shown in Fig 4.15. The display consists of two rows, with each row being capable of printing a number of characters. Typical LCDs may have 1, 2 or 4 lines with each line capable of accommodating 16, 20 or 40 characters. An LCD display with 2 lines and 40 characters is specified as 40×2 LCD. The bits DB7 through DB0 are used to specify the individual character positions. For any address, DB7 is always 1, DB6 is 0 for line 1 and 1 for line 2. Remaining DB5 through DB0 are used to refer to one of the 40 positions (0 to 39). Thus, these bits can take up the values from 00000 (decimal 0) to 100111 (decimal 39). Hence, the line 1 addresses range over 80H to A7H, while line 2 addresses range over C0H to E7H. The display consists of the following pins, grouped as per their functionality.

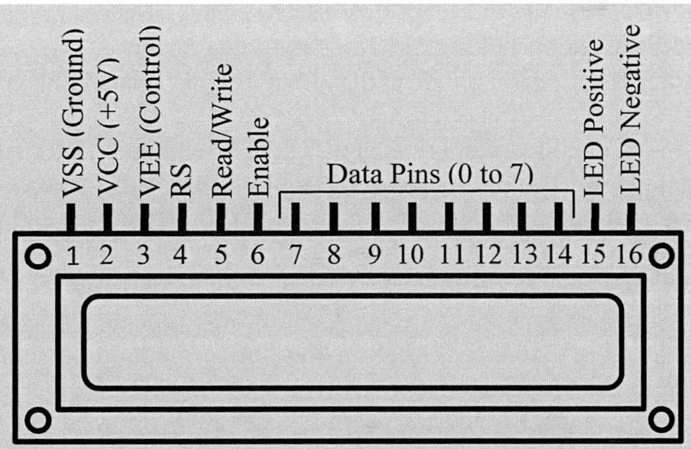

Fig 4.15: An LCD module

- **VCC, VSS, VEE:** The pins VCC and VSS provide +5V supply and ground. The pin VEE is a controllable voltage input deciding the LCD contrast.
- **RS:** *Register Select input*. The LCD module contains two important registers in it – the command register and the data register. With RS input set to zero, the instruction command code register gets selected. On the other hand with RS = 1, the data register is accessed.
- **Read/Write:** Also called **R/W**. With the pin set to zero, a writing operation is performed to the LCD registers. For reading contents of the registers, the pin needs to be set to 1.
- **Enable:** The pin, also represented as **E**, is used to latch the value present in data pins to the LCD registers. A high-to-low pulse with a minimum duration of 450ns is needed to latch the data.
- **Data Pins (0 to 7):** The 8 data lines (also marked as **DB0** to **DB7**) are used to send data to the LCD registers, or to read the content of those registers. In order to display characters/numbers, the corresponding ASCII codes are needed to be sent to the LCD with RS = 1 and R/W = 0. The Data Pin 7 has an additional functionality. Setting RS = 0 and R/W = 1, the value read at data pin 7 shows the status of the display. If this bit is found to be 1, the LCD is busy with its internal operations – no new data be sent now. On the other hand, if the bit value is found to be 0, the

Table 4.2: LCD command codes

Code (in Hex)	**Command details**
01	Clear screen
02	Return to home
04	Decrement cursor (Shift cursor left)
06	Increment cursor (Shift cursor right)
05	Shift display right
07	Shift display left
08	Display off, cursor off
0A	Display off, cursor on
0C	Display on, cursor off
0E	Display on, cursor blinking off
0F	Display on, cursor blinking on
10	Shift cursor left
14	Shift cursor right
80	Force cursor to the beginning of 1st line
C0	Force cursor to the beginning of 2nd line
38	Use 2 lines and 5×7 matrix

LCD is ready to accept further data. Thus, it is recommended that the interface routine checks the bit status before initiating any data transfer.

- **LED+, LED–:** Anode and cathode for LED backlight.

The LCD display accepts a set of commands sent to its command register for proper display of patterns. Table 4.2 shows the major commands accepted by the LCD module, the command codes and the corresponding actions. All commands are eight bit wide and sent through the pins DB0 through DB7. The commands can clear the display, move cursor to different positions on the LCD screen etc. The display is assumed to have two lines.

Fig 4.16 and 4.17 show the timing diagram depicting the behavior of various interfacing signals for the read and the write operations of the LCD command register, respectively. Thus, in both the cases, RS has been set to 0. The R/W line is set to 1 for the read operation (Fig 4.15) and 0 for the write operation (Fig 4.16). The read operation also needs a low-to-high pulse on the E line (Fig 4.15), while the write operation needs a high-to-low pulse (Fig 4.16). Typical values of Setup Time, Hold Time, Enable Pulse Width and Data Setup Time are 140ns, 10ns, 450ns and 195ns, respectively. Thus, an interface routine must take care of these minimum delays to be provided between the activation and deactivation of signals. A better method may be to monitor the DB7 line with RS = 0 and R/W = 1 to read the data bit line, after sending a command and waiting for the LCD module to be free to accept the next command.

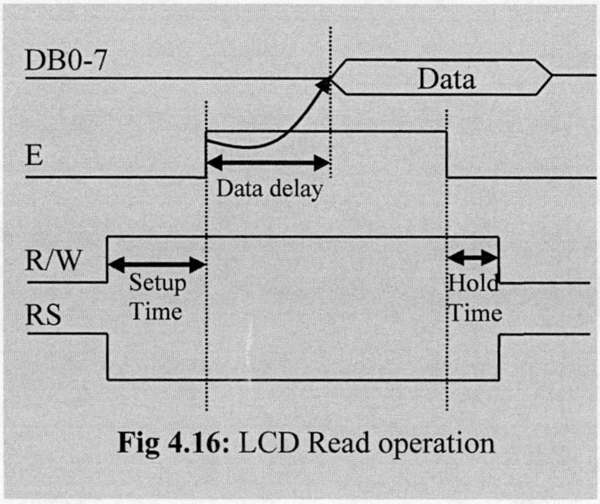

Fig 4.16: LCD Read operation

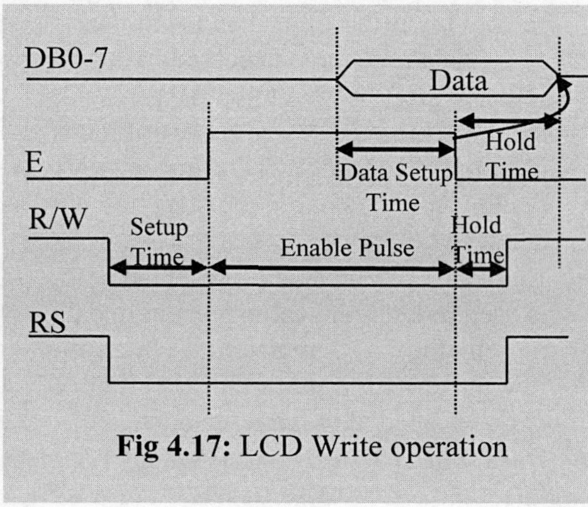

Fig 4.17: LCD Write operation

Fig 4.18 shows an interfacing of an LCD module with the 8051. The data pins DB0 through DB7 are driven by the port P1. Other important pins RS, R/W and E are connected via the port bits P3.2, P3.1 and P3.0, respectively. It is assumed that the LCD module is a 40×2 one with backlit LEDs present. The 8051 assembly language program to display the string "8051" starting at line 1, position 18 has been noted next. The program works by checking the busy flag, DB7 pin status, before issuing a command or data to the LCD.

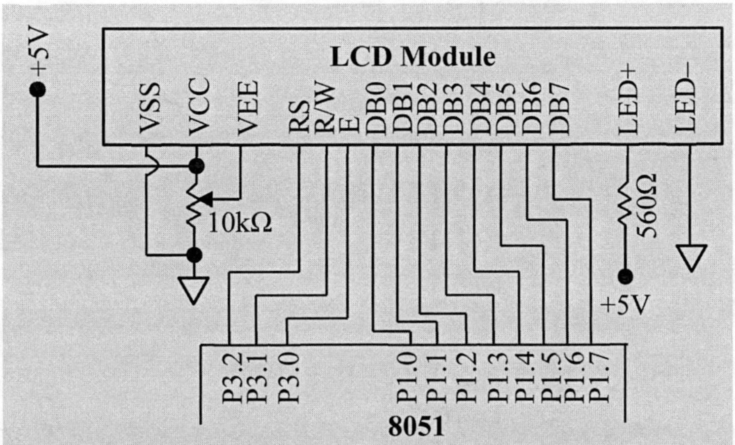

Fig 4.18: Interfacing LCD module with the 8051

```
          ORG 1000H
          MOV A, #38H         ; Initialize 2 line LCD, 5×7 matrix
          ACALL ISS_CMD       ; Issue the command
          MOV A, #0EH         ; LCD on, cursor on
          ACALL ISS_CMD       ; Issue the command
          MOV A, #01H         ; Clear LCD
          ACALL ISS_CMD       ; Issue the command
          MOV A, #92H         ; Cursor at line 1, position 18
          ACALL ISS_CMD       ; Issue the command
          MOV A, #'8'         ; Display letter '8'
          ACALL DSP_DATA
          MOV A, #'0'         ; Display letter '0'
          ACALL DSP_DATA
          MOV A, #'5'         ; Display letter '5'
          ACALL DSP_DATA
          MOV A, #'1'         ; Display letter '1'
L1:       SJMP L1             ; Remain at this position

ISS_CMD:  ACALL CHK_READY     ; Check if LCD ready
```

```
            MOV P1, A                 ; Issue the command code
            CLR P3.2                  ; Make RS = 0
            CLR P3.1                  ; Set R/W to 0 for a write
            SETB P3.0                 ; Set E = 1 for high-to-low pulse
            ACALL DELAY_RTN           ; Give a delay
            CLR P3.0                  ; Set E = 0 to latch the command
            RET                       ; Return

DSP_DATA:   ACALL CHK_READY           ; Check if LCD ready
            MOV P1, A                 ; Send data
            SETB P3.2                 ; Make RS = 1
            CLR P3.1                  ; Set R/W to 0 for a write
            SETB P3.0                 ; Set E = 1 for a high-to-low pulse
            ACALL DELAY_RTN           ; Give a delay
            CLR P3.0                  ; Set E = 0  to latch data
            RET                       ; Return

CHK_READY:  SETB P1.7                 ; Make P1.7 input to read DB7
            CLR P3.2                  ; Make RS = 0
            SETB P3.1                 ; R/W = 1 for a read operation
BACK:       CLR P3.0                  ; Set E = 0 for low-to-high pulse
            ACALL DELAY_RTN           ; Put some delay
            SETB P3.0                 ; Set E = 1 for low-to-high pulse
            JB P1.7, BACK             ; Loop DB7 is clear
            RET                       ; Return

DELAY_RTN:  MOV TMOD #01              ; Timer 0, Mode 1
            MOV TL0, #0E0H            ; Load TH and TL
            MOV TH0, #0B1H            ; 0B1E0H for 20ms delay, clock 12MHz
            SETB TR0                  ; Start timer
AGAIN:      JNB TF0, AGAIN            ; Monitor Timer 0
```

```
CLR TR0                        ; Stop Timer 0
CLR TF0                        ; Clear Timer 0 flag
RET
END
```

The corresponding C language program can be as follows.

```
# include <reg51.h>
sfr LCD_DB_Pins = P1;           // LCD data pins connected to P1
sbit RS = P3^2;                 // RS connected to Port 3, pin 2
sbit RW = P3^1;                 // Read/Write to Port 3, pin 1
sbit E = P3^0;                  // Enable to Port 3, pin 0
sbit BUSY = P1^7;               // DB7 gives the busy status

void delay_rtn( unsigned int del_val );
void LCD_Command( unsigned char value );
void LCD_Data( unsigned char value );
void LCD_Ready();
void main()
{
        LCD_Command( 0x38 );        // Initialize 2 line LCD, 5×7 matrix
        LCD_Command( 0x0E );        // LCD on, cursor on
        LCD_Command( 0x01 );        // Clear LCD
        LCD_Command( 0x92 );        // Line 1, position 18
        LCD_Data( '8' );            // Display '8'
        LCD_Data( '0' );            // Display '0'
        LCD_Data( '5' );            // Display '5'
        LCD_Data( '1' );            // Display '1'
}

void LCD_Command( unsigned char value )
{
        LCD_Ready();                // Check LCD busy flag DB7
        LCD_DB_Pins = value;        // Put value on DB pins
        RS = 0; RW = 0; E = 1;
        delay_rtn( 1 );
        E = 0;                      // High-to-Low pulse on E
}
```

```
void LCD_Data( unsigned char value )
{
        LCD_Ready();                        // Check LCD busy flag DB7
        LCD_DB_Pins = value;                // Put value on DB pins
        RS = 1; RW = 0; E = 1;
        delay_rtn( 1 );
        E = 0;                              // High-to-Low pulse on E
}
void LCD_Ready()
{
        BUSY = 1;                           // Make DB7 input
        RS = 0; RW = 1;
        while (BUSY == 1) {  E = 0; delay_rtn( 1 ); E = 1; } // Wait for BUSY = 0
}
void delay_rtn( unsigned int del_val )
{
        unsigned int x, y;
        for (x = 0; x < 1000; x++)
                for (y = 0; y < del_val; y++);
}
```

4.6 Analog to Digital Converter (ADC) Interfacing

Analog-to-Digital Converter (ADC) is a very important device that often needs to be interfaced with the 8051 to interact with the environment. While the 8051 (or any other microprocessor/microcontroller) is a digital device working with binary values of digital signals, the physical world is analog in nature. The physical signals are continuous in nature, for example, temperature, pressure, velocity, light intensity etc. A sensor/transducer can convert such signals into some equivalent electrical signals. To process the generated voltage/current signals by the 8051, it is required to convert those into digital values. An ADC performs this function. The number of bits (n) of the digital signal produced, is called the *resolution* of the ADC. The typical values of n are 8, 10, 12, 16 etc. As an ADC converts an analog signal into a set of digital values, the smallest change in the input that can effect a change in the digital output, is called a *step size*. With a resolution of n = 8, there can be 256 number of steps. Assuming the range of a voltage signal that this ADC converts, to be 5V, the step size is equal to 5V/256 = 19.53mV. On the other hand, if we need to keep the step size to say 10mV, the conversion range for this ADC will be 2.56V.

Several ADCs have been designed by different manufacturers. A typical one is ADC0808/0809 from National Semiconductor (currently, Texas Instruments). This is 8-bit ADC (n = 8). There are eight analog channels that the chip can handle in a multiplexed fashion. The two converters, the ADC0808 and ADC0809, are functionally identical except that the ADC0808 has a total unadjusted error of ±1/2 LSB and the ADC0809 has an unadjusted error of ±1 LSB. Fig 4.19 shows a schematic for the chip with the following signal line distribution.

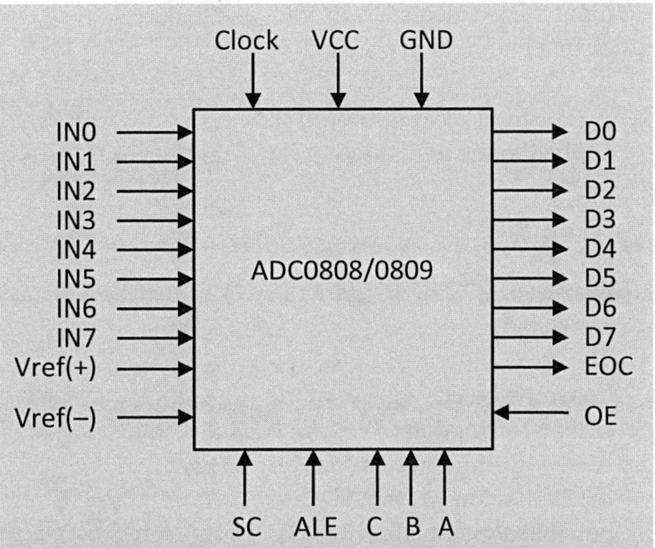

Fig 4.19: ADC0808/0809 schematic

- **VCC, GND:** The chip needs a power supply of 5 volts.
- **Clock:** Though the maximum clock speed supported by the chip is 1280 kHz, the typical clock value used is 640 kHz.
- **Vref(+), Vref(–):** These two pins set the reference voltage for the conversion process. With Vref(+) set at 5V and Vref(–) grounded, the step size is 19.53 mV, as explained earlier. Similarly, the step size can be set to other suitable values by selecting the reference voltages appropriately.
- **IN0-IN7:** These are eight analog input channels. The ADC can convert upto eight analog inputs to their equivalent digital bits by multiplexing these channels.
- **C, B, A, ALE:** These are the select inputs for the analog channels. By specifying a suitable 3-bit value to them (with C as MSB), a specific channel may be selected for conversion. A low-to-high pulse should be given to the ALE input to register the selection.
- **SC:** It stands for *Start Conversion*. A low-to-high pulse is applied to SC to initiate the analog-to-digital conversion process.
- **EOC:** The *End of Conversion* signal from the ADC indicates that the conversion process has been completed. A high-to-low transition of this line marks the completion.
- **OE:** The Output Enable (OE) input is activated to read the conversion value. A low-to-high pulse on the OE pin makes the digital value available at pins D0 to D7.

The sequence of operation for the analog-to-digital conversion process has been shown in Fig 4.20. It consists of the following steps.

1. The channel for the analog input is selected. Proper channel number is put at C, B, A.
2. A transition of low-to-high is applied in the ALE input to the ADC.
3. A low-to-high pulse is applied on the SC line to instruct the ADC to start the conversion process.
4. The ADC gives a high-to-low transition on EOC line to mark end of conversion.
5. A low-to-high transition on the OE line makes the ADC to put the digital value on D0-D7.

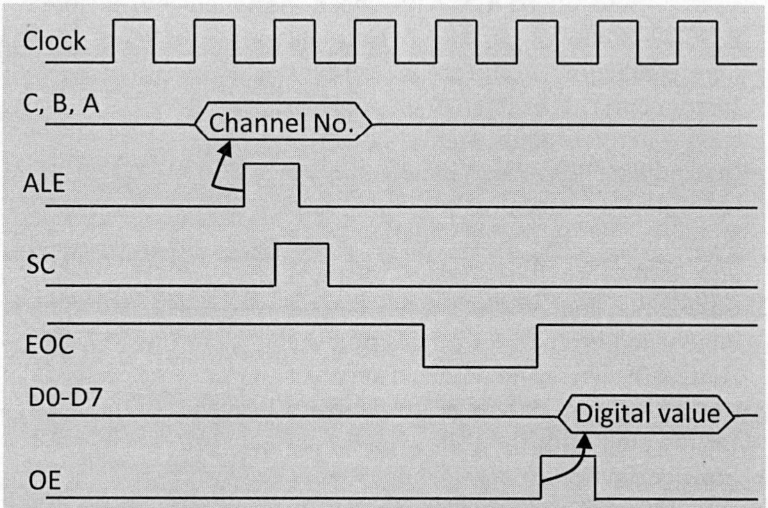

Fig 4.20: Timing diagram for ADC0808/0809

Fig 4.21 shows the connection for interfacing ADC0808/0809 to the 8051. Out of eight available analog channels, in this interface a single channel (Channel 1) has been used. The port P1 of the 8051 has been used to read-in the converted digital value. Port P2 has been used to connect to other signal lines of the ADC. Bits 0, 1 and 2 of port P2 have been used to provide proper select values needed for the input channel 1.The Vref(+) has been set to 2.56V and Vref(-) to 0 to ensure 10mV step size. Bit P2.3 controls ALE for the ADC. Bits P2.4 and P2.5 provide the output enable (OE) and start conversion (SC) for the ADC. The end-of-conversion (EOC) pin of the ADC has been connected to the port bit P2.6. The clock input for the ADC has been drawn from the crystal connected to the 8051. Since the crystal frequency is high, it is passed through four D flip-flops (with $\overline{Q}$ connected to D) to reduce it. Each such flip-flop divides the frequency by two. The VCC is connected to 5V, GND to 0 and chip select (CS) also put at zero to select the ADC chip.

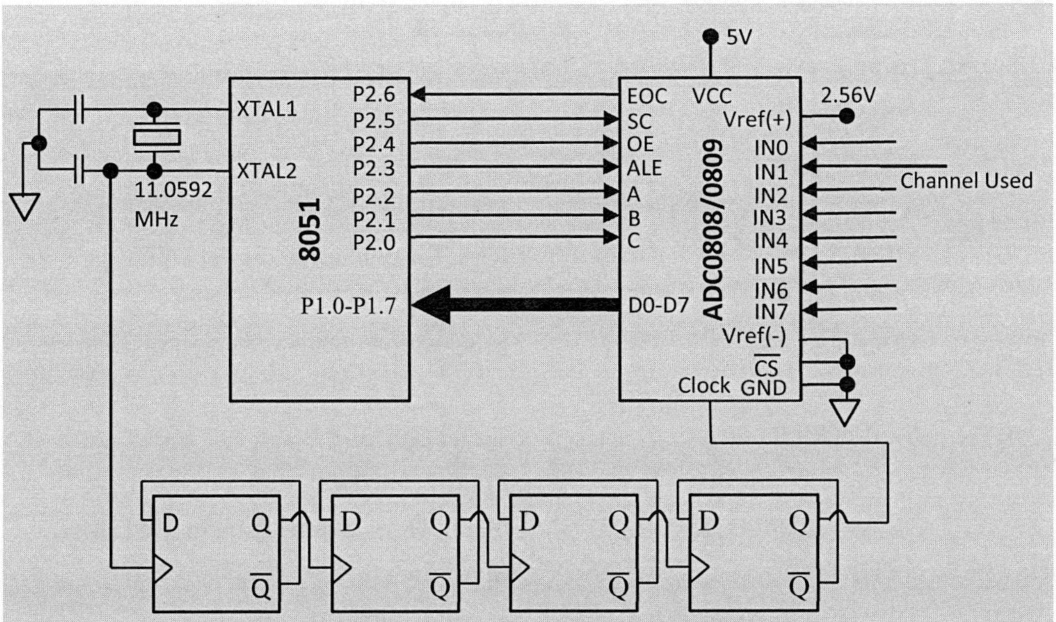

Fig 4.21: Interfacing ADC0808/0809 with the 8051

The assembly language program for interfacing the 8051 with the ADC0808/0809 has been shown in the following.

```
        ORG 1000H
        MOV P1, #0FFH           ; Configure P1 as an input port
        SETB P2.6               ; Make EOC an input line
        CLR P2.3                ; Clear ALE
        CLR P2.4                ; Clear OE
        CLR P2.5                ; Clear SC

L1:     CLR P2.0                ; Select channel 1, Set C=0, B=0, A=1
        CLR P2.1
        SETB P2.2
        ACALL DELAY_RTN         ; Put small delay
        SETB P2.3               ; Latch selection, low-to-high for ALE
        ACALL DELAY_RTN
        CLR P2.3                ; Clear ALE
```

```
            CLR P2.5                ; Clear SC
L2:         JB P2.6, L2             ; Wait for EOC to become low
L3:         JNB P2.6, L3            ; Wait for EOC to become high
            SETB P2.4               ; Set OE to high
            ACALL DELAY_RTN         ; Put delay
            MOV A, P1               ; Read the converted digital value
            CLR P2.4                ; Clear OE
            SJMP L1                 ; Proceed to convert next analog input

DELAY_RTN:  MOV TMOD #01            ; Timer 0, Mode 1
            MOV TL0, #0E0H          ; Load TH and TL
            MOV TH0, #0B1H          ; 0B1E0H for 20ms delay, clock 12MHz
            SETB TR0                ; Start timer
AGAIN:      JNB TF0, AGAIN          ; Monitor Timer 0
            CLR TR0                 ; Stop Timer 0
            CLR TF0                 ; Clear Timer 0 flag
            RET
            END
```

The C language program for the ADC interface can be as follows.

```
#include <reg51.h>
sbit SEL_C = P2^0;
sbit SEL_B = P2^1;
sbit SEL_A = P2^2;
sbit ALE = P2^3;
sbit OE = P2^4;
sbit SC = P2^5;
sbit EOC = P2^6;

sfr DIG_VAL = P1;
void delay_rtn( unsigned int del_val );
void main()
{
        DIG_VAL = 0xFF;         // Configure P1 as input
```

```
        EOC = 1;                    // Configure EOC line as input
        ALE = 0;                    // Clear ALE
        SC = 0;                     // Clear SC
        OE = 0;                     // Clear OE
        while (1) {
                SEL_C = 0; SEL_B = 0; SEL_A = 1;        // Choose channel 1
                delay_rtn(1);
                ALE = 1;
                delay_rtn(1);
                SC = 1;
                delay_rtn(1);
                ALE = 0;
                SC = 0;             // Start conversion
                while (EOC == 1);   // Wait for conversion to complete
                while (EOC == 0);
                OE = 1;             // Enable output to be read
                delay_rtn(1);
                A = DIG_VAL;
                OE = 0;
        }
}

void delay_rtn( unsigned int del_val )
{
        unsigned int x, y;
        for (x = 0; x < 1000; x++)
                for (y = 0; y < del_val; y++);
}
```

4.7 Digital to Analog Converter (DAC) Interfacing

Digital-to-Analog converter is another electronic component often interfaced with the 8051 to control the environment or output some equivalent analog quantity, corresponding to a digital value. Similar to ADC, the resolution is decided by the number of bits in the digital input. In a DAC, a digital input is specified using the bits *D0-D7* (with *D0* as the LSB and *D7* as the MSB) gets converted into an output current I_{out} as a fraction of the reference output current I_{ref}.

$$I_{out} = I_{ref}\left(\frac{D7}{2} + \frac{D6}{4} + \frac{D5}{8} + \frac{D4}{16} + \frac{D3}{32} + \frac{D2}{64} + \frac{D1}{128} + \frac{D0}{256} \right)$$

The current I_{ref} is decided by the reference voltage V_{ref} and is generally set to 2.0 mA. There can be 256 discrete current levels that can be output by an 8-bit DAC. Though DACs of higher resolution are available, those are more expensive and may not be very much useful for microcontroller based applications. The I_{out} can be converted to voltage by simply passing the current through a resistor, however, in most of the cases, an operational amplifier is used to separate the DAC from other stages.

Fig 4.22 shows the pin diagram of a very popular converter DAC0808. It has 8-bit resolution. The digital inputs are marked as A1-A8, spanning over the pin numbers 5 to 12 (with A1 as MSB and A8 as LSB). Pins 13 and 2 correspond to the positive power supply VCC and GND lines, respectively, while the pin 3 corresponds to VEE, the negative power supply. Pins 14 and 15 are the positive and negative reference voltage inputs VREF+ and VREF-. Pin 16 is for the compensation capacitor. The output is available at pin 4, marked as IO. This is a current output that needs to be converted to voltage for analog output.

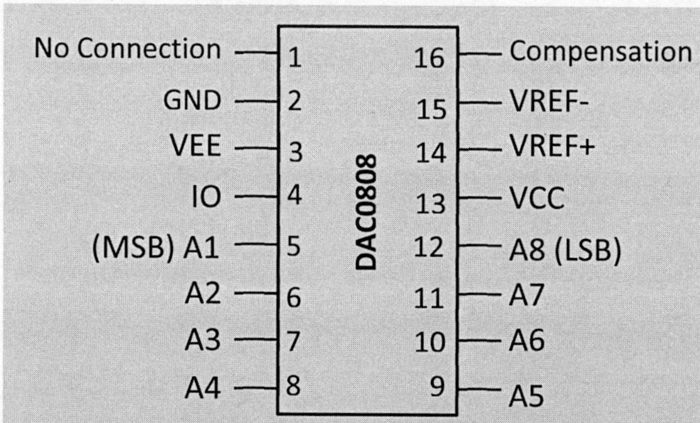

Fig 4.22: Pin layout of DAC0808

Fig 4.23 shows an interface of DAC0808 with the 8051. Port P1 of the 8051 has been used to provide the digital input to be converted to analog current/voltage. VEE has been given -15V while VCC has got +5V. VREF+ has been connected to 10V, VREF– to zero and the resistance as 5kΩ. This ensures the reference current I_{ref} to be 10mA. An operational amplifier (such as, 741), can be

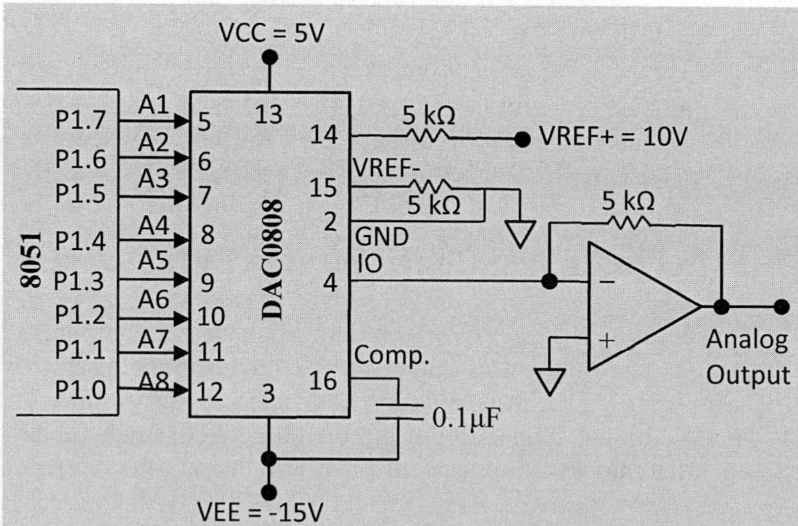

Fig 4.23: Interfacing DAC0808 with 8051

used with feedback resistance 5kΩ to convert the output current to analog voltage.

The interface shown in Fig 4.23 can be used to generate different types of analog waveforms. In the following, two examples have been noted – one to generate a triangular wave and the second one to generate a sine wave.

Example 4.2: Triangular Wave Generation. To generate triangular wave, the values 0 to 255 can be output to port P1 followed by decrementing upto 0. The digital values, when converted by the DAC will provide an analog output triangular waveform. The 8051 source code for the same has been presented next. After outputting a digital value, a small delay has been introduced to allow time to the DAC to convert the pattern. It may be noted that increasing the delay value will convert the waveform to be more of staircase in shape. The waveform can be viewed on an oscilloscope to see the shape and adjust the delay value accordingly.

```
      ORG 0
      CLR A              ; Clear accumulator
L1:   MOV P1, A          ; Send data to DAC
      ACALL DLA          ; Insert delay
      CJNE A, #0FFH, L2  ; Check if 255 reached
      SJMP L3            ; Jump to decrement
L2:   INC A              ; Increment A
      SJMP L1            ; Repeat increment
L3:   DEC A              ; Continue
      MOV P1, A          ; Send to DAC
      ACALL DLA          ; Insert delay
      CJNE A, #01, L4    ; Check if 0 reached
      CLR A              ; Clear accumulator
      SJMP L1            ; Repeat increment
L4:   SJMP L3            ; Repeat decrement
DLA:  NOP                ; Small delay routine
      NOP
      RET
      END
```

The corresponding C language program is as follows.

```
#include <reg51.h>
    void main (void)
    {
        unsigned char i;
```

```
        while (1) {
                for (i = 0; i < 255; i++) { P1 = i; delay_rtn(2); }
                for (i = 255; i > 0; i --) { P1 = i; delay_rtn(2); }
        }
}
void delay_rtn( unsigned int del_val )
{   unsigned int x, y;
    for (x = 0; x < 1000; x++)
            for (y = 0; y < del_val; y++);
}
```

Example 4.3: Sine Wave Generation. To generate a sine wave, we first need to prepare a table of the sine values of different angles in the range 0 to 360 degrees. Assuming that corresponding to zero degree, the output voltage is 5V and that the peak voltage can be at most 10V, the equation governing the sine wave is as follows.

$$V_{out} = 5\text{ V} + (5 \times \sin\theta)$$

The 10V range is covered by 256 digital levels of inputs. Thus, each level constitutes a voltage of 25.6V. Table 4.3 shows the different angles and their corresponding digital input to be sent to the DAC for generating the sine wave.

Table 4.3: Table for Sine wave generation

Angle (θ)	**sin θ**	**V_{out}**	**Digital value**
0	0	5	128
30	0.5	7.5	192
60	0.866	9.33	238
90	1.0	10	255
120	0.866	9.33	238
150	0.5	7.5	192
180	0	5	128
210	-0.5	2.5	64
240	-0.866	0.669	17
270	-1.0	0	0
300	-0.866	0.669	17
330	-0.5	2.5	64
360	0	5	128

The assembly language program for the sine wave generation is as follows. It stores the values noted in Table 4.3 and outputs those periodically to produce the sine wave. It may be noted that as the values are 30 degree apart, the generated waveform will not be very smooth. To produce a better waveform, more intermediary values are to be kept in the table and output to the DAC.

The C

```
        ORG 0
WAVE:   DB 128, 192, 238, 255,
           238, 192, 128, 64,        ;  The Table
           17, 0, 17, 64, 128
L1:     MOV DPTR, #WAVE              ;  DPTR points to Table
        MOV R2, #13                  ;  R2 holds count
L2:     CLR A
        MOVC A, @A+DPTR              ;  Get next sine value
        MOV P1, A                    ;  Output to Port P1
        INC DPTR                     ;  DPTR points to next
        DJNZ R2, L2                  ;  Go for next value
        SJMP L1                      ;  Generate next wave
        END
```

language program for the same can be as follows.

```
#include <reg51.h>
void main (void)
{
    unsigned char WAVE[ 12 ] = {128, 192, 238, 255,
                                238, 192, 128, 64,
                                17, 0, 17, 64};
    unsigned char i;
    while (1) {
          for (i = 0; i < 255; i++) {
                P1 = WAVE[ i ];
                delay_rtn(2);
          }
    }
}
void delay_rtn( unsigned int del_val )
{   unsigned int x, y;
    for (x = 0; x < 1000; x++)
            for (y = 0; y < del_val; y++);
}
```

4.8 Interfacing Temperature Sensor

Physical data from the real-world need to be converted to electrical signals for interaction with the microcontroller. Temperature is one of the very important physical quantities, monitored by the microcontroller based systems. The device used to sense the physical quantity is a *sensor*. For example, a constantan alloy (Cu-55%, Ni-45%) wire is a sensor that creates a change in its resistance when subjected to mechanical displacement. A sensor becomes a *transducer* when it can convert one form of energy into another. For example, a thermocouple is a heat sensor which is also a transducer, as in response to a change in temperature, it outputs a proportional change in the electromotive force (emf). However, the terms *sensor* and *transducer* are often used interchangeably without much differentiation.

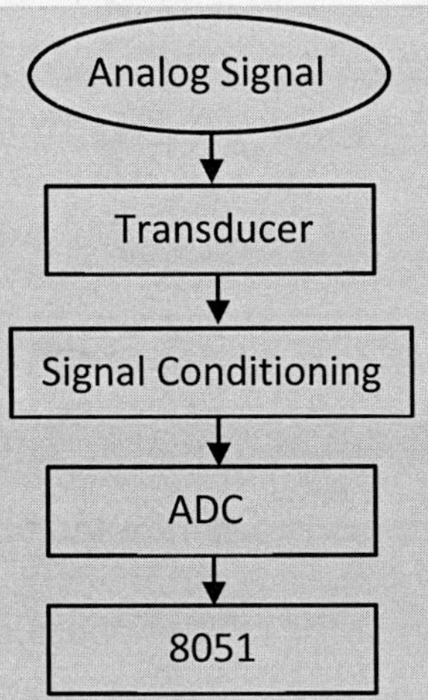

Fig 4.24: Analog signal to 8051

Most of the transducers generate output in the form of voltage, current, charge, capacitance, resistance etc. Since these are analog quantities, need to be converted to a digital value through ADC. However, it also requires some post-processing of the signal, before being fed to the ADC. This process of conversion is called *signal conditioning*. Fig 4.24 shows the intermediary steps in getting an environmental data into equivalent digital value for processing by the 8051.

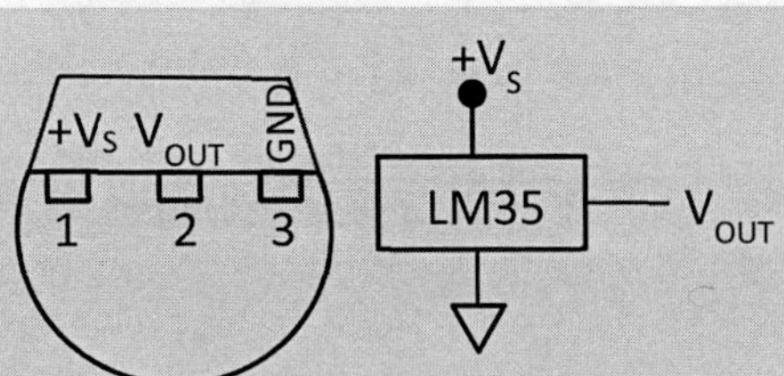

Fig 4.25: LM35 pin layout

Among the different temperature sensors, the LM35 series devices are precision integrated-circuit (IC) temperature sensors. Its output voltage is linearly proportional to the Celsius temperature, with an output of 10 mV for each degree. It is internally calibrated with temperature range of -55°C to +150°C and accuracy of 1°C-2°C. Fig 4.25 presents the pin layout of LM35. This is a three terminal device operating in the range 4-30V. The pin $+V_S$ is connected to the supply voltage, GND is the ground pin. Analog voltage corresponding to the sensed temperature is available at pin V_{OUT}. To interface the temperature sensor, it can be connected to Channel 1 of the ADC, in Fig 4.21. The pin $+V_S$ can be set to 5V, V_{OUT} is to be connected to Channel 1. Programs noted in Section 4.6 can be used to read the temperature values into the A register of the 8051.

4.9 8255 Interfacing

The chip 8255 is called a *Programmable Peripheral Interface* (*PPI*). In 8051, among the four I/O ports, only the port P1 is dedicated towards input-output operations. Rest of the three ports P0, P2 and P3 are multiplexed with several other activities, such as, interfacing external memory, timer/counter, interrupts etc. Hence, it is often necessary to have arrangement to have more I/O ports in the system. The chip 8255 is specifically used for this purpose. Fig 4.26 shows the pin layout of the chip. It is a 40-pin chip with three independent 8-bit ports, named as A, B and C. Each port can be configured as input or output. Apart from the 24 pins (PA0-PA7, PB0-PB7, PC0-PC7), the remaining 16 lines of 8255 are used for interfacing the chip with the 8051 (or any other processor). Fig 4.27 shows the grouping of pins with respect to their functionality and recommended connections. It has been detailed in the following.

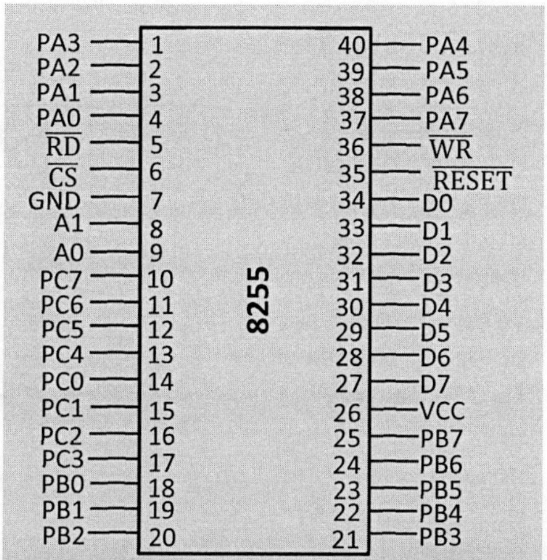

Fig 4.26: 8255 pin layout

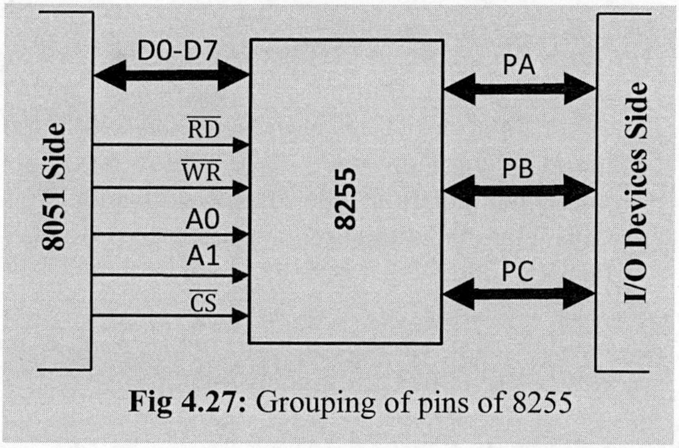

Fig 4.27: Grouping of pins of 8255

- **D0-D7:** These are data pins, generally connected to the data bus lines of the 8051 to send data to the 8255 or back.
- **$\overline{RD}$, $\overline{WR}$:** These are control signals provided by the 8051 to direct a read operation or a write operation onto the registers/ports of the 8255.
- **PA, PB, PC:** The three 8-bit ports PA0-PA7, PB0-PB7 and PC0-PC7. The ports can be configured to behave as input or output ports, independently. Out of these, port A bits can be configured for simultaneous bidirectional operation (both input and output) also. Port B can be programmed as only input or output, but not as bidirectional. Port C can be split into two parts – *Port C Upper CU* (PC4-PC7) and *Port C Lower CL* (PC3-PC0). Each of the parts of port C can be programmed to behave as input or output, independently.
- **$\overline{CS}$, A1, A0:** These lines are used to select the 8255 chip and individual ports/register within it. For any data

Table 4.4: 8255 port selection

$\overline{CS}$	A1	A0	Port/Register
0	0	0	Port A
0	0	1	Port B
0	1	0	Port C
0	1	1	Control Register
1	x	x	Not selected

transfer to the 8255, the $\overline{CS}$ must be set to low. The values of A1 and A0 will decide the port/register selection as noted in Table 4.4.

8255 Modes: The 8255 can be made to operate in one of the following modes. The mode can be selected by writing a code word to the control register. Fig 4.28 shows the bit setting needed for different modes of operation of the ports. The ports A, B and C are put into two groups. *Group A* corresponds to the Port A and the upper 4-bits of Port C (CU). *Group B* corresponds to the Port B and the lower 4-bits of Port C (CL). The mode settings are as follows.

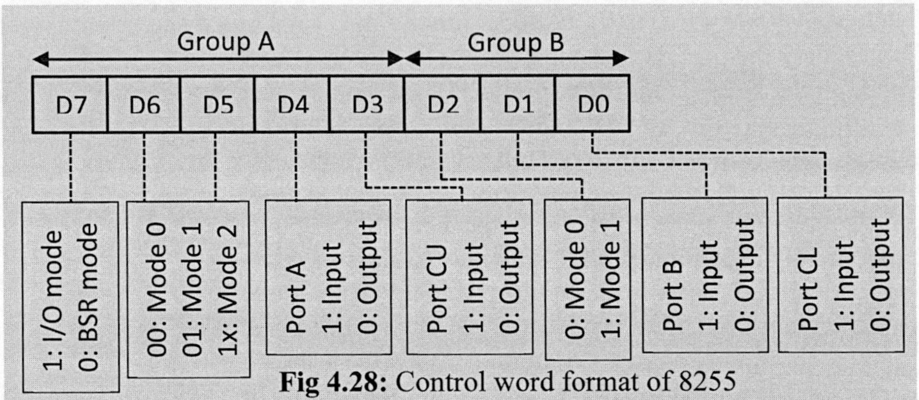

Fig 4.28: Control word format of 8255

1. **Mode 0, Simple I/O.** This mode can be used to program any of the ports A, B, CU and CL as input or output. Entire 8-bits (for A and B) or 4-bits (for CU and CL) are to be configured as either input or output, individual bits within a port cannot be programmed differently. This is the most common mode used in 8255 based port interfacing. For example, to set all the three ports in output mode, the control word should be "10000000", that is, 80H. Similarly, to set Port A as input and all the remaining three (Port B, CU and CL) as output, the control word should be "10010000", that is, 90H.

2. **Mode 1, Handshaking.** In this mode, ports A and B can be used as input or output with the port C bits providing handshaking signals.

3. **Mode 2, Bidirectional Handshaking.** In this mode, port A can be used as bidirectional I/O port with handshaking signals through port C. Port B bits can be used in either Mode 0 or Mode 1.

4. **Bit Set/Reset (BSR) Mode.** In this mode, individual bits of Port C can be programmed independently.

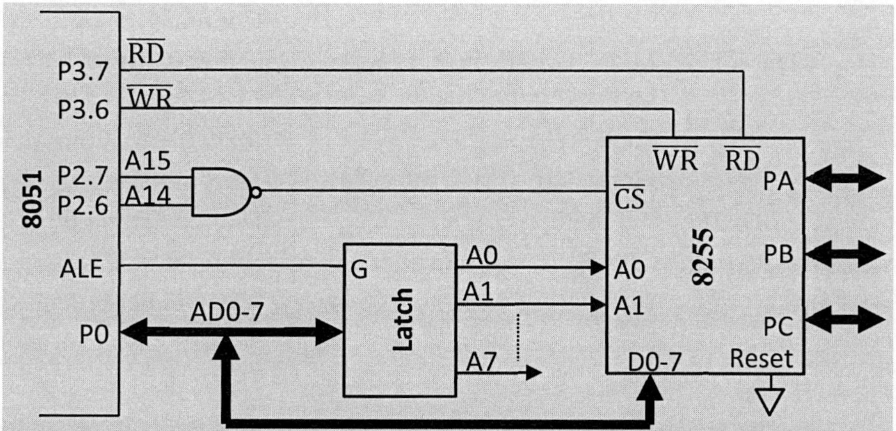

Fig 4.29: Interfacing 8255 with the 8051

Fig 4.29 shows the interfacing of 8255 with the 8051. It has been assumed that the 8255 will get selected only for addresses with A15 = A14 = 1. As shown in Table 4.4, Port A gets selected for A1 = 0, A0 = 0. Thus, for data transfer through Port A, the address should be "11xxxxxxxxxxxx00". Similarly, for the ports B, C and control register, the addresses should be "11xxxxxxxxxxxx01", "11xxxxxxxxxxxx10" and "11xxxxxxxxxxxx11", respectively. One set of addresses for the ports A, B, C and the control register can thus be, C000H, C001H, C002H and C003H, respectively. It may be noted that many more addresses are possible, as most of the bits are don't cares.

The following assembly language program can be used to output patterns to the ports A, B and C in such a fashion that the 8-bit outputs in each port are "01010101" (55H) followed by "10101010" (AAH) continually. For this, the ports are first configured as output ports by writing the control word 80H to the control register. The program then enters into an infinite loop to output the patterns. The DPTR register has been used as 16-bit address pointer for the 8255 addresses.

```
     ORG 0
     MOV DPTR, #0C003H     ;  DPTR points to control register
     MOV A, #80H           ;  Load control word
     MOVX @DPTR, A         ;  Issue control word
     MOV A, 55H            ;  Load 55H to A
L1:  MOV DPTR, #0C000H     ;  DPTR points to Port A
     MOV @DPTR, A          ;  Output to Port A
     INC DPTR              ;  DPTR points to Port B
     MOV @DPTR, A          ;  Output to Port B
     INC DPTR              ;  DPTR points to Port C
     MOVX @DPTR, A         ;  Output to Port C
     CPL A                 ;  Complement A
     ACALL DL_RTN          ;  Call Delay routine
```

```
          SJMP L1                  ;   Continue
DL_RTN:   MOV TMOD, #01            ;   Timer 0, Mode 1
          MOV TL0, #0E0H           ;   Load TH and TL
          MOV TH0, #0B1H           ;   0B1E0H for 20ms delay
          SETB TR0                 ;   Start timer
AGAIN:    JNB TF0, AGAIN           ;   Monitor Timer 0
          CLR TR0                  ;   Stop Timer 0
          CLR TF0                  ;   Clear Timer 0 flag
          RET
          END
```

The C language program for the 8255 interface can be as follows. Many of the 8051 compilers support a macro called XBYTE for external memory access. As in this case, the 8255 ports are accessed as external memory locations, the macro has been utilized.

```
#include <reg51.h>
#include <absacc.h>
void delay_rtn( unsigned int del_val );
void main()
{
        unsigned char pattern;              // Pattern to be sent to ports
        XBYTE[0xC003] = 0x80;               // Configure all ports as output
        while (1) {
                pattern = 0x55;
                XBYTE[0xC000] = pattern;    // Send 55H to all ports
                XBYTE[0xC001] = pattern;
                XBYTE[0xC002] = pattern;
                delay_rtn( 100 );           // Put a delay

                pattern = 0xAA;
                XBYTE[0xC000] = pattern;    // Send 0AAH to all ports
                XBYTE[0xC001] = pattern;
                XBYTE[0xC002] = pattern;
                delay_rtn( 100 );           // Put a delay
        }
}

void delay_rtn( unsigned int del_val )
{
```

```
            unsigned int x, y;
            for (x = 0; x < 1000; x++)
                    for (y = 0; y < del_val; y++);
    }
```

It may be noted that Mode 0 is the most common one for 8255 interfacing. Other modes are used for more sophisticated devices (such as, printers) that have bidirectional handshaking lines for interface.

UNIT SUMMARY

Interfacing input-output devices is very important for any microcontroller based system, interacting with the real-world. As the 8051 is a digital device, the simplest input device to interface is a switch while the simplest output device is a LED. As switches are mechanical in nature, debouncing is necessary to overcome the jitter. An example of more complex switch device is a matrix keyboard. A hexadecimal matrix keyboard can be interfaced using two ports of the 8051, by repeatedly scanning the rows and columns. In the display domain, LCDs have gradually replaced the LED based displays. LCD interfacing requires set of commands to be sent to it from the 8051. Analog world interfacing requires connecting analog-to-digital and digital-to-analog converters to interact with the environment. ADCs are also used to interface various sensors with the 8051. The number of I/O pins of 8051 appear to be insufficient for many applications, as most of the pins are assigned more than one function. To solve this problem, often the 8255 chip is interfaced. This chip provides three, 8-bit ports. The ports can be utilized to connect other devices to the 8051. Though 8255 has a number of modes of operations, the most common one configures the ports as simple input or output ports. This has been discussed in detail. Thus, this unit has provided a very good overview of interfacing devices and chips to the 8051.

EXERCISES

Multiple Choice Questions

MQ1. A single mechanical switch is connected to a falling edge-triggered interrupt line of a microprocessor, such that, when the key is pressed, an interrupt will be generated. The most appropriate debouncing policy for this is

(A) Hardware debouncing (B) Software debouncing
(C) Either hardware or software debouncing can be used
(D) None of the hardware or software debouncing techniques useful

MQ2. If a current limiting resistance is not used while driving an LED through the output port of 8051

(A) LED intensity may be low (B) LED may be damaged
(C) Port may be damaged (D) None of the given options

MQ3. For interfacing an LED with 8051 port, which of the following is/are safe ways?

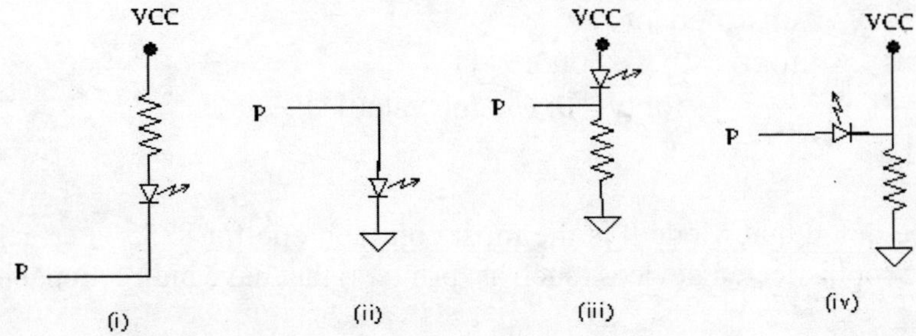

(A) (i) (B) (i), (ii) (C) (ii), (iv) (D) (ii)

MQ4. For interfacing an LED with 8051 port, if P = 1, which configuration will glow the LED?

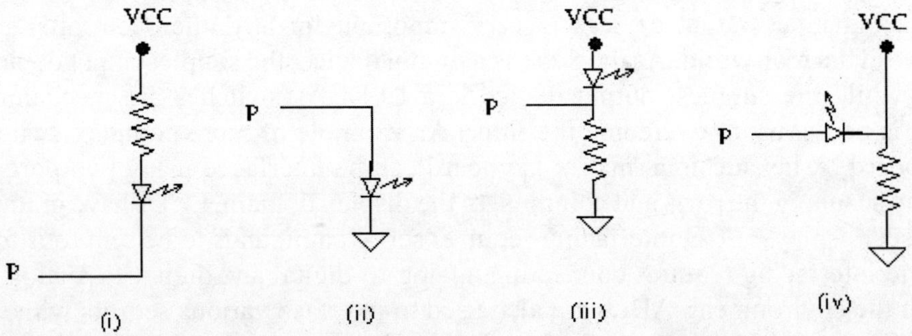

(A) (i) (B) (i), (ii) (C) (ii), (iv) (D) (ii)

MQ5. Which type of LED displays need common side to be grounded?
(A) Common anode (B) Common cathode
(C) Both common anode and common cathode (D) None of the displays

MQ6. Which type of LED displays need common side to be tied high?
(A) Common anode (B) Common cathode
(C) Both common anode and common cathode (D) None of the displays

MQ7. In Fig 4.13 if a decoder is used to produce the module selection inputs in interfacing 4 7-segment displays, the decoder should be of size
(A) 1-to-2 (B) 2-to-4 (C) 3-to-8 (D) None of the other options

MQ8. For matrix keyboard, debouncing can be implemented using
(A) Hardware techniques (B) Software techniques
(C) Both hardware and software techniques (D) None of the other options

MQ9. In a 4x4 matrix keyboard operation, software debouncing is performed by
(A) Reading each row twice
(B) Writing 0 to more than one columns
(C) Reading each row more than twice
(D) None of the other options

MQ10. For matrix keyboard, debouncing helps to
(A) Read one key when multiple keys are pressed

(B) Read a key only once avoiding vibrations
(C) Sense one key multiple times
(D) None of the other options

MQ11. A 4x4 matrix keyboard is interfaced with 8051 via ports P0 and P1. The rows and columns of the keyboard are pulled high via resistances. To check whether all keys are released,
(A) All-zero be written to P0 and P1 be read for all 1
(B) All-zero be written to P1 and P0 be read for all 1
(C) Either port can be used to write zeros while the other to read for all 1
(D) None of the other options is valid

MQ12. In a 4x4 matrix keyboard with keys 0 to F, keys are arranged on a row-major format (keys 0-3 forms first row, 4-7 second row, and so on). Rows are scanned one-by-one. If the keys 8 and F are pressed simultaneously, number of 0-bits in the pattern read at a time is
(A) 1 (B) 2 (C) 0 (D) 4

MQ13. Which display device(s) require(s) refreshing?
(A) 7-segment (B) LCD
(C) Both 7-segment and LCD (D) None of the other options

MQ14. In LCD module, busy status is reflected at pin
(A) DB0 (B) DB3 (C) DB5 (D) DB7

MQ15. In LCD devices setting RS to 0 selects
(A) Instruction command code register (B) Data register
(C) Status register (D) Control register

MQ16. The appropriate pin of a processor to which the Start Conversion (SC) line of ADC be connected to is
(A) Port bit (B) Interrupt
(C) Either a port bit or interrupt (D) Neither port bit nor interrupt

MQ17. The appropriate pin of a processor to which the End of Conversion (EOC) line of ADC be connected to is
(A) Port bit (B) Interrupt
(C) Either a port bit or interrupt (D) Neither port bit nor interrupt

MQ18. With the reference voltage as 10V, the step size of a 10-bit ADC will be
(A) 9.76mV (B) 10mV (C) 2.56mV (D) None of the other options

MQ19. Number of digital output bits of DAC0808 is
(A) 8 (B) 4 (C) 12 (D) None of the mentioned

MQ20. If an 8-bit output port of the 8051 drives a DAC to produce a sawtooth waveform, the most appropriate value to be output after 255 is
(A) 0 (B) 127 (C) 254 (D) 256

MQ21. The device converting one energy form to another is called a
(A) Transformer (B) Transducer (C) Sensor (D) Actuator

MQ22. A signal conditioning circuit is generally used before
(A) ADC (B) DAC

(C) Both ADC and DAC (D) None of the other options

MQ23. In 8255, port requiring external pull-up is

(A) A (B) B (C) C (D) None of the other options

MQ24. In 8255, control word is written to

(A) A (B) B (C) C (D) None of the other options

MQ25. In 8255, bit addressability is available with port

(A) A (B) B (C) C (D) D

Answers of Multiple Choice Questions

1:A, 2:B, 3:A, 4:D, 5:B, 6:A, 7:B, 8:C, 9:A, 10:B, 11:C, 12:A, 13:A, 14:D, 15:A, 16:A, 17:C, 18:A, 19:A, 20:A, 21:B, 22:A, 23:D, 24:D, 25:C

Short Answer Type Questions

SQ1. Explain the necessity of debouncing in switch interfaces to the 8051.

SQ2. In Fig 4.7, why is it not advisable to connect a single resistance to the LEDs instead of eight separate resistances?

SQ3. In Fig 4.8, assume that all keys are initially open. Now, if two keys in a row are pressed simultaneously, which one will be sensed? What about keys belonging to the same column?

SQ4. Explain how many 7-segment display modules can be interfaced in a multiplexed fashion.

SQ5. State the advantages of LCD over LED displays.

SQ6. State the sequence of operations in an ADC interfaced with the 8051.

SQ7. How to interface a DAC with the 8051?

SQ8. Distinguish between sensors, transducers and actuators.

SQ9. What are the modes of operation of 8255?

SQ10. State the benefits of 8255 over and above the fact that the 8051 has four ports of itself.

Long Answer Type Questions

LQ1. Design the hardware and software to interface a hex keyboard with the 8051.

LQ2. Enumerate the interfacing of an LCD module with the 8051.

LQ3. Design the hardware and software to interface a temperature sensor to the 8051 through ADC0808.

LQ4. Design the hardware and software to generate a cosine wave through the 8051.

LQ5. Show the interfacing of a 8255 chip with the 8051.

Practical Problems

PQ1. Design the hardware and software to interface 2, 8-bit DIP switches to the ports P1 and P2 of the 8051. The switch settings are to be displayed on 8 LEDs connected to the port P0, alternately.

Hint: Use the template in Example 4.1. Another DIP switch to be connected to port P2. The program should be modified to display the settings alternately to the LEDS in port P0.

PQ2. Design the hardware and software to interface a 4×4 hex keyboard. The program should work on the principle of column scanning. That is, at a time, one of the columns be made 0 and the rows be checked for a keypress in a row.

Hint: Use the template in Section 4.3. Port P1 should be an input port and P2 output port. The program be modified accordingly to reverse the role of row and column scanning.

PQ3. Design a rolling display with 4, 7-segment LED modules. It should display the numbers 0 to 9 continually. To have the rolling effect, periodically a display module should copy the digit currently being displayed by its right neighbour and the rightmost module displaying the next digit in sequence.

Hint: Use the template in Section 4.4. To have rolling effect, an "update_buffer" routine may be developed and called periodically to update the buffer content corresponding to the digits to be displayed.

PQ4. Repeat PQ3 for an LCD module.

Hint: Refer to Section 4.5.

PQ5. Design the hardware and software to interface an ADC with the 8051.

Hint: Refer to Section 4.6.

PQ6. Design the hardware and software to generate a smooth sine wave through DAC using 8051.

Hint: Refer to Example 4.3.

PQ7. Interface an 8255 chip with the 8051.

Hint: Refer to Section 4.9.

KNOW MORE

The analog-to-digital converters discussed in this unit are parallel in nature. They provide the digital output as 8-bit parallel data. This often creates problem to route all the 8 lines through the PCB, particularly if the system has a number of chips mounted on the board. A variation to this provides the converted data in serial fashion, with one bit clocked out on each high-to-low transition of the clock signal. This effectively reduces the data out pins from eight to one. A typical example of such ADC is MAX1112 which is an 8-bit serial ADC.

Similar to LM35 which is a temperature sensor working on the Celsius scale, its variant LM34 works for Fahrenheit scale. It works in the range of -50 to +300 degree Fahrenheit. These sensors are highly linear in nature. However, many sensors do not provide linearity over their entire range of operation. They require special circuitry to get a linear behaviour. The same compensation can also be done in software.

REFERENCES AND SUGGESTED READINGS

[1] S. Chattopadhyay, SWAYAM/NPTEL course on "Microprocessors and Microcontrollers", https://onlinecourses.nptel.ac.in/noc20_ee42/preview.

[2] M.A. Mazidi, R.D. McKinlay, J.G. Mazidi, "The 8051 Microcontroller: A Systems Approach", Pearson.

[3] "MCS® 51 Microcontroller Family User's Manual", https://fdocuments.in/document/8051-manual.html".

Dynamic QR Code for Further Reading

1. S. Chattopadhyay, SWAYAM/NPTEL course on "Microprocessors and Microcontrollers".
2. "MCS® 51 Microcontroller Family User's Manual", https://fdocuments.in/document/8051-manual.html".

5 Introduction to Advanced Processors and Concepts

UNIT SPECIFICS

Through this unit we have discussed the following aspects:

- *Understanding the basics of CISC and RISC architectures;*
- *Comparing the features of RISC vs. CISC;*
- *Overview of the advanced microcontroller PIC;*
- *Understanding the basics of AVR microcontroller;*
- *Overview of the ARM architecture;*
- *Features of LPC214x series of microcontrollers developed around ARM7;*
- *Input-Output programming with LPC2148 microcontroller.*

The discussion in this unit is to give an overview of advanced microcontrollers. It has started with the basics of and differences between the CISC and the RISC architecture principles. It has covered the advanced processors like PIC, AVR and ARM. It has been assumed that the reader has a good understanding of conventional processor architectures, microprocessors and microcontrollers. A good number of examples have been included to explain the concepts, wherever needed.

A large number of multiple choice questions have been provided with their answers. Apart from that, subjective questions of short and long answer type have been included. A few practical problems with solution hints have been provided. A list of references and suggested readings have been given, so that, one can go through them for more details. The section "Know More" has been carefully designed so that the supplementary information provided in this part becomes beneficial for the users of the book. This section mainly highlights the recent developments and application areas with advanced microcontrollers like ARM.

RATIONALE

This unit on introduction to advanced microcontrollers helps the reader to understand the basics of advanced microcontrollers that are in use in different applications. The requirements of such devices include less area, high performance with built-in peripheral and communication modules. The unit starts with a discussion on CISC and RISC architectures. The two philosophies have been explained with distinction between them. After that, advanced microcontrollers have been presented. In this category, first the PIC microcontroller series, PIC18F has been taken up. Another very common microcontroller comes from the AVR series. The ATmega32 series microcontroller has been illustrated to bring out the essence of the AVR family. The ARM microcontrollers have come up almost as default for the low power advanced microcontroller applications. The ARM architecture has evolved a lot – starting from the ARM1 to the advanced Cortex series. The ARM7 series is an intermediary that works well for understanding the features and acts as a link between the older and the recent processors of ARM. ARM7 architecture has been discussed in sufficient detail. A particular implementation of ARM7, LPC214x series has been presented along with the input-output programming features that can make the reader understand the basics and capabilities of the series. Thus, the unit gives bird's-eye-view of advanced microcontroller based system design.

PRE-REQUISITES

Electronics: Units 1, 2, 3, 4 of the book

UNIT OUTCOMES

List of outcomes of this unit is as follows:

U5-O1: State the basic features of CISC and RISC architectures

U5-O2: Compare between the features of RISC and CISC

U5-O3: Enumerate the internal architecture of PIC microcontrollers

U5-O4: Enumerate the internal architecture of AVR microcontrollers

U5-O5: State the features of ARM

U5-O6: Enumerate the ARM7 architecture

U5-O7: Develop hardware and software for I/O programming with LPC2148

Unit-1 Outcomes	***EXPECTED MAPPING WITH COURSE OUTCOMES*** *(1- Weak Correlation; 2- Medium correlation; 3- Strong Correlation)*					
	CO-1	***CO-2***	***CO-3***	***CO-4***	***CO-5***	***CO-6***
U5-O1	2	-	-	-	-	2
U5-O2	2	-	-	-	-	3
U5-O3	2	-	-	-	-	1
U5-O4	2	-	-	-	-	1
U5-O5	2	-	-	-	-	3
U5-O6	1	-	-	-	-	3
U5-O7	1	-	-	-	-	3

5.1 Introduction

In order to get some fruitful computation done, a processor interacts with the memory for instructions and data. The instruction set supported by a processor is fixed at its design time. Thus, the processor designer has the liberty to make the processor powerful enough to handle complex operations by its individual instructions directly. This increases the complexity of the processor hardware design. The alternative approach for the designer may be to support simple machine instructions only by the processor, while the complex operations of high-level languages are to be realized by a group of machine instructions. Here, the job of translating complex high-level operations into a sequence of simple processor instructions, is carried out by optimizing compilers. Both the approaches are effective, however, needs special care at the hardware and/or software level.

For example, consider a high-level multiplication operation "$a = a \times b$", where a, b are memory locations. In continuation to the discussion above, the following two approaches may be taken for its realization.

1. The multiplication of two memory operands may be implemented directly in the hardware, via a machine instruction,

   MULT a, b ; $a = a \times b$

   However, to implement it in hardware, the operands a and b are to be brought into CPU registers first. The register contents are then multiplied, storing the result in some third register. Content of this third register is then copied back to a. The primary advantage of the approach is that the high-level language compiler does not need to do much work, since matching machine instruction is directly available and all sub-operations are taken care of by the processor itself. Of course, the overall multiplication instruction takes a number of clock cycles.

2. The other option may be to have the machine instruction MULT working only on CPU registers, loading and storing of operands being taken care of by separate LOAD and STORE instructions. The approach makes the processor hardware simple, however, the job of the compiler increases significantly as it has to determine the best possible instruction subsequence to realize a high-level operation.

The first approach is commonly known as *Complex Instruction Set Computer* (*CISC*) while the second one is known as *Reduced Instruction Set Computer* (*RISC*). A computer's performance ability is often expressed by the following equation.

$$\frac{time}{program} = \frac{time}{cycle} \times \frac{cycles}{instruction} \times \frac{instructions}{program}$$

The CISC approach attempts to minimize the number of instructions per program, while the RISC approach attempts to reduce cycles per instruction. The CISC sacrifices the number of cycles per instruction, while RISC sacrifices the required number of instructions per program. The following example illustrates the situation better.

Example 5.1: Consider a program with 80% instructions simple and 20% complex. For CISC implementation, let each simple instruction take 4 cycles and complex instructions 10 cycles, cycle time being 100 ns. For RISC implementation, simple instruction takes one clock cycle. Also, let any complex operation take on an average, 12 simple instructions. Cycle time for RISC is assumed to be 75 ns.

Then, time needed by the CISC processor to execute a program with 10^6 instructions will be given by,

$$(10^6 \times 0.80 \times 4 + 10^6 \times 0.20 \times 10) \times 100 \times 10^{-9} = 0.52 \text{ sec.}$$

The time needed by the RISC processor for the same program will be about,

$$(10^6 \times 0.80 \times 1 + 10^6 \times 0.20 \times 12 \times 1) \times 75 \times 10^{-9} = 0.24 \text{ sec.}$$

Thus, in this case, the RISC processor is expected to accomplish the program in less than half the time needed by the CISC processor.

5.2 Features of CISC

The main features of CISC processors are as follows.

1. CISC processors support a large number of instructions, typically more than 200. The instructions are complex in nature. The complexity comes primarily from the amount of computation done in the individual instructions. For example, an instruction may compute "$s = s + a_i \times b_i$" to facilitate multiply-accumulate type operations. However, the instruction, in turn, includes a multiplication and an addition, which are much simpler in nature. Many different data types may also be supported for the operands, such as, *byte*, *word*, *double word* etc.

2. Supports addressing modes, some of which may be quite complex in nature. Apart from the direct, indirect and immediate modes (as for the 8051), a CISC processor may support auto-increment and auto-decrement modes among others. These modes are similar to the indirect mode with the additional feature of index register being incremented (for auto-increment) or

decremented (for auto-decrement) automatically, after accessing a memory location. These are useful for operations that modify each element of an array. However, this makes the instruction format complex and require additional time/hardware to modify the index register.

3. Direct hardware implementation of high-level language constructs. Typical high-level languages (such as, C) support constructs like *if-then-else*, *switch-case*, *loop* etc. Converting them to machine language is cumbersome and often introduce additional machine-level instructions as overhead to ensure proper flow-control. To reduce this software overhead, many CISC processors provide facilities to realize these constructs directly in the hardware. This increases the hardware complexity.

4. The controller for the processor is generally implemented using microprogramming techniques. Microcoding of new instructions provide the flexibility of making CISC machines upwardly compatible: a new computer would run the same programs of earlier computers, as the instruction set of the new processor is a superset of the same for the earlier processors. However, microprogrammed control units are slower than complete hardwired units.

5. Small code size for programs. As the individual instructions are complex, they can correspond to more computation. Thus, the size of the user program is expected to be less.

6. Instruction decoding is complex. This happens due to the requirement of supporting large number of instructions with non-uniform format. Having more addressing modes makes the problem of decoding further difficult.

7. Less number of general purpose registers. Many of the operations are performed with the operands present in memory only. The result is also stored in memory. This reduces the requirements of general purpose registers. To support special instructions, some additional special purpose registers may get introduced.

Example 5.2: Let us consider the *Intel i486* as an example of a typical CISC processor. It is a 32-bit integer processor along with an on-chip floating-point unit. The processor supports 235 instructions of size varying from 1 to 12 bytes. Eleven different addressing modes are supported. There are eight general-purpose registers. Instructions are executed following different execution models: *register-register*, *register-memory* and *memory-memory*. As the decoding of instructions become a significant problem, instruction execution is divided into five pipelined stages: *Fetch*, *Decode1*, *Decode2*, *Execute* and *Write-Back*.

Though the CISC processors may possess the advantages of compiler simplification, smaller program size and expected faster program execution (due to hardware solution for complex operation), there are several disadvantages also, as listed next.

1. Large number of complex instructions require complex hardware, escalating the area, delay and power requirements of the associated circuitry. More number of decoding steps in *i486* is a clear indication in that direction.

2. Complex instructions are introduced in CISC to match with instructions available in high-level languages. However, a small mismatch between them may turn the complex machine instruction to be mostly useless. The problem gets aggravated further if a number of high-level languages are to be supported. One complex instruction of CISC may not match with variations in similar instructions across all high-level languages supported. As a result, the compiled program may become inefficient.

3. Compiler simplification may not always be achievable. Optimizer may find it difficult to realize the intended computation of a high-level language program by using individual machine instructions which themselves are not very simple and uniform in nature.

4. Advantage of small program size may not be very beneficial as the cost of memory chips is declining at a rapid rate. Moreover, with the increasing instruction size (for example, upto 12 bytes in *i486*), overall code size reduction may not be significant.

5. As instructions are highly non-uniform in terms of size and execution time, supporting instruction pipelining becomes an issue.

5.3 RISC Processors

In the last section, we have seen CISC approach to solve the problem of efficient execution of high-level language programs by the processor. It has been observed that the approach has several drawbacks, as well. The other extreme in processor design is to have a simple instruction set in which all instructions are of same size and takes same amount of time (typically, one cycle) to execute. This second approach is followed in designing the *Reduced Instruction Set Computer* (*RISC*) processors. The main characteristics of a RISC processor are as follows.

1. It possesses a small number of simple instructions only. Simplicity comes in terms of size of the instruction and its execution time. Instruction size is kept such that it can be fetched in a single memory access, that is, memory word size.

2. Compared to CISC architecture, the controller in a RISC processor is often hardwired. This makes it possible to run the processor fast. CPU also takes less silicon area and possibly less power/energy to execute programs.

3. Execution of operations follow register-register model. As a result, the operation could be completed in a single cycle. Only LOAD and STORE instructions refer data in memory. Such architectures are also known as *load-store* architecture.

4. Only simple addressing modes are supported. This reduces the instruction complexity significantly.

5. A large number of registers is made available to the programmer. Variables and intermediate results of a computation are stored in registers, so that repeated loading from memory is not needed. Similarly, local variables and parameters of a procedure are allotted space in CPU registers.

Example 5.3: Let us consider the RISC processor SPARC. This is a 32-bit processor having an integer unit and a floating point co-processor. It has only 69 basic instructions. There are 40 to 520 general purpose registers, each of width 32 bits. The registers are grouped into 2 to 32 overlapping register windows. A register window is assigned to a procedure. Thus, it is ensured that the registers of the calling procedure are not inadvertently modified by instructions in the called procedure. The overlapping of windows of caller and called procedures help in passing parameters and return values between them. Fig 5.1 illustrates the idea in which a Level *m* procedure has called another one (at level *m*+1). Temporary registers of level *m* procedure have been overlapped with the parameter registers of the called procedure at level *m*+1. Thus, parameters need not be passed separately to the called procedure, these are already available in its register window.

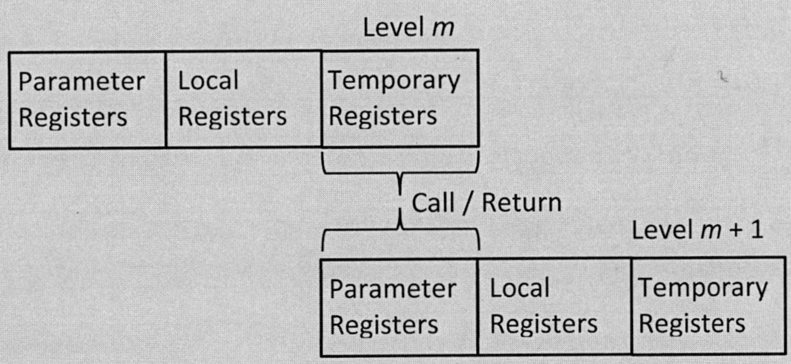

Fig 5.1: Overlapping Register Windows

However, RISC is also not free from all disadvantages. The following issues need to be taken care of.

1. An operation of high-level language may need multiple machine instructions. This effectively increases the number of memory accesses for certain applications.

2. Assembly language programming may be a problem, as individual instructions are not powerful enough to directly realize an operation of high-level language.

3. Despite their advantages, RISC chips require software support. In particular, availability of a good optimizing compiler that can utilize the instruction set effectively, is a must for the success of RISC technology.

4. Some of the CISC features, like hardware support for loop, copying a chunk of data from a source memory block to a destination memory block etc. are required by the programming community.

Table 5.1 summarizes the major differences between the CISC and the RISC architectures. However, neither RISC nor CISC has come up as a better alternative. As a result, the microcontrollers and other processors being designed in the recent time are tried out to have the better features of both the alternatives incorporated into them. In the following we shall look into three such advanced microcontrollers – PIC, AVR and ARM.

Table 5.1: CISC vs. RISC

Feature	***CISC***	***RISC***
No. of instructions	Large, 120-350	Small, less than 100
Data types supported	More	Less
Addressing modes	Large	Few
Instruction format	Variable	Fixed
Operands	Register, Memory	Register
Clocks per instruction	Variable 1-20	Fixed to 1 due to pipelining
General purpose registers	8-32	Large
Control Unit	Microprogrammed	Hardwired

5.4 PIC Microcontroller

PIC – Programmable Interface Controller, microcontrollers are one of the popular set of RISC based processors, introduced in the year 1993 by the *General Instruments*. These have been widely used in different applications, including smartphones, audio accessories and advanced medical devices. There are different variants of PIC, however, PIC18F constitute the advanced one. In the following, we shall concentrate on the PIC18F series only. Fig 5.2 shows the pin configuration of the PIC18F452.

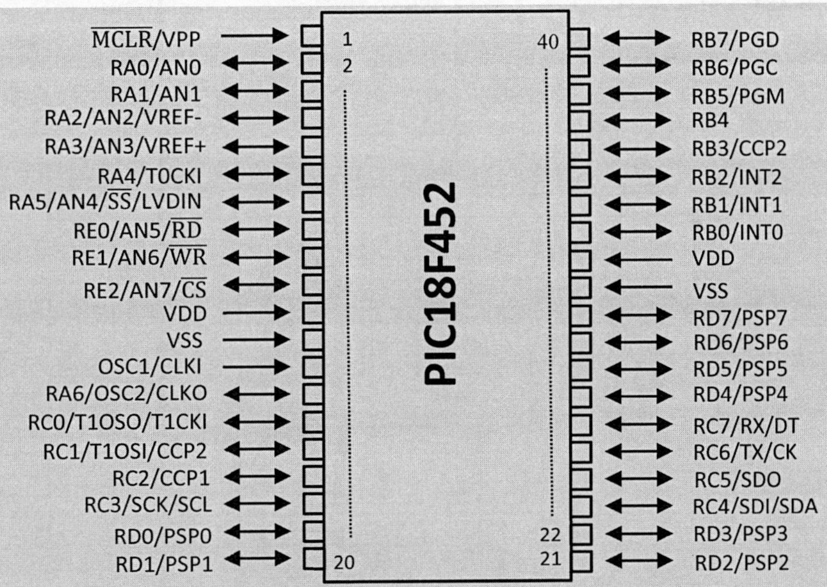

Fig 5.2: Pin Configuration of PIC18F452

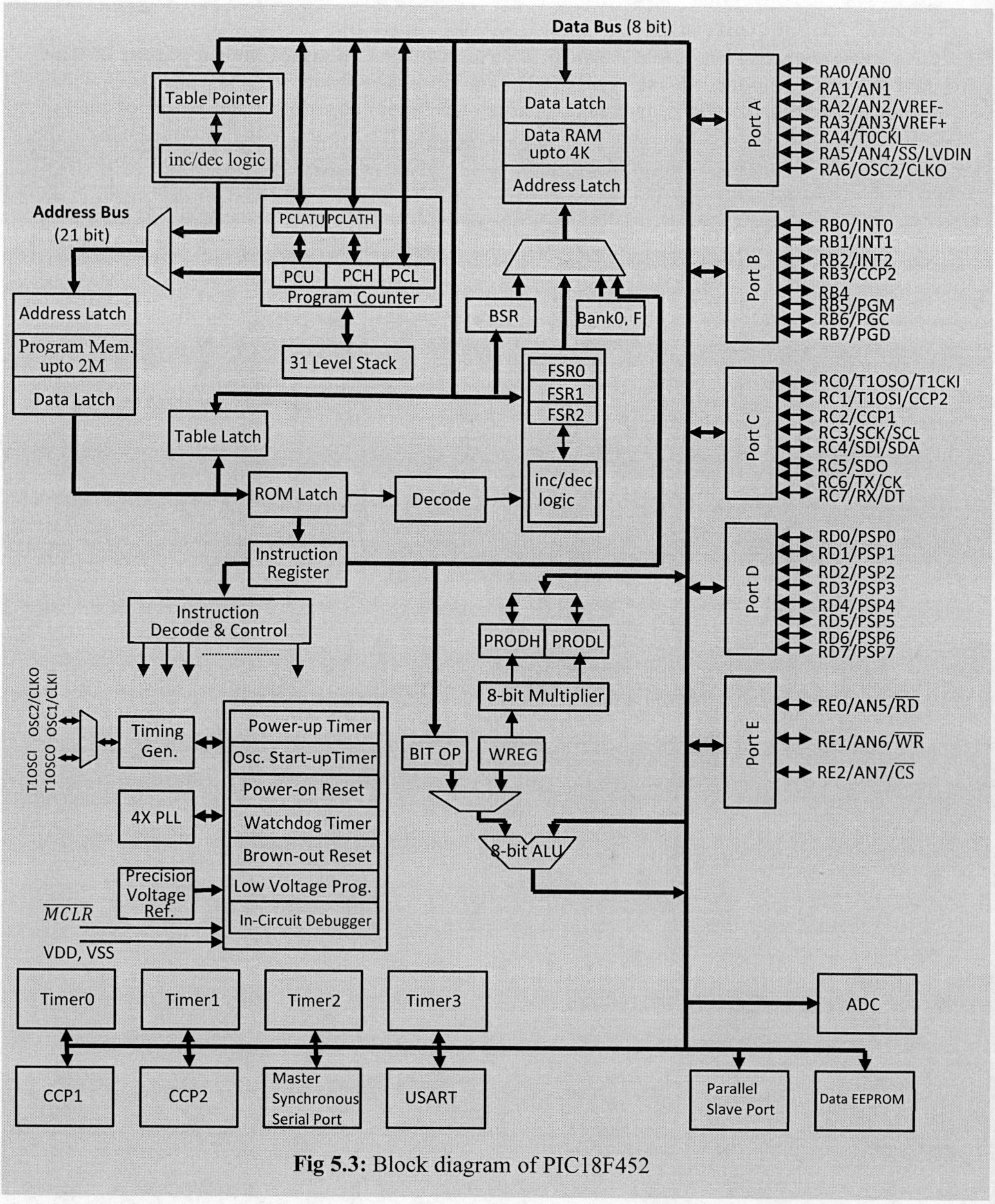

Fig 5.3: Block diagram of PIC18F452

Fig 5.3 shows the internal block diagram. It has an 8-bit CPU, 2 Mbyte program memory, 256 bytes to 1 kB EEPROM, upto 3968 bytes of on-chip SRAM, 4kB to 128 kB flash program memory. Sophisticated timers are available that can perform functions, such as, input capture, output compare, pulse width modulation, real-time interrupt and watchdog timer. Several serial communication protocols are supported, namely, *Serial Communication Interface* (*SCI*), *Serial Peripheral Interface* (*SPI*), *Inter-Integrated Circuit* (*I2C*) and *Controller Area Network* (*CAN*). A 10-bit *Analog-to-Digital converter* (*ADC*) is available. The CPU can operate at upto 40 MHz crystal oscillator. Further, instruction pipelining is used to increase the performance of the processor to one instruction per cycle. The microcontroller follows *Harvard architecture* in which the program and the data memory are separate. The two memories have their individual address and data buses. The policy allows simultaneous access for data and instruction in program execution.

The CPU contains an 8-bit ALU, an 8-bit working accumulator register (WREG) and an 8-bit multiplier. The lower byte of the 16-bit multiplication result is stored in the PRODL register, higher order 8 bits in PRODH. The program memory address is 21-bit wide, corresponding to a maximum of 2 MB space. However, the PIC18F452 has only 32 kB program memory, requiring 15-bit address bus only – 6 bits are left unused. Instructions stored in the program memory are either 2-bytes or 4-bytes wide with the least significant byte always stored at an even address. A table pointer is used access tables and data stored in the program memory. A 31-level stack stores the return addresses from subprogram calls and interrupts. The stack is not part of any other memory and is controlled separately by a 5-bit stack pointer, initialized to 0, on reset. The data memory is of size upto 4 MB with a 12-bit address bus. In PIC18F452, the data memory size is 1536 bytes, organized as 6 banks of 256 bytes each. This makes the lower part of the data memory, the upper part being dedicated to *special function registers* (*SFRs*). The SFRs control the operations of peripheral units (such as, timers/counters, ADC, interrupts, serial communication and so on), selection of clock sources, watchdog operations etc. The SFRs are programmed during the programming of the flash memory.

PIC18F series of microcontrollers have a number of I/O ports. The actual number of ports and the number of port pins in each of them vary with the specific microcontroller in use. PIC18F452 has five ports – PORTA, PORTB, PORTC, PORTD and PORTE with their capacities as noted in Table 5.2. For each port bit, the operations possible are as follows.

- Set direction – input or output
- Set output value
- Read input value

Table 5.2: Ports in PIC18F452

Name	Bits	Function
PORTA	7	Digital I/O, analog input, ADC reference voltage, Timer clock, SPI slave select
PORTB	8	Digital I/O, External interrupts, CCP, PGM, PGC and PGD interface
PORTC	8	Digital I/O, Timer, External interrupts, CCP, SPI, USART interface
PORTD	8	Digital I/O, PSP
PORTE	3	Digital I/O, analog input, PSP interface

- Set output value and read back the latched value

Each port has a TRIS*x* register to control the direction and a LAT*x* register to latch data output for each bit (*x* = A, B, C, D, E).

5.4.1 Timers

The PIC18F452 has four timers named as Timer0, Timer1, Timer2 and Timer3. An overview of the timers is presented next.

Timer0: This timer can be made to operate either in 8-bit mode or in 16-bit mode. It supports 8-bit programmable prescaler. The clock source can be internal or external. Thus, it can act both as a timer and a counter. The timer is capable of generating interrupt on overflow. The SFR T0CON controls the operation of this timer.

Timer1: This is a 16-bit timer controlled by the SFR T1CON. It can also work as a timer or a counter. The prescalar value can be 1, 2, 4 or 8 only.

Timer2: It is an 8-bit timer that has a *Period* register associated with it. An interrupt is generated when the timer value becomes equal to the Period register value. The timer has programmable prescalar and postscalar.

Timer3: It is similar to Timer1 in operation.

5.4.2 Capture/Compare/PWM Modules (CCP)

Two CCP modules are present in the PIC18F452. The modules work in conjunction with timers 1, 2 and 3 to provide the capture, compare and pulse width modulation (PWM) operations. Each CCP module has two registers – CCPR*x*L and CCPR*x*H (*x* = 1, 2). CCP1 and CCP2 are controlled by the CCP1CON and CCP2CON registers, respectively.

Capture: In *capture mode*, a CCP module acts like a stopwatch. The time corresponding to the occurrence of an event is recorded, however, the clock continues to run (unlike stopwatch that stops on occurrence of the event). The 16-bit time value of Timer1 or Timer3 (depending upon the control register setting) is captured into CCPR*x*H:CCPR*x*L.

Compare: In this mode, the 16-bit content of CCPR*x*H:CCPR*x*L is compared continually with the Timer1 or Timer3 value. For CCP1 module, when a match occurs, RC2/CCP1 pin gets affected. The change in the pin is programmable to become high, low, toggle, no change or to generate an interrupt. RB3/CCP2 pin gets affected for CCP2 compare operation.

PWM: The CCP module can be made to produce a pulse width modulated output at CCP1 or CCP2 pin. It's operation is controlled by Timer2. The period and duty cycle can be specified. The timer values, CCPR*x*L and CCP*x*CON registers are to be loaded accordingly.

5.4.3 Analog-to-Digital Converter Module

The PIC18F family contains a 10-bit ADC that can support multiple analog channels. In PIC18F452, there are eight channels AN0-AN7 shared by the pins of ports PORTA and PORTE. The SFR ADCON0 and ADCON1 controls the operation of the ADC. The converted digital values are made available at ADRESH (higher order 2-bits) and ADRESL (remaining 8-bits) registers. If enabled, an interrupt is generated at the completion of the conversion process. To connect an analog source to any of the analog input pins AN0 to AN7, it is recommended to ensure that the source resistance is limited to 2.5 kΩ.

5.4.4 Interrupts

The sources of interrupts in the PIC18F452 can be classified into two categories – core interrupt sources and peripheral interrupt sources. The core interrupt sources include the following.

- External interrupt pins, such as, INT0, INT1 and INT2.
- Any of the PORTB pins changing states (this also includes INT lines).
- Timer 0 overflow.

The following interrupt sources are considered to be of type peripheral interrupts.

- Parallel slave port read/write
- ADC conversion completion
- USART receipt/transmit
- Synchronous serial port
- CCP1 and CCP2
- Timer1, Timer2 and Timer3 overflows
- EEPROM/Flash write
- Low-voltage detection
- Bus collision

The interrupts can be grouped into two groups by the programmer – *high priority* and *low priority*. All the high-priority interrupts vector to address 00008H, whereas all low-priority interrupts jump to the address 00018H. There are a number of registers controlling the operation, enabling/disabling of interrupts.

5.4.5 Addressing Modes

The PIC18F processors support the following four addressing modes.

- *Register Direct*: The instruction uses an 8-bit value to directly identify the register. For example, in the instruction "movwf 0x20, A", copies the WREG register to the data register 0x20.
- *Immediate*: The operand value is directly specified in the instruction. For example, the instruction "addlw 0x10" adds the value 0x10 to the WREG register.
- *Inherent*: The operand is implied in the instruction. For example, in the instruction "andlw 0x3C", the value 3CH is ANDed with the WREG. Here, the operand WREG is inherent.
- *Indirect*: Here, a special function register is used as a pointer to the actual data register. For example, in the instruction "movwf INDF0", INDF0 gives the indirect operand.

Thus, PIC18F provides a limited set of addressing modes with 2- and 4-byte instruction format. Detailed discussion about the instruction set of PIC18F is beyond the scope of the book. The readers may look into the references noted at the end of the unit for more detail.

5.5 AVR Microcontroller

The AVR (*Advanced Virtual RISC*) was introduced in 1996 by Atmel Corporation, the first one in the series being AT90S8515. AVR microcontrollers are available in three varieties – *TinyAVR*, *MegaAVR* and *XmegaAVR*. Out of these, MegaAVR is the most popular variant. A summary of the three variants has been presented in Table 5.3. AVR is an 8-bit RISC based microcontroller executing most of its instructions in one cycle. It is about four times faster than PIC and also possesses different power-saving modes. The key features of the ATMega32 AVR are as follows.

Table 5.3: Comparison of AVR Series Microcontrollers

Series	*Pins*	*Flash size*	*Remarks*
TinyAVR	6-32	0.5-8 kB	Small
MegaAVR	28-100	4-256 kB	More peripherals
XmegaAVR	44-100	16-384 kB	Direct memory access, Event system

- 2 kB Static RAM
- 32, 8-bit general purpose registers
- 32 kB Flash
- 1 kB EEPROM
- Programmable USART
- 10-bit ADC with 8 analog channels
- One 16-bit, two 8-bit timer/counter
- SPI interface
- 32, programmable I/O limes
- Four PWM channels
- Programmable watchdog

- On-chip boot program

Fig 5.4 shows the pin diagram for ATMega32. It has 40 pins. Two pins are for power supply and ground. Pins 12 and 13 are for oscillator. Pin 9 is the reset pin. Three pins are dedicated to the power supply and reference for the internal ADC. There are 32 I/O pins arranged into 4 groups of 8-bit ports. Port A can be used for digital I/O or as eight analog input channels. Timer 0 and Timer 2 are 8-bit timers, while Timer 1 is a 16-bit timer. It supports SPI, I2C and USART standards. Fig 5.5 shows the block diagram of ATmega32.

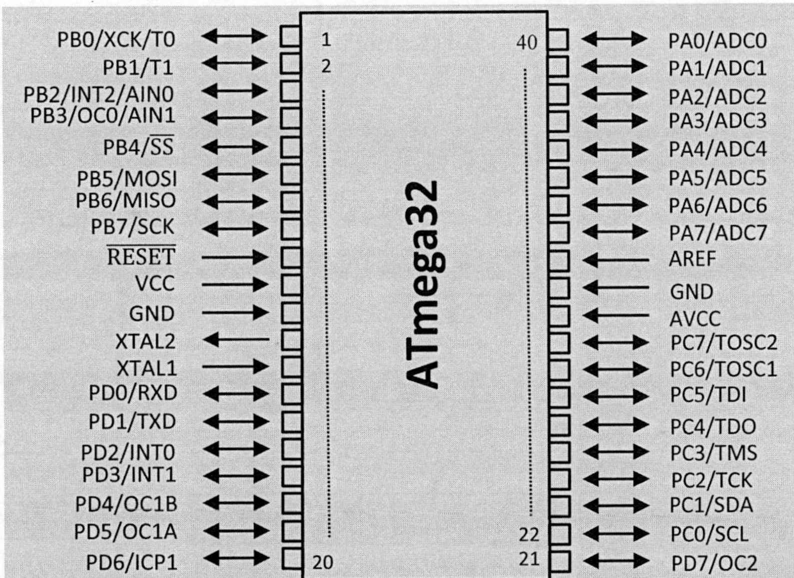

Fig 5.4: Pin Configuration of ATmega32

ATmega32 has on-chip analog comparator, an interrupt has been assigned to it that is generated based on the results of comparison. Three external interrupt pins are supported. Sensing of the interrupts are also programmable. The device can operate at a frequency from 1 to 16 MHz. As noted earlier, most of the instructions take one clock cycle, while multiplication takes two clock cycles. On-chip debugging facilities are available through *JTAG Boundary Scan*. There are 32, 8-bit general purpose registers in the ATmega32, named R0-R31. There are three 16-bit registers X, Y and Z. These registers overlap with the general purpose registers R26 to R31. The three registers could be used as address pointers, or to contain data values wider than 8 bits. The Z register could be used to access the program memory. The registers available in the ATmega32 programmer model have been listed in Table 5.4. The SRAM locations are used as

Table 5.4: Programmer Model

Category	*Name*	*Number*	*Size*	*Function*
General purpose working register	R0-R31	32	8 bit	Store data
Address pointer	X,Y, Z	3	16 bit	Address pointer
Stack pointer	SP	1	16 bit	Stack access
Program counter	PC	1	14 bit	Address of instruction
Status register	SREG	1	8 bit	Status information

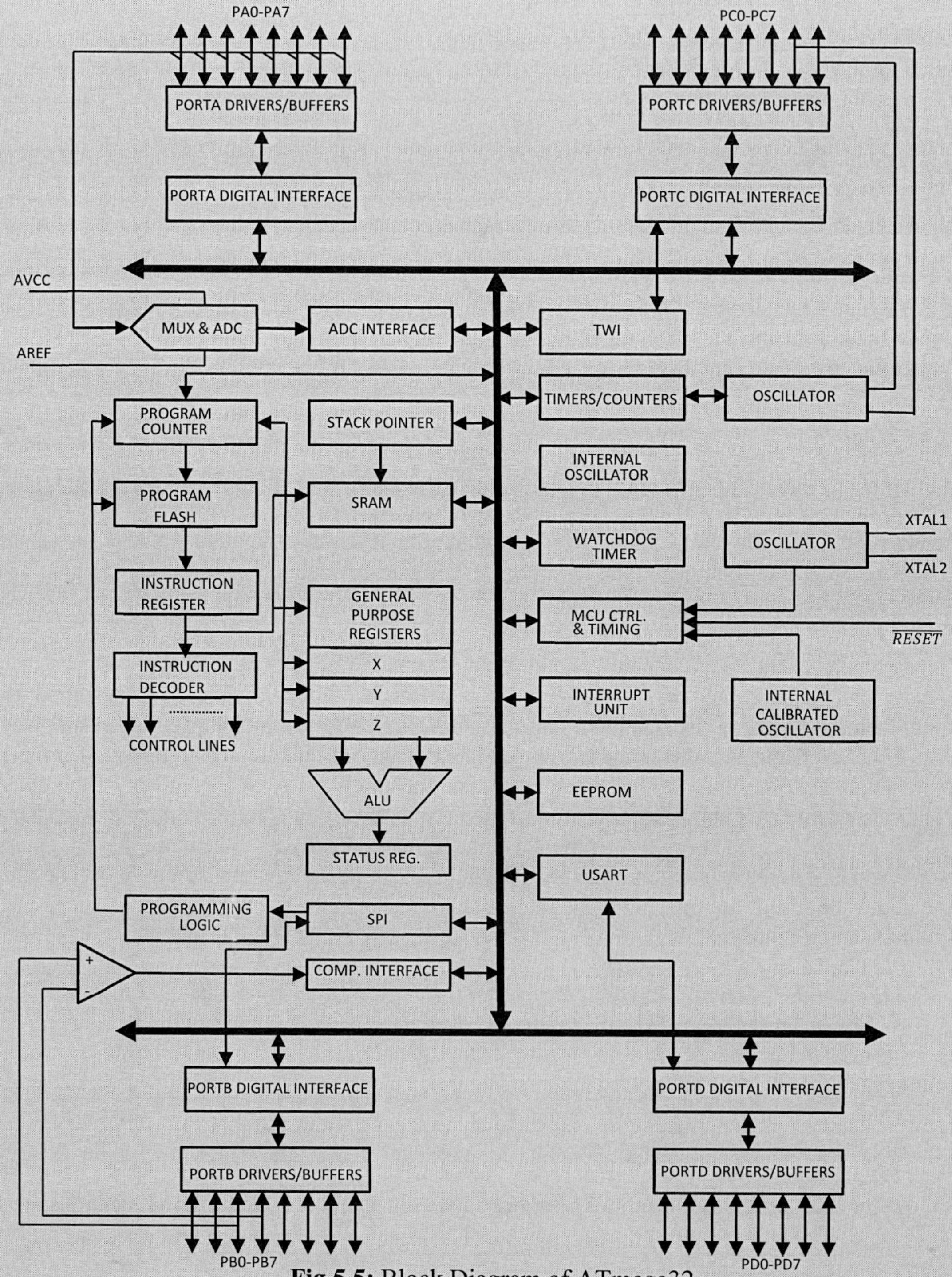

Fig 5.5: Block Diagram of ATmega32

follows. The 32 general purpose registers occupy the SRAM locations from 00H to 1FH. I/O ports span over the locations from 20H to 5FH, user data from 60H to 85H.

5.5.1 Addressing Modes

The ATmega32 processor supports the following addressing modes.

- *Immediate*: Data encoded into the instruction itself. Operand is available in the Flash, the program memory. For example, in the instruction "ldi r16, 0x56", the operand 56H is put as part of it. This is a marked deviation from Harvard architecture which says that the data is available only in the data memory.
- *Direct:* These are two-word instructions. One word specifies the address of the data memory space. For example, the instruction "lds R1, *K*" where *K* is a 16-bit data memory address.
- *Indirect with displacement:* In this case, along with an address pointer (X, Y or Z), a displacement is also mentioned. For example, "ldd R1, Y+*q*" instruction copies the content of memory location Y+*q* to R1.
- *Indirect with pre-increment:* The content of the address pointer register is incremented before accessing the addressed memory location. For example, in the instruction "ld R1, +X", X is first incremented. The memory location pointed to by this new X register content is copied to R1.
- *Indirect with post-increment:* Similar to pre-increment, however, register increment takes place after accessing the memory. For example, an instruction of this category may be "ld R1, X+".
- Similarly, there are indirect access modes with pre- and post-decrement operations.

Now that we have seen three different microcontrollers, namely 8051, PIC and AVR, Table 5.5 presents a comparison between them. The 8051 is one of the very simple microcontrollers. However, the features available in it have been extended in the advanced controllers. Also, in the advanced microcontrollers, many of the frequently used peripherals have been included, so that overall footprint of the system remains small.

Table 5.5: Comparison of 8051, PIC, AVR

Feature	*8051*	*PIC*	*AVR*
Speed	Slow	Moderate	Fast
Memory	Small	Large	Large
CISC/RISC	CISC	RISC	RISC
ADC	No	Yes	Yes
Timers	Yes	Yes	Yes
PWM	No	Yes	Yes

5.6 ARM Microcontroller

The ARM microcontroller is a 32-bit RISC processor developed by the *ARM Corporation*, previously known as *Acron RISC Machine*. However, ARM Corporation does not produce any processor chip. Rather, the production of systems built around ARM based CPU is licensed to various companies, such as, NXP, STMicroelectronics, Texas Instruments, to name a few. The licensee can develop their own processors compliant with the ARM instruction set. The following are some of the notable features of the ARM architecture.

- The ARM architecture is very simple. As a result, it requires less number of transistors in the chip. As a whole system is built on a chip (called, *System-on-Chip*, *SoC*), more space on the chip is made available to realize memory and other peripherals. The silicon die can accommodate more amount of memory and various associated logic modules, such as, ADC, Timers/Counters, SPI, I2C, USART, and so on.
- Very carefully designed instruction set architecture with pipelined design that optimizes the power consumption. As a result, the ARM has become almost the default choice for low-power applications.
- Supports two instruction sets. The default 32-bit instruction set is called the ARM instruction set. However, another 16-bit instruction set, called THUMB, has been made available that results in better code density and further power reduction.
- Performance is often much higher than other contemporary advanced processors, possibly with CISC architecture.
- The design of the architecture is highly modular. In the entire design, only the integer pipeline, responsible for integer arithmetic is mandatory. The designer has the choice to take other modules (for example, real arithmetic), based upon the requirements.
- Built-in JTAG debug port and on-chip embedded in-circuit emulator support full debugging.

The first version of the ARM, ARM1 was introduced in 1985 as a 26-bit RISC processor. The 32-bit RISC processor, ARM7 was introduced in 1992. After that several other processor architectures have been introduced over the years, namely ARM7, ARM8, ARM9TDMI, ARM10, ARM11, Cortex etc. To have a basic understanding of the ARM architecture, we shall look into the ARM7 architecture in more detail.

5.6.1 ARM7 Architecture

Fig 5.6 shows the block diagram of the ARM7 CPU. It has 32-bit address and data buses. An important point to note here is the direction of the ALE signal. Since the address and data buses are totally separate, there is no necessity of demultiplexing them, as in 8051. ALE signal may be used by the external memory/device to instruct the CPU to keep the address lines content valid on the bus. This will help in interfacing devices requiring the address to be valid more than one clock cycle. Internally, the processor possesses a large number of registers, following the RISC philosophy. It has 31 number of 32-bit registers accessible by the users. There are six status registers used in different modes of operation of the processor (explained later). A dedicated address incrementer module is responsible to increment the address after every access. To make the arithmetic operations faster, an efficient 32-bit ALU has been included. The ALU has been relieved of the operations like multiplication and logical shifting. A dedicated multiplier module implementing the Booth's multiplication algorithm has been incorporated. Shifting and rotation

operations are done by a barrel shifter module. It may be noted that one of the operand to the ALU comes through the A bus from the registers. The other operand, coming from the B bus passes through the barrel shifter module first. This enables shifting/rotation of the second operand before carrying out the operation. ARM7 supports three stage pipelined execution of instructions, similar to the classical *fetch-decode-execute* pipeline. In this structure, while the first instruction reaches the execute stage, a second one will be in decode phase, while a third instruction will be memory fetch stage. The uniform size and similar execution time for the instructions aid in smooth realization of the pipeline. In ARM7 pipeline, the execute stage is heavily loaded. It has the responsibilities to read the operands, perform ALU operation and write back the result. To have further balance between the stages, the later versions of ARM processors contain 5, 6 and 8 stage pipeline structures.

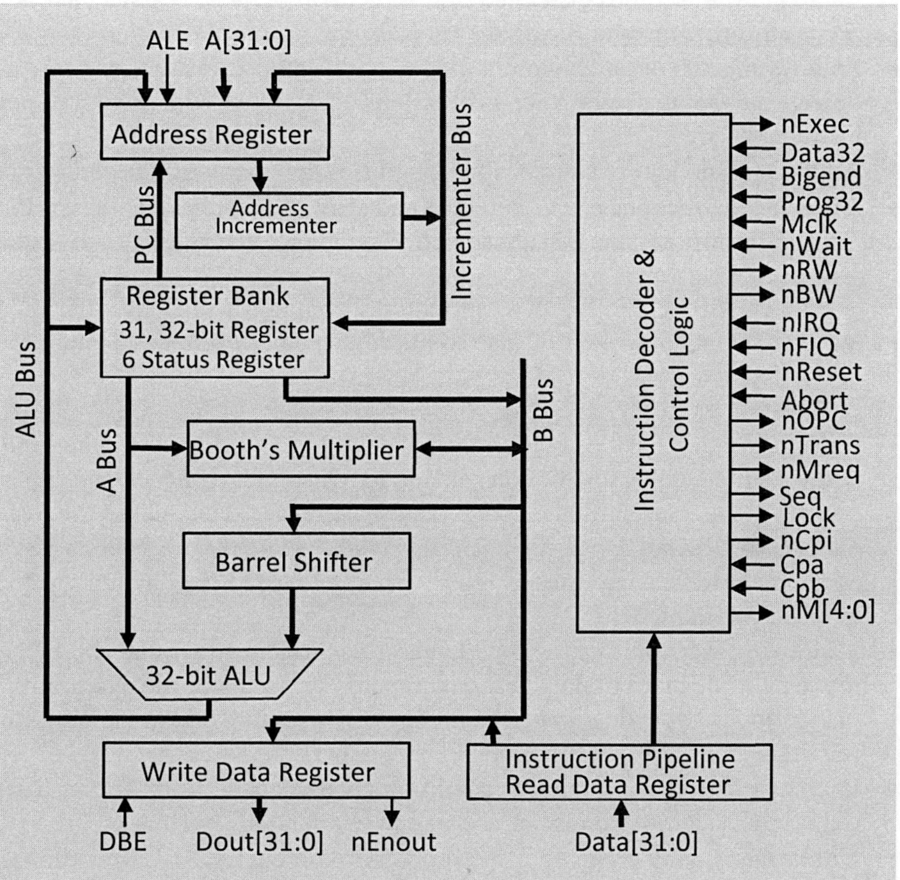

Fig 5.6: Block Diagram of ARM7

5.6.2 Instruction Set Architecture

The ARM7 is a typical RISC architecture with several enhancements close to CISC that enhances performance further. The RISC features of ARM7 are as follows.

- Large uniform set of registers having 16 general purpose registers accessible by the user. Such set of uniform registers is called a *register file*.
- Follows a *load/store* architecture model. In this model, instructions carrying out data operations operate only on registers. Such instructions do not work with memory operands. Memory access instructions are *load* and *store* only.
- Addressing modes are simple. This simplifies the instruction decoding stage.
- All ARM instructions are 32-bit wide and most of them have a regular three-operand encoding. This uniformity enhances balance between the pipeline stages.

Interestingly, along with the features common to the pure RISC processors, ARM has included some features of CISC also to improve the performance. Some such features are noted in the following.

- Each instruction has been given the capacity to control the ALU and the shifter. For example, while a simple ADD instruction can add two operands, if necessary, the instruction can also get one of its operands shifted through the use of shifter. This makes the instruction more complex – closer to CISC.
- Supported addressing modes have been enhanced by including the autoincrement and autodecrement modes.
- Multibyte load/store instructions have been introduced so that the CPU may be instructed to move multiple bytes of data between memory and register file. Naturally, time for executing the instruction is dependent upon the number of bytes moved – a violation of equal execution time requirement of RISC instructions.
- Each instruction has a four bit condition code attached to it. The instruction will get executed only if the specified condition is satisfied (elaborated later).
- Unlike many other processors, instructions involving the ALU operations, may or may not affect the status flags. For example, pure ADD instruction does not affect the status flags. To ensure that the status flags get affected, ADDS instruction has to be used.

5.6.3 Registers and Mode of Operation

The ARM processors can work in one of the six modes, namely, *User mode, Fast Interrupt Processing (FIQ) mode, Normal Interrupt Processing (IRQ) mode, Supervisor (SVC) mode, Undefined (UNDEF) mode* and *Abort mode*. The user mode is for normal execution of user programs. A program in user mode can make a system call to reach the supervisor mode. There are two types of interrupts supported by the ARM – fast and normal. In response to fast interrupt, the processor reaches the FIQ mode, whereas for normal interrupts, it is the IRQ mode. The undefined mode is entered if the received instruction code part is not understandable by the processor. Abort mode corresponds to memory fault.

Each mode has got its associated set of registers. There are 16 general purpose registers R0-R15 in the user mode. Out of these, R15 is the program counter, however, unlike other processors, the R15 can also be manipulated as a general purpose register. There is no stack defined by default in ARM. If necessary, user has to implement stack as part of the program. The register R13 is conventionally used by the users as stack pointer. In the absence of stack, for subprogram call and return, the register R14 is used as the *link register*. In a procedure call, the current program counter value (that is, the return address) is automatically copied into the R14 register. To implement a return from the procedure, the R14 register is copied into R15. Each mode has got its own copy of R13 and R14 registers. Apart from that, each mode has a status register of its own. All modes, except the user mode has a register to save the content of the status register of its previous mode. The FIQ mode has additional set of registers for R7-R12 also. This helps in writing the service routines using the additional registers only which eliminates the necessity of saving and restoring registers used by the interrupt service routine.

5.6.4 ARM Instructions

The ARM processors support the following two instruction sets.

1. ARM – standard 32-bit instruction set
2. THUMB – 16-bit compressed instruction set

The instructions belonging to the ARM instruction set are executed directly by the processor. However, the THUMB instructions are first decompressed and converted to equivalent ARM instructions which are then executed by the processor. Since THUMB instructions are shorter, two THUMB instructions occupy one memory word. This provides code density better than many of the CISC processors. However, the execution speed suffers. Table 5.6 presents a summary of the ARM instruction categories.

Table 5.6: ARM Instruction Set Summary

Category	Description	Example	Remarks
Data Processing	32-bit Addition, Subtraction, Multiplication	• ADD R1, R2, R3; R1 = R2 + R3 • ADD R1, R2, R3, LSL #2; R1 = R2 + R3*4 • ADDS R1, R2, R3; R1 = R2 + R3 with status flags affected	• 1st operand and destination are registers • 2nd operand may be a register or immediate value, may be shifted or rotated • Limited values for immediate operand

Byte Data Transfer	Transfer data between memory and registers	•LDR R0, [R8]; R0 = Mem[R8] •LDR R0, [R1,-R2]; R0 = Mem[R1 – R2] •LDR R0, [R1,#4]; R0 = Mem[R1 + 4] •LDR R0, [R1,#4]!; R0 = Mem[R1 + 4], R1 = R1 + 4	• 1, 2 or 4 bytes data transfer • Base plus offset can be used • Auto-increment supported
Block Data Transfer	Multi-byte data transfer between memory and registers	•LDMIA R12!, {R0-R11}; Load 48 bytes of data from memory buffer pointed to by R12 to registers R0-R11 •STMIA R13!, {R0-R11}; Store 48 bytes of data from registers R0-R11 to memory buffer pointed to by R13	• Data transfer between 1-16 registers to/from memory • Lowest register number to/from lowest memory address • Can implement stack or bulk data movement
Multiplication	Integer multiplication with 32/64 bit results	•MUL R0, R1, R2; R0 = R1 * R2 •MULA R0, R1, R2, R3; R0 = R1 * R2 + R3	• Source and destination separate registers • R15 not usable • For each pair of bits in source, 1 clock plus 1 clock to start • *Early terminates* if source becomes zero
Software Interrupt	Interrupts the CPU via program instruction	•SWI #*n*, *n* is a 24-bit number	• Control jumps to SWI interrupt vector • Value of *n* ignored by the processor • Realizes system calls, a total of 2^{24} calls possible
Branching	Branch to a different location	•B <*target*>; Branch to *target* •BL <*target*>; Branch to *target* with PC+4 saved in R14	• Relative branching only • Jump within ±32 MB • BL used for subroutine • Subroutine return by copying R14 to R15

All ARM instructions can be executed conditionally. For this, a condition code may be prefixed with the instruction. The instruction gets executed only if the status flags satisfy the specified condition. For example, the instruction "EQADD R1, R2, R3" has the effect of R1 getting R2 + R3 only if the equality condition is satisfied. Else, though the instruction reaches the CPU and goes into the execution phase, effect is similar to a "no operation". Availability of this facility eliminates small branching in the program, the code becomes more of a straight line one and augments the pipeline performance. The following example clarifies the point.

Example 5.4: Consider the high-level code fragment given below.

```
if R1 = R2 then
  R3 = R4 + R5
else
  R3 = R4 – R5
```

In the following, two tentative assembly codes are shown. The left one does not assume the existence of conditional instructions, thus some additional branch instructions got created. The code on the right side uses conditional instructions that results in a straight line code. For the code in the left side, if the equality condition is satisfied, the processor, after executing "JE L1" has to wait for the instruction at L1 to be available to it. The prefetched instruction "SUB R3, R4, R5" is not the correct one to be executed in that case. This problem is commonly known as *pipeline stall*. Such problems do not occur with the right side code.

```
    CMP R1, R2                  CMP R1, R2
    JE L1                       EQADD R3, R4, R5
    SUB R3, R4, R5              NESUB R3, R4, R5
    JMP L2
L1: ADD R3, R4, R5
L2:
```

It may be noted that conditional branching can be implemented using conditional execution of branch instructions, in a similar fashion.

Though the ARM instruction set has many interesting features, there is a marked deviation from the contemporary processors in terms of stack, conditional execution and software interrupt support. The other instruction set, THUMB contains 16-bit instructions and are stored in the memory in a compressed form. The THUMB instructions are executed unconditionally, excepting the branch instructions. While using THUMB, the user has unlimited access only to the registers R0-R7 and R13-R15. The total

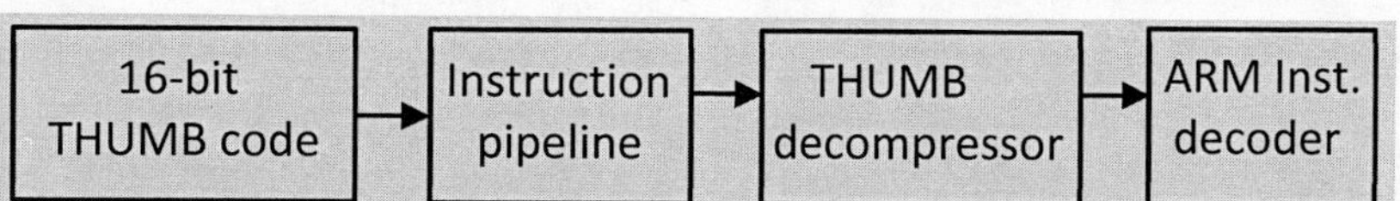

Fig 5.7: THUMB to ARM conversion

number of software interrupts is limited to 256. Similar to other conventional processors, PUSH and POP instructions have been included in the THUMB set. Upon reset, the processor enters into ARM instruction set mode. To use THUMB mode, the user program should execute a "BX <*target*>" or "BLX <*target*>" instruction. The processor will expect the THUMB instructions to start from the *target* address. The BX/BLX instruction should also be used to come back to ARM instruction set mode from THUMB. However, the THUMB instructions are not directly executed by the ARM processor. After reaching the instruction pipeline, the THUMB instruction goes through a decompressor to get converted into its equivalent ARM instruction, and get executed thereafter. The situation has been shown in Fig 5.7. However, programs written in THUMB requires less memory space due to compression. THUMB also consumes upto 30% less power than ARM code, in general, while ARM code is about 40% faster than THUMB. In a typical system, ARM instruction set should be used for on-chip memory, containing small speed-critical routines, while THUMB should be used with off-chip memory for non-critical routines.

Example 5.5: Consider the problem of finding the maximum of a set of numbers stored at a memory buffer starting at address pointed to by R3. Register R2 holds the count of the number of numbers in the buffer. The following is the assembly language code for the problem. The largest number be available at R1.

```
      EOR R1, R1, R1          ; Clear R1 by XORing
      CMP R2, #0
      BEQ OVER                ; Block empty, done
L1:   LDR R3, [R0]            ; Get next data
      CMP R3, R1              ; Compare
      BCC L2                  ; Skip if R1 is bigger
      MOV R1, R3              ; Else get larger in R1
L2:   ADD R0, R0, #4          ; Increment R0 for the next number
      SUBS R2, R2, #1         ; Decrement R2
      BNE L1                  ; If count still not zero, goto L1
OVER:                         ; R1 has the largest
```

5.6.5 LPC214x – An ARM7 Implementation

In this section, a typical implementation of ARM7 architecture, LPC214x has been discussed. LPC214x series of microcontrollers are very popular due to their tiny size and low power consumption, particularly for devices that require miniaturisation. There are five different microcontrollers in the series, namely LPC2141/42/44/46/48. A comparison between the devices has been presented in Table 5.7. It comes as a quad-flat package. There are 8-40kB of SRAM and 32-512kB flash memory. USB 2.0 is supported. One to two on-chip 10-bit ADCs provide a total of 6-14 analog channels. Some variants have on-chip 10-bit DAC as well. Two 32-bit timers/counters are available with four capture and four compare channels. There is a 6-channel pulse width modulation module and an watchdog timer. Interfaces like SPI, SSP, I2C, USART are available for communication. A real-time clock module with independent power supply has been provided in it. Upto 21 external interrupt pins are available. Fig 5.8 shows the block diagram of the LPC214x microcontroller.

Table 5.7: Comparison across LPC214x devices

Device	*SRAM (kB)*	*Flash (kB)*	*No. of ADC channels*	*No. of DAC channels*
LPC2141	8	32	6	-
LPC2142	16	64	6	1
LPC2144	16	128	14	1
LPC2146	40	256	14	1
LPC2148	40	512	14	1

5.6.6 I/O Port Programming for LPC2148

LPC2148 has got two General Purpose I/O (GPIO) ports, namely, Port 0 (P0) and Port 1 (P1). Both the ports are 32-bit wide, however, for P1, the bits 16 to 31 are only available for input/output. All bits of P0 are available for I/O, however, these pins also have several functions multiplexed to them. As a result, the actual number of I/O pins available, depends upon the application in hand which may use other modules of the chip as well. For example, pin P0.21 also acts as PWM5 (Pulse Width Modulation), AD1.6 (ADC), CAP1.3 (Capture input for Timer1, Channel 3). For Port 0, 28 out of 32 pins can be configured as bidirectional. P0.24, P0.26 and P0.27 are unavailable. P0.30 can be used as output pin only.

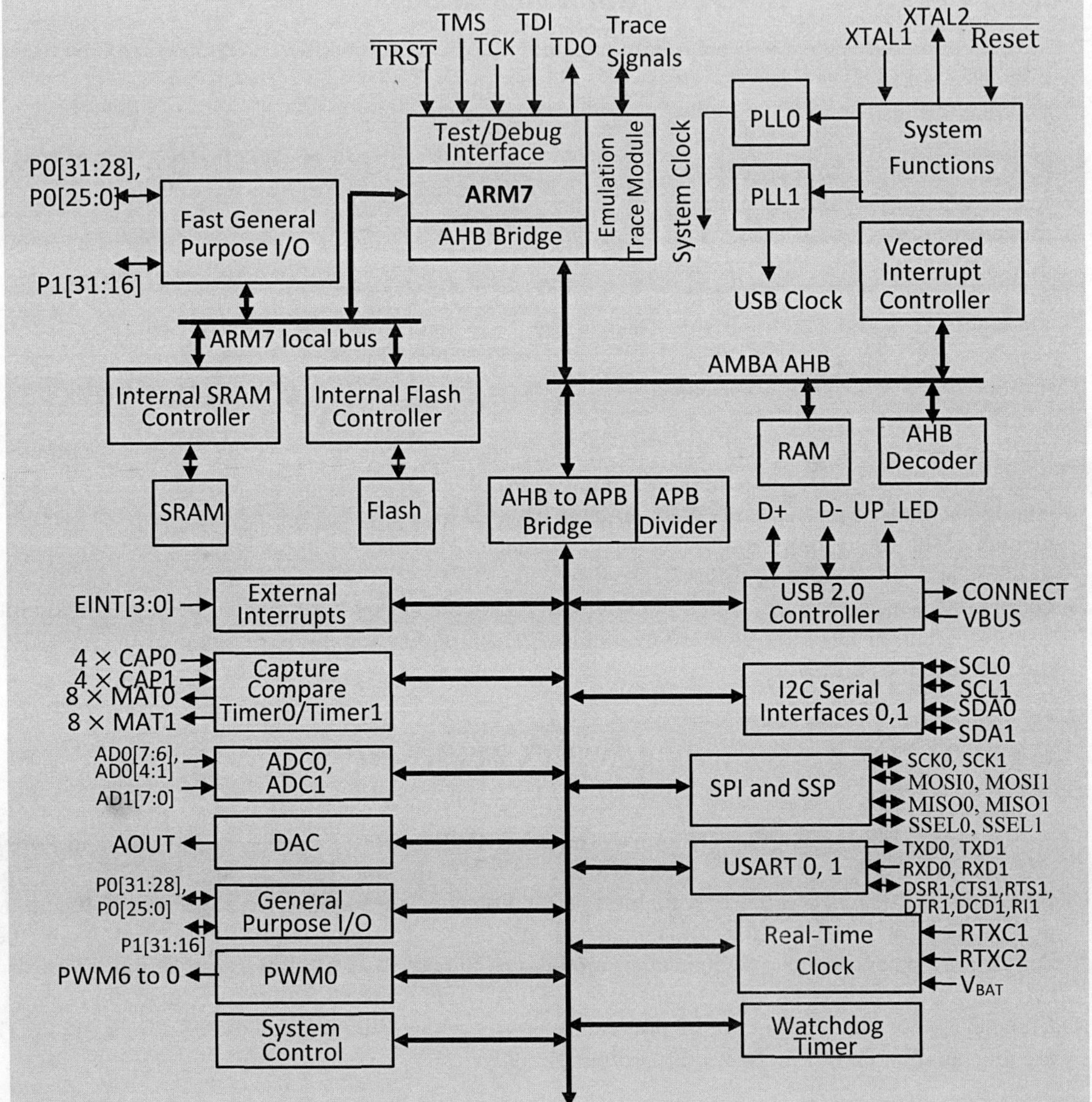

Fig 5.8: Block Diagram of LPC214x

Table 5.8 shows the important registers and their settings for GPIO operations. The registers need to be programmed properly to get the I/O operations done. The registers control the functionality of the pins, I/O directions, setting and resetting of bits. Individual bits can be programmed separately. In particular, for I/O operation, first the direction of the port bit be set. For example, the setting "IO0DIR = 0x04" will configure the Pin 2 of Port 0 (P0.2) as output and other bits as input. For an input operation, the IO*x*PIN register can be read. However, for output operation, to write a 1, corresponding bit of IO*x*SET register should be set to 1. To output a 0, the bit in IO*x*CLR be set to 1. After a port pin has been written with some value, the value can be read from the IO*x*PIN register bit.

Table 5.8: Registers for I/O Port Programming

Register (x = 0, 1)	*Functionality*
IO*x*PIN	Register can be read to get the current state of the GPIO pins.
IO*x*DIR	Controls direction of port bits. Setting a bit to 0 makes port pin to act as input, 1 makes the pin output.
IO*x*CLR	Drives the corresponding pin to 0.
IO*x*SET	Drives the corresponding pin to 1.

Example 5.6: Consider the problem of setting P0.14 pin to high first and then low. The C code fragment for it is as follows.

```
IO0DIR |= (1 << 14);        // P0.14 set as output pin
IO0SET |= (1 << 14);        // Output high to P0.14
IO0CLR |= (1 << 14);        // Output low to P0.14
```

Next, we shall look into two more examples of GPIO operations. The first example assumes two LEDs connected to Port 0 pins 0 and 1. When the program is executed, the LEDs will blink. In the second example, a switch and an LED are connected to port pins 0 and 1 respectively. When the switch is closed, the LED will glow.

Example 5.7: Two LEDs are connected to port pins P0.0 and P0.1. The LEDs should blink continually. The complete C program for the purpose is shown next.

```
# include <lpc214x.h>
void Delay_rtn(void);
int main(void)
{
    IO0DIR = 0x3;       // Configure P0.0 and P0.1 as output
```

```
        while (1)
        {
            IO0SET = 0x3;     // Turn LEDs on
            Delay_rtn();
            IO0CLR = 0x03;  // Turn LEDs off
            Delay_rtn();
        }
    }
    void Delay_rtn(void)
    {
        int a, b;
        b = 0;
        for (a = 0; a < 2000000; a++) b++;    // Do something, else compiler may
                                              //  remove the loop
    }
```

Example 5.8: A switch is connected to P0.0, an LED to P0.1. The LED should glow whenever the switch is closed. The corresponding C program is shown next.

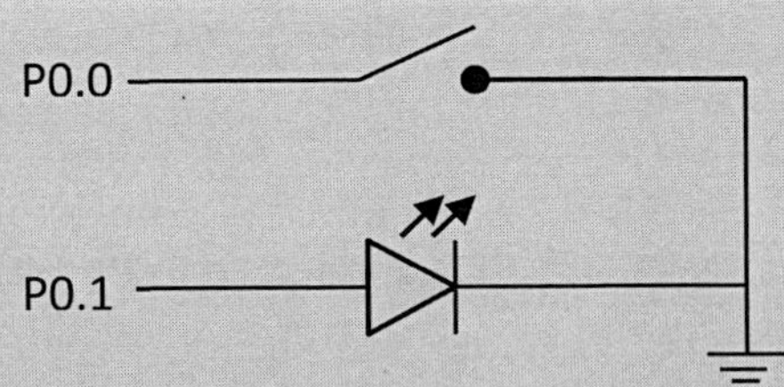


```
# include <lpc214x.h>
int main(void)
{
    IO0DIR &= ~(1); // Make P0.0 input
    IO0DIR |= (1<<1);  // Configure P0.1 as output
    while (1) {
        if (!(IO0PIN & (1))    // Becomes true if P0.0 = 0
            IO0SET |= (1 << 1);  // Drive P0.1 high
        else
            IO0CLR |= (1 << 1);  // Make P0.1 low
    }
}
```

UNIT SUMMARY

Though 8051 is one of the very popular microcontrollers, its usage is now limited due to the introduction of several new microcontrollers. All these architectures could be classified to be CISC or RISC. A clear discussion on the features of RISC and CISC processor architectures has been presented that also distinguishes between the two. Among the advanced microcontrollers, three examples have been taken up. The first one is PIC. In this category the advanced series PIC18F has been discussed. This has been followed by the AVR microcontrollers. The AVR also has a number of series. Among them, ATmega32 is the most popular one and has been discussed in the unit. Among the recent microcontrollers targeting low power applications, ARM is now almost the choice, by default. Again, ARM has a number of processor architectures. The most advanced being the Cortex series. However, for better understanding, ARM7 architecture has been taken up. Several companies have different implementations of the ARM7. The one, LPC214*x* by the NXP is a very popular processor. The I/O programming with this processor has been discussed that will enable the reader to carry out interfacing assignments comfortably. More detailed discussion on each of these processors and series are beyond the scope of the book. The readers are requested to look into the references for the same.

EXERCISES

Multiple Choice Questions

MQ1. CISC processors attempt to minimize
- (A) Instructions per program — (B) Cycles per instruction
- (C) Both A and B — (D) Neither A nor B

MQ2. RISC processors attempt to minimize
- (A) Instructions per program — (B) Cycles per instruction
- (C) Both A and B — (D) Neither A nor B

MQ3. Which one is not a CISC feature
- (A) Large number of registers — (B) Large number of instructions
- (C) More addressing modes — (D) None of the other options

MQ4. Which one is not a RISC feature
- (A) Large number of registers — (B) Hardwired controller
- (C) More addressing modes — (D) None of the other options

MQ5. In a load-store architecture, memory is accessed by
- (A) Load — (B) Store
- (C) Both Load and Store — (D) None of the other options

MQ6. Which architecture has more dependency on software for better performance
- (A) RISC — (B) CISC
- (C) Both RISC and CISC — (D) None of the other options

MQ7. Size of address bus in bits for PIC18F series is
(B) 16 (B) 21 (C) 24 (D) None of the other options

MQ8. PIC18F can work upto crystal frequency
(A) 10MHz (B) 20MHz (C) 30MHz (D) None of the other options

MQ9. Port bit width of port A of PIC18F processor is
(A) 7 (B) 8 (C) 15 (D) 16

MQ10. Number of timers in PIC18F is
(B) 2 (B) 3 (C) 3 (D) 4

MQ11. The mode in which a timer works as a stopwatch is
(B) Capture (B) Compare (C) PWM (D)None of the other options

MQ12. The high priority interrupt vector in PIC18F is
(B) 00008H (B) 00010H (C) 00016H (D) 00018H

MQ13. Number of timers in ATmega32 is
(A) 1 (B) 2 (C) 3 (D)4

MQ14. In AVR, the registers X, Y and Z overlap with
(B) R0-R5 (B) R16-R21 (C) R26-R31 (D) None of the other options

MQ15. Bit width of address pointers in AVR is
(A) 8 (B) 16 (C) 32 (D) 64

MQ16. The address pointer that can be used to access program memory in AVR is the register
(A) X (B) Y (C) Z (D) All of the options mentioned

MQ17. Width (in bits) of Timer 2 in ATmega32 is
(A) 8 (B) 13 (C) 16 (D) None of the other options

MQ18. In AVR, the start address of GPRs in memory is
(A) 00H (B) 20H (C) 60H (D) None of the other options

MQ19. Width of instructions in the THUMB instruction set, in number of bits is
(A) 16 (B) 32 (C) 48 (D) None of the other options

MQ20. ALE signal in ARM processor is
(B) To the processor (B) From the processor
(C) Not present (D) Bidirectional

MQ21. The register that acts as program counter in ARM is
(A) R13 (B) R14 (C) R15 (D) None of the other options

MQ22. The register useful for making subprogram calls in ARM is
(A) R13 (B) R14 (C) R15 (D) None of the other options

MQ23. Conditional execution of instructions in ARM helps in improving
(B) Pipeline performance (B) Stack overflows
(C) Loop implementation (D) None of the other options

MQ24. In LPC2148 the register responsible for setting direction of I/O ports is
(B) IO*x*DEP (B) IO*x*PIN (C) IO*x*SET (D) None of the other options

MQ25. ARM instruction to change instruction set is
(B) BX (B) XCH (C) THUMB (D) None of the other options

Answers of Multiple Choice Questions

1:A, 2:B, 3:A, 4:C, 5:C, 6:A, 7:B, 8:D, 9:A, 10:D, 11:A, 12:A, 13:C, 14:C, 15:B, 16:C, 17:A, 18:A, 19:A, 20:A, 21:C, 22:B, 23: A, 24: D, 25: A

Short Answer Type Questions

SQ1. Enumerate the features of a CISC processor.

SQ2. Enumerate the features of a RISC processor.

SQ3. What role does a compiler play in the choice of RISC vs. CISC processors?

SQ4. How does the overlapping register windows help in subprogram call?

SQ5. Distinguish between RISC and CISC processors.

SQ6. Enumerate the I/O ports of PIC18F series of processors.

SQ7. How are the *Capture* and *Compare* operations carried out by the timer modules?

SQ8. Compare between *Tiny*, *Mega* and *Xmega* AVR series.

SQ9. Compare the features of 8051, PIC, AVR and LPC2148 ARM microcontrollers.

SQ10. Enumerate the non-RISC features of ARM processors.

Long Answer Type Questions

LQ1. Discuss the advantages and disadvantages of RISC and CISC processors.

LQ2. Discuss the architecture of PIC18F452 microcontroller.

LQ3. Elaborate the architecture of AVR ATmega32 microcontroller.

LQ4. Enumerate the ARM7 architecture and compare the same with the 8051.

LQ5. Discuss the internal structure of the LPC2148 microcontroller.

Practical Problems

PQ1. Write an assembly language program for ARM processor to find the minimum of a set of numbers.

Hint: Refer to Example 5.5.

PQ2. Modify the code in Example 5.7 so that alternate LEDs glow at a time.

Hint: Refer to example 5.7.

PQ3. Modify the code in Example 5.7 so that the LEDs connected to the 8 least significant bits of port show the number stored in the variable *kount*, initialized at the program development time.

Hint: Refer to Example 5.7.

PQ4. Modify the program in Example 5.8 so that there are two switches – SW1 and SW2. Pressing SW1 will turn ON the LED, pressing SW2 will turn the LED OFF. If both the switches are pressed, SW1 will have higher priority, turning the LED ON.

Hint: Refer to Example 5.8.

PQ5. Modify the program in Example 5.8 so that there are two switches – SW1 and SW2 and two LEDs – L1 and L2. In SW1 is closed, L1 will glow. If SW1 is open, L1 will also be OFF. Similarly SW2 controls the LED L2. However, if both the switches are closed, both L1 and L2 will blink continually till both the switches are released.

Hint: Refer to Example 5.8.

KNOW MORE

Beyond ARM7, some more ARM processors have been introduced, namely, ARM8, ARM9TDMI, StrongARM, ARM10 and ARM11. The latest development in the ARM family is the introduction of ARM Cortex processors. It has three families. The *Cortex-A* corresponds to application processors with third party applications. The *Cortex-R* are embedded processors supporting real-time signal processing and control applications. The microcontroller series is marked as *Cortex-M.* This series is fully programmable in C and possesses only two modes – user mode and supervisor mode. It has one non-maskable interrupt and upto 240 prioritizable interrupts.

REFERENCES AND SUGGESTED READINGS

[1] S. Chattopadhyay, SWAYAM/NPTEL course on “Microprocessors and Microcontrollers”, https://onlinecourses.nptel.ac.in/noc20_ee42/preview.
[2] S. Chattopadhyay, “Embedded System Design”, PHI Learning.
[3] H.W. Huang “The ATMEL AVR Microcontroller Mega and Xmega in Assembly and C”, Delmar, Cengage Learning.
[4] M. Rafiquzzaman, “Microcontroller Theory and Applications with the PIC18F”, Wiley.

Dynamic QR Code for Further Reading

S. Chattopadhyay, SWAYAM/NPTEL course on “Microprocessors and Microcontrollers”.

CO AND PO ATTAINMENT TABLE

Course outcomes (COs) for this course can be mapped with the programme outcomes (POs) after the completion of the course and a correlation can be made for the attainment of POs to analyze the gap. After proper analysis of the gap in the attainment of POs necessary measures can be taken to overcome the gaps.

Table for CO and PO attainment

Course Outcomes	Expected Mapping with Programme Outcomes (1- Weak Correlation; 2- Medium correlation; 3- Strong Correlation)						
	PO-1	**PO-2**	**PO-3**	**PO-4**	**PO-5**	**PO-6**	**PO-7**
CO-1							
CO-2							
CO-3							
CO-4							
CO-5							
CO-6							

The data filled in the above table can be used for gap analysis.

Index